GODFREY RUBENS

W. R. Lethaby

WILLIAM RICHARD LETHABY

HIS LIFE AND WORK 1857–1931

The Architectural Press: London

For Kelly William and Emma

First published in 1986 by the Architectural Press Ltd,
9 Queen Anne's Gate, London SW1H 9BY

© Godfrey Rubens, 1986

BRITISH LIBRARY CATALOGUING IN PUBLICATION
DATA

Rubens, Godfrey
William Richard Lethaby: his life and work
1857–1931.
1. Lethaby, W. R.   2. Artists—England—Biography.
I. Title
709′.2′4   N6797.L4/
ISBN 0 85139 350 0

Designed by Peter Ward

Imprint, the typeface used in this book, was designed at
the Central School of Art and is based on Caslon Old
Face

Typeset by Stratatype, London

Printed in Great Britain by Dotesios Printers Ltd,
Bradford-on-Avon

CONTENTS

ACKNOWLEDGEMENTS

I would like to thank the following people for their help in the preparation of this book: Dorothy Bosomworth, Peter Banham, Alan Crawford, Derek Dyne, Roger Gill, Joan Heddle, John Harvey, Margaret Holden-Jones, the late Priscilla Johnston, Roger Keene, the late Sidney Loweth, Elizabeth Nicholson, John Myers, David Martin, the Hon. Sara Peel, Thomas Paine, Roger Powell, the staffs of the RIBA Library and Drawings Collection, Celia Rooke, the late H. V. Molesworth Roberts, Andrew Saint, Elsie Seatter, the late Arthur Llewellyn Smith, Roger Thorne, the late Lawrence Tanner, Lynne Walker and A. B. Waters. I am particularly grateful to John Brandon-Jones for his generous loan of material and to Frances Stevens for her patient advice and faith in the subject without which this study could hardly have been completed. Much of the research was carried out with the aid of a University of London Leon Fellowship.

SOURCES OF ILLUSTRATIONS

1 Bodleian Library; **2,3** Author; **4** St Anne's Museum, Barnstaple; **5,6** Author; **7,8,9,10** Private collection; **11** *Building News*, vol. 36, 1879, p.170; **12** *The Architect*, vol. 22, 1879, p.334; **13** *Building News*, vol. 36, 1879, p.268; **14** *The Builder*, vol. 14.1, 1881, p.138; **15** Author; **16,17,18** Private collection; **19** Author; **20** *Building News*, vol. 42, 1882, p.204; **21** Private collection; **22** R.A.; **23** *Building News*, vol. 41, 1881, p.328; **24,25,26** Private collection; **27** *The Architect*, vol. 28, 1882, p.329; **28** R.I.B.A. Drawings Collection; **29,30** R.A.; **31,32,33** Private collection; **34** Andrew Saint; **35** V&A; **36** Martin Harrison; **37** V&A; **38** A.I.S. 1st ser. no. 137, *The Architect*, vol. 39, 1888, p.39; **39** Private collection; **40** V&A; **41** Tate Gallery; **42** R.I.B.A. Library; **43** Author; **44** A.I.S. 2nd ser., nos 328, 329, *The Architect*, vol. 45, 1891, p.115; **45** Private collection; **46** V&A; **47** A.I.S. 2nd ser., no. 230, *The Architect*, vol. 43, 1890, p.327; **48** Private collection; **49** A.I.S. 2nd ser., no.195, *The Architect*, vol. 43, 1890, p.87; **50** A.I.S. 2nd ser., no. 293, *The Architect*, vol. 44, 1890, p.335; **51** Coalbrookedale Museum; **52,53** Author; **54** N.M.R.; **55,56,57,58,59** V&A; **60** Private collection; **61** A.I.S. 2nd series, no. 164, *The Architect*, vol. 42, 1899, p.299; **62** *Studio*, vol. ix, 1896, p.199; **63** N.M.R.; **64** *Studio*; **66** Author; **67** John Brandon-Jones; **68** R.I.B.A.; **69** John Brandon-Jones; **70** Author; **71** R.I.B.A.: **72,73** John Brandon-Jones; **74** Author; **75** John Brandon-Jones; **76** R.I.B.A.; **77,78,79,80** John Brandon-Jones; **81** Author; **82** John Brandon-Jones; **83** Joan Hoddle; **84** Andrew Saint; **85** Author; **86,87,88,89,90** John Brandon-Jones; **91** Author; **92,93,94,95,96,97,98** John Brandon-Jones; **99** R.I.B.A.; **100** H. Muthesius; **101** W. Curtis Green; **102** J. Ruskin; **103,104** *Architectural Review*; **105** Private collection; **106** Author; **107,108,109** John Brandon-Jones; **110,111** Elsie Seatter; **112,113,114** Author; **115,116** J. Ruskin; **117** J. Ruskin; **118** R.I.B.A; **119,120** John Brandon-Jones; **121** Author; **122,123** Sources unknown; **124** Author; **125** Private collection; **126,127,128,128,129** V&A; **130,131,132** *Architecture, Mysticism, and Myth*; **133** Author; **134** Private collection; **135** L.C.C. Technical Education Board Gazette; **136,137** Author; **138,139** Private collection; **140,141** Tate Gallery; **142,143** Author.

CHAPTER ONE

EARLY YEARS

PLATE I.   Barnstaple, Devon. Watercolour by G. Shepherd, 1823. Lethaby wrote, 'I have found a view of my own town of Barnstaple – a kind little town seated in a smiling "landskip". There is something in these birthplaces and cradle homes which attacks our very heart strings, and I never look at this town of mine from the outside without that "O Jerusalem" feeling.'

WILLIAM RICHARD LETHABY WAS BORN ON 18 JANUARY 1857 IN BARNSTAPLE, A NORTH DEVON TOWN BUILT IN A WIDE FERTILE VALLEY AT THE UPPER END OF A TIDAL ESTUARY, WHERE THE

rivers Taw and Torridge meet and flow westward into the Bristol Channel. Long after, remembering his birthplace, Lethaby wrote:

> The vision of the Town that opened to one approaching it by Sticklepath was of touching beauty, it remained so still as I remember it . . . In the olden days, the narrow thread of causeway and bridge directed over the river towards the lowly gray town, out of which rose the sharp lead spire, the front fringed with masts and the background of pleasant hills must have been a scene of extraordinary beauty even for fair England.[1]

Up to the middle of the nineteenth century, the town had altered little. For centuries it had been the market town and principal port of north Devon, with a thriving shipbuilding industry and a worldwide commerce. Everything, including, in the latter days, the products of the new manufactures – lace, pottery and furniture – had to travel by sea from one of the four quays. At the time of Lethaby's birth, the old commercial ways were changing. A series of events, principally the coming of the railway, was to transform the old town and its way of life. It was a slow process, hardly discernible while Lethaby was a boy; but in the end the railway strangled the port and it is not easy nowadays to imagine Barnstaple as Lethaby remembered it,

> with a Customs House and Bonded Stores on the Quay. I remember the sea-going ships and the romance they gave to the Town. Fine vessels were built; on the slips close to the West end of the Bridge. I can recall the noble frames and the hammering of caulking and the excitement of being on a barque, I think when she was launched about sixty years ago. After launching they were brought to Queen Anne's Quay where final fitting out was done.

> Two memories come back to me; leaning against a big vessel, floating on the tide I found that after a time she gently swung away from the Quay, which gave me a notion of the slow action of forces which I have never forgotten. Again I asked a sailor of this or another ship where they were going. 'Valparaiso', he replied. On some festival, the Queen's Birthday or the like, the ships along the Quay had out all their bunting and as the evening came, hoisted lanterns. As seen from Anchor Wood bank it was a joyous sight.[2]

The Lethabys could trace their ancestors in Devon back to the sixteenth century, and some believed beyond, to the Dane Hubba son of Lethabrook, who had landed at nearby Appledore in the tenth century. Many, like the boy's grandfather William Lythaby – there are several spellings of the name – were

PLATE 2.   Richard Pyle Lethaby, Lethaby's father.

agricultural labourers, but one of his sons, Richard Pyle Lethaby (Lethaby's father) became a skilled craftsman. How he learned the carving and gilding trade is unknown, but it seems most likely to have been in London where there were other members of the family in the wood business with whom he could have lodged. Perhaps it was there that he met and married Mary Crago, in about 1850. The date is uncertain because the marriage was not registered, perhaps because it took place in a Bible Christian Chapel. In March 1851, presumably seeking lodgings, he travelled to Pilton, a village on the outskirts of Barnstaple[3] where, in the following December, his wife bore him a daughter, Emmeline Shapcot.[4]

From a formal photograph taken on a visit to Exeter, and also from his obituary,[5] we get a clear impression of him (Plate 2). He was the very pattern of the respected and respectable working man, so much admired by his sober fellow Victorians – authoritarian, unbending, devout, a fine and careful craftsman with a head for business, but a Radical nevertheless. Sometime before 1850 he had joined the Bible Christian Society, whose rules, though modelled on those of the Wesleyans, were far more restrictive and puritanical. Soon he was a lay preacher and trustee of both the first Bible Christian Chapel, opened in 1885, and the second, a new church. Pouring in his energies as he did, he must have figured large in the affairs of the Society and contributed much to the successful effort to establish it in Barnstaple. From its earliest days it had been a folk church; though it embraced yeoman farmers and small shopkeepers, its chief strength came from 'Hodge', the country labourer, society's poorest class. Gradually transformed from a revivalist movement, it became an institutionalized church with an established order of service, but was still characterized by extempore prayers and sermons with violent images of damnation, hell-fire and revelation. Its main difference, which set it at first sharply apart from the orthodox Methodist Connexion, was that its members, like the Primitive Methodists, were actively involved in radical politics. When the Barnstaple Liberal League was founded, after the Second Reform Bill had given the vote to the majority of working men, Richard Pyle Lethaby was elected to the committee and played a part in the successful attempt to clean up parliamentary elections, then corrupt affairs run on 'beer, bribes and intimidation'.[6]

Throughout the years that Richard Pyle lived in the town he worked for John Ley, a carver and gilder, whose house and workshop were on the original quay. In about 1860 Ley opened a fine art gallery, where he sold ornamental gilt frames of every kind and 'the best selection of engravings and chromo-lithographs'.[7] A few years later the young Richard (who was known as 'Willem' in the early days), must have been a frequent visitor and have come to know at least something of popular art. It is tempting to think that it may have been here that he first met Alexander Lauder, his future employer, when he came seeking a frame for his latest painting. By then Richard Pyle had become foreman and may have carried on the business after Ley's death, for, at his own, he left £800 – no small sum even for a skilled craftsman.

In the early years of their marriage the Lethabys had lodged with the Leys at 2 The Strand, but by

PLATE 3.   2 Ebberley Lawn, Barnstaple, Lethaby's home from about 1860.

1857 had moved to Grosvenor Street in the upper part of the town where William Richard, their only son, was born. Shortly afterwards they acquired a house, 2 Ebberley Lawn (Plate 3), not far away, where Richard Pyle was to live out his life. Once part of a horse barrack, it had been converted into a terrace of eight neat little houses, so that when another terrace was built opposite and a pair of entrance gates added at one end it became, as it still is, an elongated and tranquil square. Ebberley Lawn stands at what were then the town's outskirts, on rising ground which climbs behind the house to Font Hill and to Dartmoor, ten miles away.

Life in the devout, sober little household, crowded with Mrs Lethaby's lodgers and constrained by the strict rules of the Connexion, revolved around chapel affairs. They would have eaten plain food, worn drab, homely clothes and had few diversions, certainly nothing that could be called amusements. The boy William Richard found it narrow and restricting and, though loyalty to his family almost prevented any complaint, he seldom spoke, even in later life, about his childhood. All he permitted himself to say was, 'When I was young children were expected to have their hair nicely brushed and to sit still, to "be seen and not heard". Wise children know better; they really want to be doing things and to be put "in the way of doing them".'[8] He was convinced that it was by making toys that he had unconsciously broken through. As so often happens with children, one of the most important and liberating influences came from something which to an adult might seem trivial; in his case from the accidental fact that a certain Mr Websdale was a friend of the family.

Had it not been for one little chance, that some toys stirred my interest . . . I don't see how I should have been allowed to squeeze through life.

It happened in this way. When I was about four or five this nice man, who would amuse me by cutting out with scissors the shapes of animals in thick paper or cardboard, used to visit our house. If I had gone to bed, which, of course, I usually had, a few would be done and set out, on their legs, on a little table and I had them in the morning. There were horses, best loved things, cows with horns, camels with humps and elephants with 'trunks'. They would all stand upright on their legs after they had been bent, – two on this side and two on that. Then there were snakes, rather frightening, but cut in a spiral and pulled out, they were amusing, and there were cocks and hens, geese and the like, which would stand if a biggish piece of card were left at their feet and bent at the right angle. The paper creatures were very well done, for Mr Websdale was an artist. I must say his name with gratitude, although probably no one on earth, except myself, remembers him across the chasm of years . . . We rigged ships, made peepshows and I contrived a kaleidoscope and made a kite.[9]

One of his rare presents, another game called Tangram, also made a great impression:

This toy was a great joy to me and it made me familiar with notions about shapes, triangles,

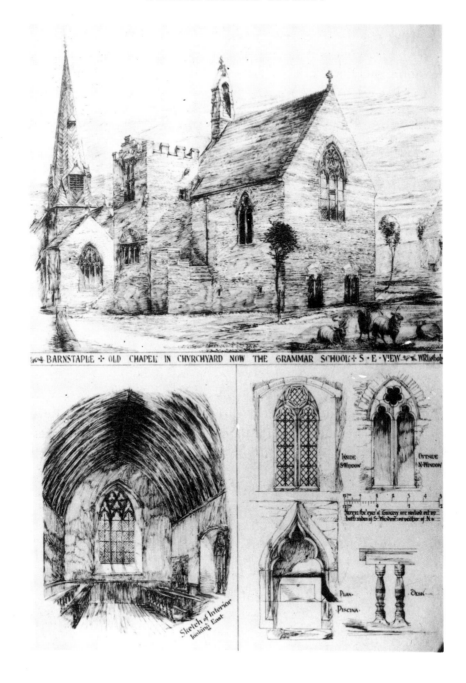

PLATE 4. The Grammar School, Paternoster Road, Barnstaple.

squares, divisions and fitting together; what we call geometry. It is quite wonderful the
teaching that may be got out of it and it must have been designed by a mathematical sage.[10]
Lethaby was to become in later life a skilful geometer, and sound geometrical knowledge is a notable factor
in his early work.

Lethaby's mother died when he was thirteen. Virtually nothing is known about her but it is likely that
she countered the severe authoritarianism of her husband by being discreetly indulgent to her children.
There is a glimpse of her playfully warning the little boy against the likely consequences of yet another
helping of pie, and giving in to him when he countered with 'It'll be worth it!'. She even tolerated the
occasional truancies when he was bored with school, and compounded her leniency by allowing him to
stay in bed. Perhaps she satisfied her conscience by remembering the schoolmaster's assurance that,
whatever her son might do, he was always top of the class.[11]

Lethaby's formal education began at an institution run by a Plymouth Brother, from which he went
on to the local grammar school in Paternoster Road which dated from the sixteenth century, and included
John Gay among its former pupils. Housed in a rather dilapidated fourteenth-century building and
formally a charnel house (Plate 4), it had suffered the fate of most of the endowed grammar schools. It was
much run down, had few pupils, and was conducted by one aged teacher, the Reverend Johnston, who
was also chaplain to the workhouse, the gaol and the infirmary.[12] He seems to have taught little beyond the
three Rs, a smattering of the Classics and some drawing, all this by what Lethaby called book rote:
'Arithmetic and grammar and what they call history were horrid bores and mostly gibberish to me'.[13]

Fortunately, Lethaby's education was not to remain solely in the hands of the Reverend Johnston. In
1868 Lethaby, newly elected a free member of the Barnstaple Literary and Scientific Institute, attended its
first 'Night Drawing Class for Artisans and Children over the age of twelve', and entered upon the
mechanical and arduous curriculum which he would pursue for many years.[14] This class, organized and
controlled by the Department of Science and Art, was part of Henry Cole's national system of art
education. Uniformity was maintained by the issue of a precise syllabus ('The National Course of
Instruction for Government Schools in Great Britain'), and by the Government supplying all the
equipment. Much of the syllabus, which divided the learning-process into twenty-three artificial and
progressively arduous stages, consisted of drawing-exercises similar to those in William Dyce's dull
Drawing Book, which was also widely used, and drawing from plaster casts.

The sixty students of the twice-weekly class would have started with Stage 1, Linear Drawing, which
comprised geometry, linear perspective, simple technical drawing, copying other drawings or diagrams
and sciography (the technique of shading an outline drawing to suggest modelling). As unpromising a
programme, one might think, as that of the grammar school! Much, however, depended on the quality of
the teacher, and Barnstaple's was a good one. At the end of his first year Lethaby won the first of the many

PLATE 5. Mantelpiece in glazed terracotta, by Alexander Lauder. Designed for his own house, 'Ravelin', Barnstaple, and probably fired at his pot works, the North Devon Art Pottery in Barnstaple.

prizes he was to gain over the next decade,[15] some of them awarded by the Institute and others by the Department, for art, geometry, mathematics and building construction.

In later life, Lethaby was to spend much time attacking this system of education; but to a child conditioned by the severity of a Bible Christian household its rigours would have given no cause for protest. On the contrary, he found it 'exact, complete and systematic',[16] and pursued it so successfully that his progress was marked not only by the string of prizes but also by a first-class pass, at the age of seventeen, in the difficult examination of Stage 1 in the Department of Science and Art Building and Construction Course.

By that time, however, he had already been for three years under a very different influence, that of Alexander Lauder, to whom he had been articled at the age of fourteen.[17] If Lauder was fortunate in his talented apprentice, so too was the boy in his master. It was rare to find a man of Alexander Lauder's calibre in a place like Barnstaple; perhaps that is why he was twice elected mayor. A competent watercolourist and an enthusiastic, if poor, writer of Ossianesque verse, which he illustrated and published at his own expense, Lauder had a wide interest in education and the building crafts. He 'used to insist that all the men working on his own buildings should have an understanding of one another's craft, so that each might feel that he was building a house and not just practising carpentry, bricklaying or plumbing'.[18]

He delighted, moreover, in decoration, the variety and vigour of which enlivened his sound but rather unimaginative structures: '[Lauder] revelled in craftsmanship and would decorate many of the houses he built with huge sgrafitto murals, terracotta friezes and high relief ceramic tiles, all carved or modelled with his own hand'.[19]

He established a brickworks, which also made decorative terracotta, much of which he modelled himself (Plate 5), and he founded the Devon Art Pottery. Among local landowners he seems to have built up quite a large architectural practice; a devout Methodist, he also designed without charge a number of schools and chapels for the Connexion in London and Devon.[20] Thus, for Lethaby the pupil, the seeds were sown in adolescence of both the early decorative exuberance and the later concern for education which are so evident in the overall picture of his life.

There is little direct, but considerable circumstantial evidence of some of the work Lethaby did for Lauder. Between 1871 and 1878, a period coinciding with Lethaby's years in the office, Lauder published eight designs for chapels and churches.[21] He had published none before this period, and only one other, very different in its style of drawing, appeared many years later.[22] The dates are suggestive, and the following considerations also make it likely that Lethaby did a great deal of work on the designs. First, Lauder seems to have had no great interest in structural problems, that is, in architecture for its own sake: the style of his drawings, which hardly contain any representations of buildings, is quite unlike that of the

PLATE 6.   Wesleyan Chapel, New Cross Road, London, designed by Lauder, 1876. A perspective drawing signed by Lethaby. The chapel was bombed in the last war and subsequently demolished.

published designs. Secondly, though only one of the five perspectives among them is actually signed by Lethaby, all are similar in style and consonant with that interest and skill in this type of technical drawing for which he was later noted (Plate 6). Since three of the perspectives are of chapels in the London area, it was probably in connection with their construction that he visited London in 1875, and took the opportunity to make a drawing of the north transept of Westminster Abbey – an early beginning of his long association with that building.[23]

In the last year of his apprenticeship, Lethaby spent much of his spare time working on drawings for an important competition organized by *Building News,* which had already published some of his studies.[24] Maurice Adams, its architectural editor, had announced in 1877 that the paper was to extend its efforts in architectural education by starting a Designing Club with the object of promoting the 'faculty of Design'.[25] At a time when there were few architectural schools, no properly organized architectural education and no central examinations, many young architects were to owe their chance of success to the Club and to the helpful and kindly criticism given them by Adams, one of the best perspective artists of his day. To inaugurate the Club, Adams promoted a competition with the modest prize of £5. At intervals throughout the year a number of subjects (twenty-one in all) were set, and to qualify for the prize competitors had to submit at least twelve designs.

In January 1878 the paper announced that the prize had been won by W. R. Lethaby of Barnstaple, using the pseudonym 'Début'. The prize-winning designs, wrote Adams, 'have usually been marked not only by considerable refinement as well as feeling, but by some originality'.[26] Seventeen of Lethaby's nineteen designs were published.[27] There is a noticeable discrepancy between the competence of the plans, elevations and sections and the less assured technique of the freehand sketch perspectives, the earlier examples of which are scratchy and badly drawn. It is also interesting to observe a change in style: up to about the middle of 1877 most of the designs are Gothic in character, but after that point they are classical. All the designs manifest a strong interest in geometry, but the severe neo-classicism of the later ones prompts a suspicion that the designer may have discovered Schinkel (Plates 7, 8, 9, 10).

These designs epitomize all that Lethaby had learned in Barnstaple. From the Institute classes he had acquired his skill in mechanical drawing, knowledge of geometry and proficiency in the 'styles'. His father first, and subsequently Lauder, had given him an understanding of craftsmanship and construction, which he had supplemented by making the numerous studies of local churches and other buildings of which his sketchbooks are full. Finally, from close reading of the architectural press he had gained a knowledge of architectural fashions.

The gifted young man had known nothing but success; at each step he had swept up every prize within his reach; and success had made him ambitious, for he went on competing for these marks of

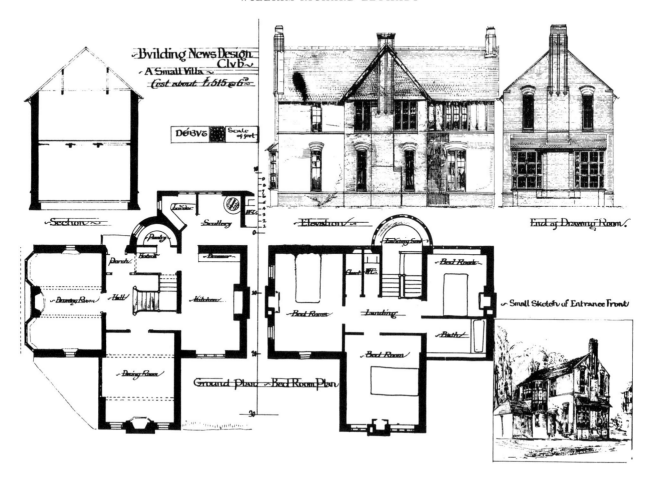

PLATE 7.   Design for a small villa. One of four illustrations submitted for the *Building News* Designing Club competition in 1877 (see also Plates 8, 9 and 10), it was considered 'too piquant for a villa'; the plan – a cross – made for a 'haphazard arrangement' of the interior.

achievement. It must also have made him restless, for the year following the completion of his apprenticeship is marked by a variety of employers and locations.

His first move, to the office of Richard Waite in Derbyshire, would have offered a change of scene but little else to an adventurous and questing spirit; for Waite, a solid citizen, seems to have been a prosperous but unexciting designer, though he was something of an expert in the field of agricultural building, which received little attention from architects. Lethaby had received sound training in this kind of work: for

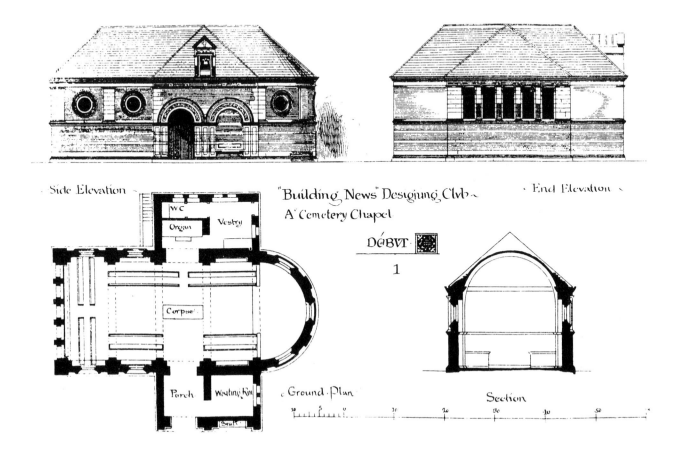

Side Elevation "Building News" Designing Club End Elevation

A Cemetery Chapel

DEBVT

1

Ground Plan   Section

PLATE 8.   Design for a cemetery chapel. The editor of *Building News* commented on 'the almost deathlike serenity of line and feature in the classical style . . . although the idea was not, to some minds, sufficiently suggestive of a Christian burial'.

when he was in Lauder's office he learned to design farm buildings 'which had to *work* and work efficiently, as an engine or a pump must',[28] and it was probably this training that had recommended him to Waite. During this short time in Derbyshire, he served his employer well, for his hand is evident in the designs which won for Waite three prizes in just over a year. Nearly all that is known of Waite's work is contained in a letter he wrote in 1879, in which he discusses his prize-winning Dairy Show design for a Homstead for eighty cows: '[This makes the third] I have won for farm plans and buildings in thirteen

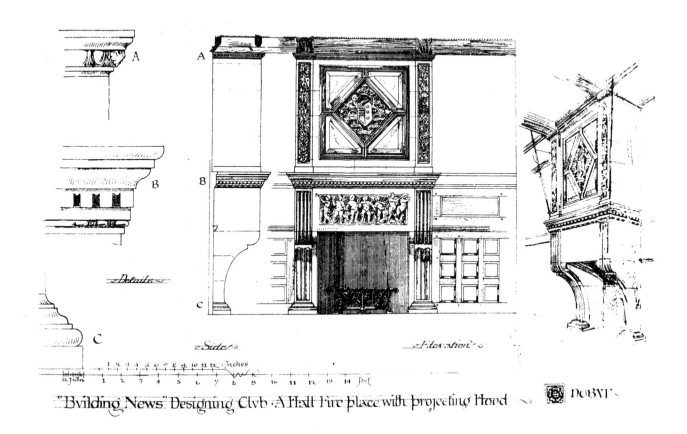

PLATE 9. Design for a hall fireplace. Considered to be 'a very characteristic and pleasing sketch . . . it evinced meaning . . . and bore the impress of a cultivated taste in a semi-classical spirit'.

months, viz: one in September, 1878, for a moveable cattle-shed at the Derby Agricultural Society's Show; one at the Kilburn Royal Show, 1879, farm plans; one at Dairy Show, 1879, farm plans'.[29] The last two were published, together with a design for a farmhouse near Tamworth.[30] Two of the drawings are perspectives signed by Lethaby; a third, for the 1880 Dairy Show, was probably done by him after he had moved to London. The young man's ability to turn architectural plans into sparkling representational views – or 'perspectives' – of the design must have succeeded in presenting the master's ideas in a visible

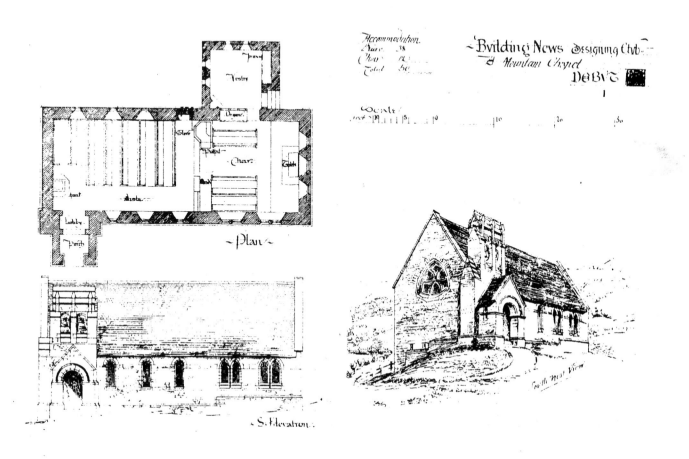

PLATE 10.   Design for a mountain chapel. 'Ingenious, picturesque
and suggestive', it was thought to be very successful.

form immediately attractive to the judges. *Building News* gave detailed technical descriptions of the designs, and praised them for their indications of durable structure and efficiency. Introducing the first of them, the paper noted: 'Good plans of farm buildings are very seldom to be found in books of reference, so that we have from time to time endeavoured to supply the want by giving particulars of the kind whenever an example worthy of being taken as a model comes before us.'[31] In less than a year, Lethaby was back in Barnstaple, working on his designs for the RIBA Soane Medallion. But, short as it was, the spell in

PLATE II.   Early seventeenth-century house in Warwick, Derbyshire.

Derbyshire had produced some fine work, particularly topographical drawings (Plate II). He was stimulated by both man-made and natural sights. At this period, many fine timber-frame and other interesting houses were still to be found in and around Derby, and one of the most impressive was Haddon Hall, about twenty-five miles from his employer's house. Almost as soon as Lethaby arrived he was over there, making drawings. He was interested too in the furniture and decoration of this great house, which was to keep its attraction and significance for him. A decade later, when he was on holiday with his friend Ernest Gimson, the two men paid it an enjoyable and rewarding visit. At about the turn of the century he chose it as the setting for what must have been one of the great moments of his life: it was here that he proposed to Edith Crosby, who was to become his wife.[32] As for nature, it is to the short Derbyshire period that we owe the following delightful account of an incident on a country walk:

It is curious, but I think the biggest single impression of beauty I ever had was from a muddy puddle. It was on a yellow, clayey road in Derbyshire, when, after a swiftly passing storm of rain brilliant sunshine made all diamond bright. Coming out from shelter I felt the refreshment, vitality and wonder of it; drops still fell from the foliage and miniature rivers ran down the ruts of the road. Then I came to my puddle, which may have been two feet over and two inches deep, filled with diluted mud. It was still and reflected the heavenly blue above in the most amazing way; there was something in the contrast of the little sea and its yellow, sunlit shore, which made the blue appear more intense than the sky itself. Somehow the puddle seemed a mirror of the whole immensity; it was a vision of the essence of beauty.[33]

Between January and March 1879 Lethaby worked in the office of another architect, T. H. Baker, who had a small, domestic and, from what slender evidence there is, undistinguished practice in Leicester.[34] But he too may have had his hour of vicarious distinction through the work of his young assistant, for in 1880 *The Architect* published three designs for Nonconformist chapels (Plate 12), with a note that they were part of a series which would be published shortly by T. H. Baker and W. T. Toppott who, it was claimed, had made a special study of this subject.[35] No ecclesiastical building by either man has been found, nor anything to support the claim. This is, however, just the sort of enterprise Lethaby would have welcomed and was well equipped to bring about. But in the end nothing came of the project and the fact that the book was never published makes plausible the supposition that Waite, a devout Methodist, loaned his clerk to Baker for this specific job and that when it was abandoned after only three months Lethaby returned to Derby.[36] Just before he left Leicester, however, the Royal Institute of Architects had announced that he had been awarded the Soane Medallion for 1878–9.[37] This was for the design of a 'Building to Accommodate Four Learned Societies' in which each of them had to be provided with a library, a council room, a committee room, writing and reading rooms for members, a secretary's office, a clerk's office, lavatories, etc., and a lecture theatre capable of accommodating 300 people to be used in common by each society. The site was supposed to be on the Thames Embankment. Lethaby adopted a courtyard plan, modelled on a Renaissance palace partly to complement Somerset House which would have been further along the Embankment and partly because, '[it] would lend itself most readily to equality in arrangement of the four sets and to efficient lighting and privacy'[38] (Plate 13). *Building News* published the drawing and found the design

a very clever work exhibiting considerable power and artistic feeling . . . In plan . . . the blocks are ingeniously disposed symmetrically about a centre axis and considerable skill is evinced in the outline and grouping of the parts, despite some obvious defects in detail. The buildings are

PLATE 12.   Design for a Nonconformist chapel. Unsigned perspective accredited to T. H. Baker and W. T. Toppott of Leicester but believed to be largely by Lethaby.

Selected Design ⊗ BY W.R.LETHABY

SOANE MEDALLION COMPETITION

A HOUSE for the LEARNED SOCIETIES

PLATE 13. 'A Building to Accommodate Four Learned Societies', 1879. RIBA Soane Medallion, 1878–9.

comprised within a long quadrangle, there being three transverse and four side blocks, leaving two inner courts . . . Reading and writing rooms are on the upper floor, and occupy the two main transverse buildings, each with its own entrance and staircase, while the ground floor is devoted to Council room, secretaries' and clerks' offices. The connecting side blocks are made the libraries, while the building in the rear is the Lecture theatre, T-shaped in plan which echoes the plan of the courtyards with the seats arranged curvilinearly, and with side entrances from the inner courts. We admire the manner the staircases, which form large circular bayed ends towards the courts, are planned, but the lobby and entrances look ill lighted on plan and the clerks' entrance somewhat tortuous. The arrangement of the first floor is much better. The landing and vestibules are architecturally managed, and the rooms are pleasingly broken by bays, which externally produce a very piquant grouping, especially toward the river front-age . . . Less to our taste is the side elevation; the centre hipped roof portion harmonizes ill with the lateral bays of the libraries, which are carried up too high, and are filled with an unmeaning kind of lozenge panelling in the gables.[39]

Of his choice of Renaissance style ornament Lethaby wrote, 'The chief intention . . . was to do without an order, and to obtain some originality without the eccentricities of later developments'. This resulted in a restrained and formal decorative scheme, more or less Renaissance in character and some sculpture, like the herms supporting the entablatures of the societies' entrances and the five figures standing above the river front entrance. Here *Building News* thought the details were 'particularly refined [being] French Renaissance of the type . . . between the sixteenth century and the Grand Monarque though some of the details are incoherent enough to belong to that of Henry IV'.[40]

Winning this prize – the most prestigious student award – must have strengthened his belief that designing rational cowsheds for Waite was not in his stars, and encouraged him to look around for a more satisfying job. Accordingly, by July 1879 he was off to London. He went initially in the hope of working for William Butterfield, by whom he was interviewed; but 'the fine old man' wrote a letter of rejection. Far from being impressed by Lethaby's success in the *Building News* competition, which had been mentioned at the interview, he said he believed that 'competitions were upsetting to quiet and steady work'.[41] But Lethaby also suggested another reason for the rejection: that Butterfield had taken exception to one of his more astonishing designs, that for a cemetery chapel.[42] (See Plate 8.)

Having arrived in London, it seems that Lethaby decided to stay on and see what opportunities offered themselves. 'At the outset', wrote Maurice Adams,

like many another architectural assistant, he had to rely on temporary engagements, and sometimes 'took in washing', a similar avocation to that among young barristers . . . It was in

PLATE 14.   New vestry hall and offices, Westminster, London.

this way that I became personally acquainted with Lethaby, who . . . often assisted me in this commercial side of professional practice and perspective making . . .

The following amusing incident . . . exemplifies how this traffic betimes was managed. A limited competition happened to be held for an important municipal building, very familiar nowadays to all Londoners. One of the firms . . . chosen to submit designs . . . applied to me to prepare their scheme. I happened at the moment to be too busy . . . so got Lethaby to make a design . . . In due course they won the competition, the design . . . being excellent had served their purpose; but the firm that secured the commission let Lethaby's plans 'go hang', and the

33

PLATE 15. Norman Shaw memorial, New Scotland Yard, 1914.
Designed by Lethaby and modelled by Hamo Thornycroft. Terracotta.

well known existing hall and premises bear no sort of resemblance to the scheme chosen by the assessor.[43]

The competition mentioned can be identified with some degree of certainty: it was for the new vestry hall and offices for the United Parishes of St Margaret and St John in Westminster, now known as Caxton Hall, and was won by the firm of Lee and Smith of Westminster on the strength of Lethaby's design (Plate 14). Subsequently, however, most of its somewhat bizarre historicism disappeared and the existing building only resembles the original design in a general way.

Thus, in less than two years after completing his apprenticeship, Lethaby had sampled a variety of employers, had won coveted awards, and had some work published. He was now ready for an important and stabilizing move, and the opportunity was soon to arise.

At about this time, Norman Shaw (Plate 15), then the most successful designer of Victorian country houses, was looking for a new chief assistant. He wanted a man with special abilities as a draughtsman, for

PLATE 16.   Lethaby, probably taken just after he came to London.

he attached much importance to the quality of his office drawings. Perhaps Adams, who was just then working on Shaw's Bedford Park designs, had shown him some of Lethaby's drawings, which already bore signs of being inspired by Shaw's work. Shaw was delighted with the drawings. He one day appeared in his office with one of them,

> and showing it to his staff said, 'What do you think of this? I am going to write and ask him to come here' – and so Lethaby came to London. This was in the summer of 1879. He was at that time twenty-two years of age. I have been told, by those that met him, that he was shy and retiring and was at first overawed by the presence of the great man into whose office he had come.[44]

Lethaby's abilities must have impressed Shaw deeply for, in succession to Ernest Newton, he was made chief assistant and put in charge of Shaw's large office. To be given at his age such a position over the heads of such talented young men as Edward Prior, Mervyn Macartney, Arthur Keen and Gerald Horsley was a triumph and a challenge.

35

In October 1880 Lethaby moved to an attic at 20 Calthorpe Street, WC1, which was to be his home for the next ten years. Being now well launched on his career, he could almost certainly have afforded better quarters, but frugality must have become second nature. It is consistent with the care which he showed in later life for his clients' money, accounting scrupulously for the last halfpenny. How different from Shaw, whose costs frequently exceeded his estimates!

CHAPTER TWO

CHIEF ASSISTANT

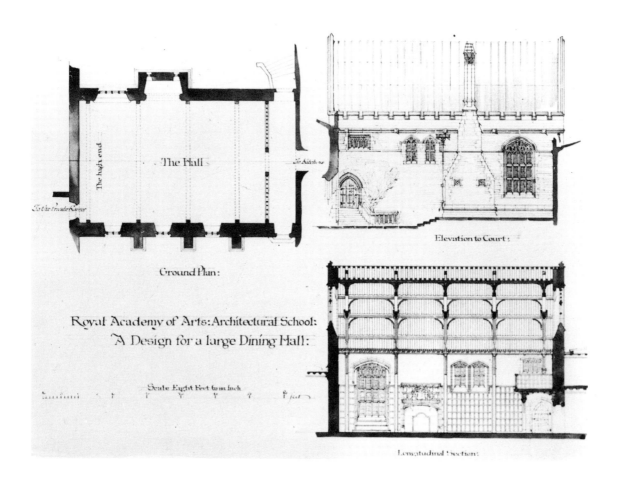

The high end

The Hall

To the Inner Court

To the Kitchen

Ground Plan:

Elevation to Court:

Royal Academy of Arts: Architectural School:
A Design for a large Dining Hall:

Scale Eight Feet to an Inch

feet

Longitudinal Section:

PLATE 17.   R.A. Schools design for a large dining hall.

DURING THE 1880S, LETHABY GREW FROM AN UNKNOWN PROVINCIAL TO A SOPHISTICATED AND LEARNED ARCHITECT WITH A GROWING REPUTATION AMONG THE COGNOSCENTI AS ONE OF

the new stars in the architectural firmament. It was for him a period of intense enquiry and development during which most of his ideas about himself, society and, not least, architecture underwent considerable change. The basis for this dynamic process was his long and fruitful association with Norman Shaw.

Shaw, then at the height of his career, had an office at the north-east corner of Bloomsbury Square, where he occupied three rooms on the ground floor of a fine eighteenth-century house, now destroyed. Even by the standards of the day his drawing-office, which lacked any mechanical aids, was old-fashioned, and business was conducted in a relaxed manner. Unlike most Victorian architects Shaw gave his staff a great deal of freedom, treating them all, Lethaby tells us, as younger friends.

> There was never any pressure or excitement. If drawings were not finished one night they would do 'tomorrow', and (this is literally true) I never heard him speak a word of anger all the twelve or thirteen years I had the delight of working (with plenty of play) for him.[1]

Lethaby found Shaw 'not only a man of high gifts, but . . . a delightful person. To work with him was all pride and pleasure . . . he was amazingly generous and loved to praise [his clerks] whenever he could.'[2] Their unique relationship approximated to that of junior and senior partner, for, however genial with all his staff, to no other assistant did Shaw extend the freedom enjoyed by Lethaby. Robert Schultz Weir and Arthur Keen, both former clerks of Shaw, and Beresford Pite, an architect in a position to know what he was talking about, provide first-hand evidence. Weir wrote that Shaw gave Lethaby 'a free hand in detailing his work'[3] and Keen that

> the collaboration . . . was an ideal one; Shaw with his enterprise and resource [and] his unequalled power of sheer independent design . . . and Lethaby with his unrivalled knowledge of style and detail, his fine taste and sense of fitness, his superb draughtsmanship and his unfailing instinct for right building.[4]

In Pite's words,

> Shaw had the largeness to let Lethaby loose upon his buildings . . . that Shaw loved and valued Lethaby and gave him liberty in dealing with his work was the real estimate of his quality.[5]

To his other qualities the new chief assistant added a talent for leadership and ran Shaw's office like clockwork; he 'must have had a good business ability . . . for in spite of letters always, and details commonly, being sent away from the office uncopied, the buildings were duly successfully completed with singularly little friction or difficulty'.[6] Weir, who came to work in Bloomsbury Square in 1884, said Lethaby had done

> everything that a kindly nature could think of to make my entry into the office as pleasant as possible. Coming from a hard-driven Scotch office I was at first rather taken aback by the amount of larking that went on, generally under Lethaby's leadership, but between times a surprising amount of work was got through. It was all a new and at first a somewhat strange experience for me, but the keenness and enthusiasm being contagious I soon fell in with the spirit of it all and Lethaby taking me in hand and putting me on the right footing, in a few months I had, under his guidance, qualified for entry into the R.A. Schools.[7]

Another clerk remembered the kind of prank that Lethaby, who loved cricket, got up to. One hot summer's afternoon, work, so Lethaby felt, was not going with sufficient spirit. He improvised a game of cricket with T squares for bats and an india-rubber for a ball. Shaw returned in the middle![8] History does not record the principal's words.

Shaw expected his clients to treat Lethaby as they would treat him. If they did not there was certain to be trouble, as the following incident illustrates. W. A. Tyssen-Amhurst, for whom Shaw had agreed to rebuild Didlington Hall, called at Bloomsbury Square; finding only Lethaby there, he said he would not be fobbed off with a mere minion. Immediately Shaw wrote telling him to take his business elsewhere, and it was only after many delays that the quarrel was eventually patched up.[9]

From his first day in the office, Lethaby

> entered upon his duties with a degree of courage and apparent confidence that seemed at the time remarkable in a man of his age. He was quite prepared to do anything from eighth-scale sections to full-size drawings of ornament or perspectives in ink or colour, but his draughtsmanship at first was free and loose in comparison with that in vogue in the office – the clean, crisp pencil and ink work in which Horsley and Hardy followed Shaw so closely; the looseness, however, was more apparent than real . . . and his details were far more than mere working drawings; they were in all cases a definite contribution to the artistic completeness of the design, and done with unquestioning loyalty to the original drawings.[10]

In the making of perspective representations of projected buildings he was also highly skilled, working with a quite astonishing speed and accuracy. On one occasion he drew out in detail the façade of a large and complicated building in one evening, and even after going to Shaw he continued to make such representations for others.

This evidence, reinforced by a careful examination of the office drawings, confirms the view of Andrew Saint who concludes, in his excellent biography of Shaw, that 'the plans are inevitably Shaw's, critical details are frequently Lethaby's and the elevations which remain in doubt, must have resulted from intimate collaboration'.[11] To a large degree it was this detailing which gave Shaw's buildings their characteristic colour and texture, a richness which resulted from Lethaby's great sensitivity to the nature of building and decorating materials.

By examining Lethaby's ideas as represented in his own work and statements at the time, it is possible to discover in what way, if at all, he influenced Shaw in his moves towards classicism.

Lethaby's first drawings, careful studies of architectural details in north Devon, and perspective views of Lauder's rather turgid neo-Gothic chapels, began appearing in the architectural press when he was seventeen, but attracted little notice until two years later, at the time of his winning the *Building News* competition. The 'Début' drawings fascinate because, like the first faint but clear statements of a theme, they are harbingers of ideas that were to become dominant in later life. One of these is a love of solid geometry, expressed in the simple rational purity of some of the designs, which is foiled sharply by the rich decoration of others. Another is his religious feeling, discernible though less easy to identify. In this connection may be noticed the oddity of his choosing a cruciform shape – the ultimate Christian symbol – for his plan of a family house (see Plate 7). The intention is clear, the design probably unconscious. At first he designed mostly in Gothic, but for the latter part of the period he chose the Renaissance, which marked the beginning of his love affair with that style.

These were followed almost immediately by the design for the 'Building to Accommodate Four Learned Societies' for the Soane Medallion which, though obviously influenced by French palace design was, with its astylar scheme of wall decoration, an attempt at an original statement broadly within the language of classicism. After coming to Bloomsbury Square, however, the influence of Shaw's style became more marked, until 1883 when a purer form of classicism began to appear in his work. The most important of the earlier designs are some studies done in the R.A. Schools, others for the Goldsmiths Hall and finally one for a school.

The first of these was a School's design for a hall probably produced in one of Shaw's classes, built of stone with an open timber roof in a Tudor style (Plates 17 and 18). Shaw's design for Adcote perhaps influenced this design just as it influenced another, also made at the Academy, for a town house (Plate 19). In the latter, however, though the plan is Shavian, the decoration of the oriels, the mullion and transom windows and the four gables shows some independent thought, foreshadowing things to come.

G. E. Street, who taught Lethaby for a while, was also a passing influence; Lethaby found his 'earnestness, powers and good looks convincing'.[12] Indeed, so convinced was he that for a moment his enthusiasm was kindled and he produced a design for a bishop's tomb in thirteenth-century Gothic which won a prize (Plate 20).[13] This was but a flirtation; he soon decided that Gothic was to be measured up, admired and sketched – but not imitated. *Vive la Renaissance* was Lethaby's cry; and in 1882 this phrase

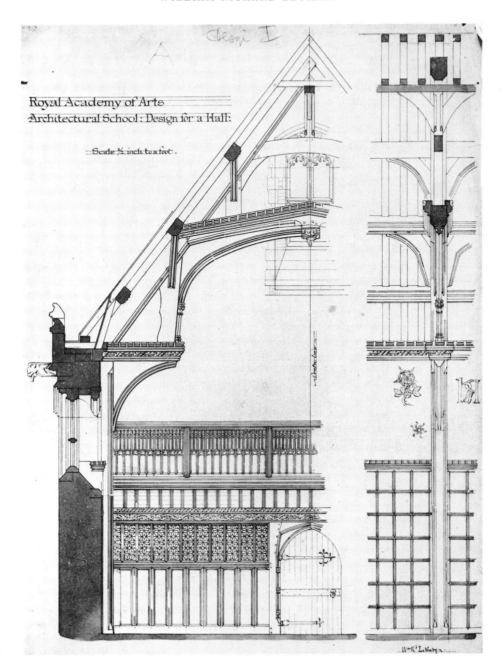

Royal Academy of Arts
Architectural School: Design for a Hall.

Scale ½ inch to a foot.

PLATE 18.   R.A. Schools design for a hall.

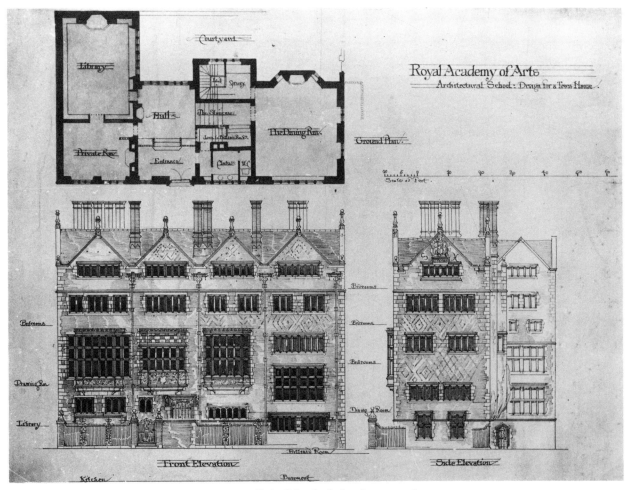

PLATE 19. R.A. Schools design for a town house.

was the *nom de guerre* he chose to put on four silverware designs sent in for the Goldsmiths Hall competition (Plates 21, 22).

For these designs it was to the Anglo-Flemish and London forms that he turned for inspiration. One piece, a salad bowl (Plate 22) based on a Flemish maser, won a £15 prize; but it is less interesting than the taut and lively silver fruit dish. Nor could his enthusiasm for the Renaissance be more clearly shown than by the measured drawing of the mid-sixteenth-century tomb of the Flemish Count de Borgnival (Plate 23). This was, ironically, one of the drawings with which he won the Pugin Travelling scholarship! 'I am a great admirer of the Renaissance', declared Lethaby in a lecture of 1883, adding that the attacks on it by

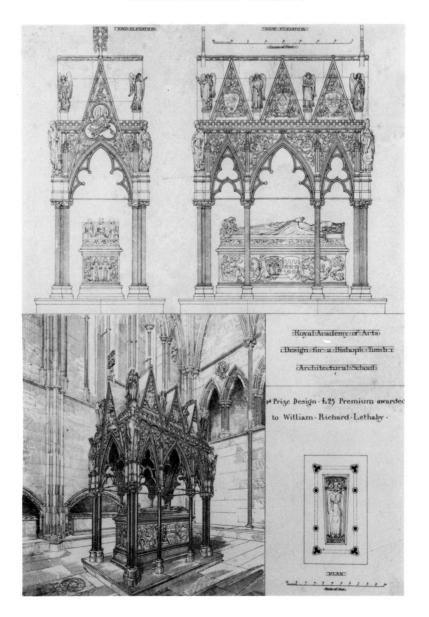

PLATE 20.   A bishop's tomb (R.A. Prize). 'The subject is set by the Visitor, and has to be done within three months (three evenings a week) . . . the students had the advantage of the criticism of Mr Waterhouse and the late Mr Street . . .' 'The intention,' wrote Lethaby, 'was to work in the style of the Earliest Decorated work before the conventional crocket was used, and the materials supposed were Purbeck marble for the shafts, arches and mouldings, the carved parts being of soft stone wholly gilt and the effigy of alabaster, painted and gilt.'

44

PLATE 21.   Fruit dish, 1882.

PLATE 22. Salad bowl. Goldsmiths Hall Competition design.

PLATE 23. Tomb of the Count de Borgnival, 1881. From a cast in the South Kensington Museum, this drawing was submitted as part of Lethaby's successful attempt to win the Pugin Memorial Travelling Scholarship.

47

Pugin and Ruskin were 'illogical and inconclusive'. He contemptuously dismissed Pugin and his 'utility doctrines' with the assertion that his arguments could with equal justice be returned on his own head. As for Ruskin's moral criticism of corruption and heartlessness, '[it] can surely have little weight when he admires so profoundly the painting and sculpture of the same age, which is part of the same development as architecture, and practised by the same men'. At the conclusion of this lecture he described two traditional styles as appropriate for modern English architecture:

> The one, which I will call the Classic, is derived, through Inigo Jones, from a study of the Roman School of Bramante and Michael Angelo . . . To this school belonged Wren, Hawksmoor and Gibbs. It is essentially a London style. The other is what has been called the Elizabethan, and is closely allied to Dutch and German work much of which might, without any violence to our own national traditions, be embodied in English work.[14] (Plates 24, 25, 26.)

PLATES 24, 25 and 26.   Ewer and dish (Goldsmiths Hall Competition design). Lethaby won a prize of £35.

GOLDSMITHS HALL : 1883
Design for Ewer and Dish in Silver :

DETAIL of EWER.

PLATE 25.

PLATE 26.

All that survives of the entry made by Lethaby, Macartney and Newton for the St Anne's School competition is Lethaby's elevation of the entrance façade (Plate 27). It seems exactly to depict the kind of Northern Renaissance style described above and presumably the outcome of the practise he proposed, which is described below.

When Lethaby started work for Shaw in the late summer of 1879, the most important of the many jobs already in progress was the scheme for the rebuilding of Flete, H. B. Mildmay's great country house in Devon. Soon after construction began, Shaw contracted a mysterious illness which was to keep him relatively inactive for nearly two years, until towards the end of 1881, when, for no obvious reasons, it disappeared. Much responsibility was therefore thrust on to Lethaby, a formidable challenge for a young

PLATE 27. St Anne's School, Streatham, 1884. A competition entry by Macartney, Newton and Lethaby.

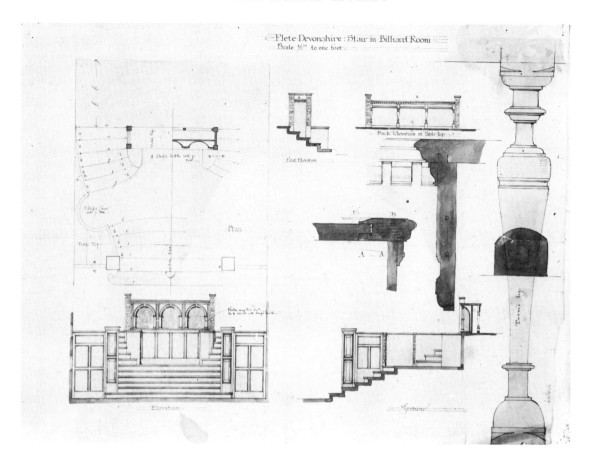

PLATE 28.   Flete, Devonshire. Stair in billiard room (½in.:1ft).

and inexperienced man. But he met it with joy; at once he was down on the site directing the work and designing all manner of fittings – woodwork panels, doorcases, fireplaces, the beautiful organ case for the reconstructed saloon and the stair in the billiard room (Plate 28). The friezes and ceilings, like the rest, are decorated with various versions of Jacobean 'antique work', which Henry Peacham, one of Lethaby's favourite authors, had described as, 'an unnatural or unorderly composition for delight's sake, of men, beasts, birds, fishes, flowers, etc., without rhyme or reason, for the greater variety you show in your invention the more you please'.[15] Somewhat similar in style was the decoration of Shaw's Alliance

PLATE 29.   The Alliance Insurance Building, St James's Street, London, 1882. Lethaby's drawing of Shaw's design.

Insurance building in St James's Street, London (Plate 29). 'It is', wrote Arthur Keen, 'one of the most fully detailed buildings in London, and remarkable for the way in which richness was secured without loss of breadth. Lethaby made most of the drawings for it . . . the first was made by Shaw himself . . . but all the detail work was done by Lethaby'.[16]

The most outstanding of the decorations in this style was the drawing-room chimney-piece for Cragside (Plate 30), the great house Shaw was building for Sir William Armstrong in Northumberland. The influence of his visit to the Loire Valley the previous year seems obvious too, but Lethaby himself probably thought of it as typically English. This style was, he argued in his first lecture, not so much an overlay of Italian detail on an earlier one, as was French work,

> but more of a radical change with squareness and symmetry in the composition, and nearly always an order . . . Other features are found . . . such as the obelisk form used as a pinnacle, rustication, etc., of the former, and strap work, quaint arabesques, curved gables, nondescript animal and human forms, and swags of fruit of the latter.

Then came his recipe for modern architecture:

> My views . . . [are] that, while keeping ourselves open to all new ideas to be gathered from French or any other styles, we should work in our own traditions, inclining as much as may be to purism, [here he is presumably referring to the antique] but admitting the truth of Bacon in the 'Essay on Beauty', when he says there is no exquisite beauty without some strangeness in its proportion.[17]

In Shaw's later churches Lethaby designed many of the wooden fittings, turning again to a modified form of the carved wooden decoration of the English Renaissance. A good example is the reredos for the Harrow Mission Church in Latimer Road, Harrow, where Lethaby designed many other works. Its general form repeats in a modified way the gabled façade of 42 Netherhall Gardens, a Shaw house of about the same date, which was probably designed by Lethaby, and the frame is decorated with a fretted and pierced classical scroll, though the motif is the formalized English wild rose, which was to become Lethaby's favourite decorative motif. The only designs Lethaby made that could be called Gothic were the tracery windows for Shaw's churches, but these, though they undoubtedly show a great understanding of mediaeval architecture, are primarily compass exercises of the kind he delighted in. James Heath, the builder of Shaw's church All Saints', Leek, noted in his diary: 'Myself, son and the Foreman are setting out the templates for north and south chancel windows. The tracery is very fine indeed. Mr W. L. Sugden says Mr Lythaby [sic] is the finest architectural draughtsman in the world.'[18]

His own work, which is of course especially revealing, since it was made largely to please himself, was, during this time, more adventurous and more exotic; he adopted a Hellenistic simplicity, inspired by

PLATE 30.   Drawing room chimney-piece, Cragside, Rothbury, Northumberland. The house was designed by Shaw for Sir William Armstrong, but Lethaby did much of the detailing, including this chimney-piece in white marble.

PLATE 31.   Design for the decoration of a room in panelling and paint.

the fashionable evocations of domestic life in ancient Greece by such painters as Leighton and Alma Tadema, whose house the members of the St George's Art Society had made a point of visiting (Plate 31). In his 1884 Goldsmiths Hall designs when he used the pseudonym 'Argentier', there appears the first hint of this new influence (Plates 32, 33). They comprise a toilet set consisting of a jewel casket, a hand mirror and a trinket tray and a toilet glass, which has two Greek silver coins set into its silver frame, in the manner of William Burges.

The expression of the classical architectural forms of simple geometrical solids appears at this time too, if we are to believe that the Shaw-attributed designs for the two lodge cottages at Shavington Hall are also his (Plate 34). Japanese art provided him with other forms to be explored, which first appear in the jewel casket; but a stronger influence still, though at first glance less evident, is that of Burges again. Burges's work on the borderline between fantasy and eclecticism and his decorations worked out to illustrate poetic themes must have attracted Lethaby. He never lost his fascination for Burges (Plate 35), describing him forty years later as 'play-acting, yet . . . earnest and thorough, a real make-believer'.[19] He

56

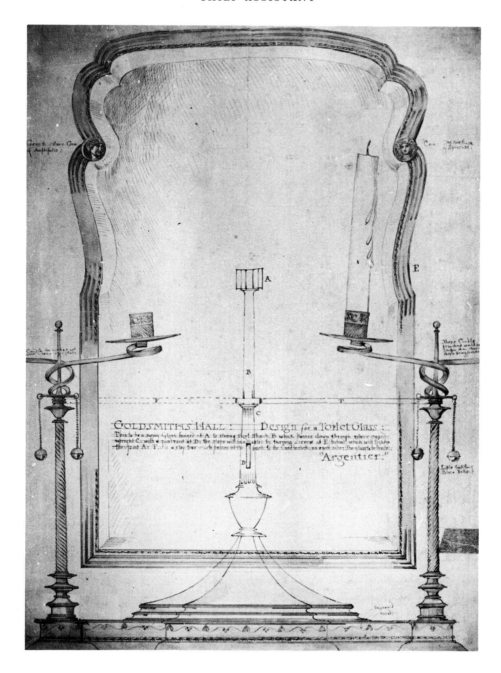

PLATE 32.   Design for a toilet glass.

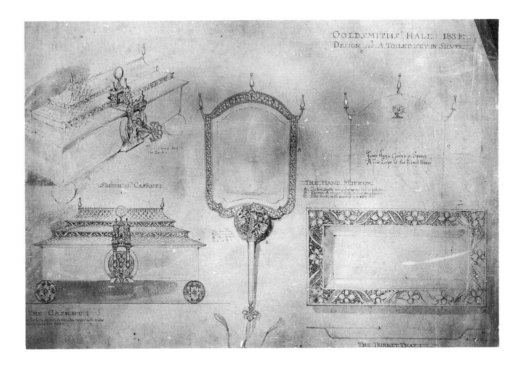

PLATE 33.   Design for a toilet set (Goldsmiths Hall Competition design).

went on to recall his still vivid impression of a visit to the Tower House, which Burges had built for himself. His description, which must convey something of his own state of mind at the time, reads:

> The house was exactly as he had made and furnished it – massive, learned, glittering, amazing . . . It was strange and barbarously splendid; none more than he [Burges] could be minutely intimate with the thought of old art or more saturated with a passion for colour, sheen and mystery. Here were silver and jade, onyx and malachite, bronze and ivory, jewelled casements, rock crystal orbs, marble inlaid with precious metals; lustre iridescence and colour everywhere; vermillion and black, gold and emerald; everywhere device and symbolism, and a fusion of Eastern feeling with his style.[20]

The hastily scribbled record of that visit and a drawing he had made of the gatehouse and drawbridge of Chaumont are the two sources[21] for the design of the fastening for the jewel casket mentioned above which, with its Japanese temple form, is bizarre indeed but no more so than any of Burges's own juxtapositions in miniature.

PLATE 34. Shavington Hall Lodge Cottage, Shropshire, 1885. One of a pair of cottages originally attributed to Shaw as part of his reconstruction of Shavington Hall. The general symmetry and four-squareness of the design suggest it to be the work of Lethaby.

PLATE 35. Chimney-piece. The Tower House, Holland Park, London, designed by William Burges. Drawing.

At about the same time as these experiments were going on, a far more complex idea was forming in Lethaby's teeming brain. One day in 1884, he was attending a ceremony in the parish church of St John the Baptist, Symondsbury, Dorset: the marriage of his friend Prior to the daughter of the vicar. This was probably the point of origin for an important commission, since it was in that year that the Udall family asked Lethaby and Prior to design a memorial window for the church (Plates 36, 37). Prior designed the four-light tracery and Lethaby the glass. Prior based his stonework on the existing fifteenth-century windows; but there was no local precedent for the complex, almost caballistic way in which Lethaby piled up the symbols of the Four Evangelists, one above the other, so that the earlier form is represented above the later one. Its meaning, rather like an acrostic, can be read across or up and down and was explained in Lethaby's laconic note scribbled on one of the cartoons:

Reading the window upwards we have these:
The Garden of Eden and its reference to the Fall
The Gospel
The Four Beasts around the Throne
The Cherubim
The Throne
Reading across – the Gospel History.[22]

The scheme was taken from 'The Four Evangelists', a chapter in Mrs Jameson's *Sacred and Legendary Art*; it is encyclopaedic in the sense that Lethaby has fitted into it most of the ways described in that book of depicting the fathers of the church. His note does not explain the significance of the four columns at the head of the window, but they must be a representation of the passage with which Mrs Jameson opened the chapter: 'On the Four Evangelists as witnesses and interpreters of a revealed religion the whole Christian church may be said to rest as upon four majestic pillars'. Lethaby's iconographic scheme is in fact exactly foreshadowed in Mrs Jameson's summing up, in which she described in historical sequence exactly how the ways of representing the Evangelists had changed:

First we have the mere *fact* – the four scrolls or four books . . . next the *idea*; the four rivers of salvation flowing from on high to fertilize the whole earth. Thirdly the *prophetic* symbol; the winged cherub of four-fold aspect. Next, the *Christian* symbol, the four 'beasts' in the Apocalypse, with or without angel wings . . . Then the *human* personages, each of venerable or inspired aspect as becomes the teacher and witness; and each attended by the scriptural emblem – no longer an emblem but an attribute – marking his individual vocation and character . . . and holding his gospel.[23]

This window not only deserves attention as a remarkable work of art; it also illustrates the stage

PLATE 36.   Stained-glass window depicting the Four Evangelists, St John the Baptist, Symondsbury, Dorset, 1885. The window was presented by the Udall family in memory of their parents.

PLATE 37.   St. Matthew. Stained-glass cartoon, full size. Pencil and wash.

Lethaby had reached at that time (1884) in his theory and practice. A decade later he would have regarded putting a modern window into an ancient building as an act of vandalism; but there is no evidence that the commission at this time occasioned him any moral conflict. He did not produce, as Prior had done, a 'Neo-Gothic' solution, for he already thought the style a dead duck. Instead, in what seems to have been a study of Burges's ways, he turned for inspiration to contemporary literature and art (particularly Burne-Jones's painting 'The Days of Creation'), and for execution to Worrel, Burges's own stained-glass maker.[24] Nor, I think, does the window conflict with his interest at that period in classicism. The design he evolved for the Four Evangelists was the curious outcome of an essentially rational and, for the 1880s, modern approach, combined with a wilful striving to be original.

Poetry was another source of inspiration and from it came the most strange and disturbing drawing ever done by Lethaby. This was 'The Beryl Shrine' (1889) (Plate 38), intended as an illustration of Rossetti's poem *Rose Mary*, a long, melodramatic 'romance' heavy with guilt, desire and punishment, and laden with decorative detail of the kind which abounds in Pre-Raphaelite poetry. Perhaps the idea for the drawing came to Lethaby from Joseph Knight, who, in his *Life of Rossetti* (1887) had written: 'The picture of Rose Mary passing by the secret path her feet had not trodden before, to the altar, and her destruction of the beryl, would supply a fine subject for a painting which Rossetti might have painted.'[25]

Rossetti's description of the Shrine reads,

The altar stood from its curved recess
In coiled serpent's life likeness:
Even such a serpent evermore
Lies asleep at the world's dark core
Till the last Voice shakes the sea and shore.

From the altar-cloth a book rose spread
And tapers burned at the altar head:
And there in the altar-midst alone
Twixt wings of sculptured beast unknown
Rose Mary saw the Beryl-stone.

Firm it sat 'twixt the hollowed wings,
As an orb sits in the hand of kings.

O'er the altar-sides on either hand
There hung a dinted helm and brand:[26]

But Lethaby's illustration differs in several important respects from the poem. It shows a column standing

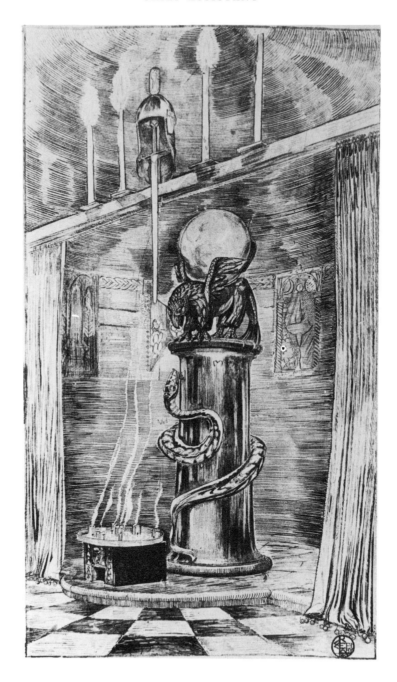

PLATE 38. 'The Beryl Shrine', an illustration to Dante Gabriel Rossetti's *Rose Mary*.

at the centre of a semicircular niche. A serpent is coiled round it, and standing at the top, with the Beryl (a magic crystal sphere) between its wings, is an Assyrian-looking monster. The serpent, which has human lips and eyes, owes nothing to Rossetti.

It originated in a sketch and a quotation from John Keats's poem, *Lamia*, which are found together in one of Lethaby's note books.[27] Because of its relevance to Lethaby's drawing the whole passage, which describes the Lamia, is given here but Lethaby himself only copied down those words within brackets.

> [*a palpitating snake,*
> *Bright, and cirque-couchant in a dusky brake.*
>
> *She was a gordian shape of dazzling hue,*]
> *Vermilion-spotted, golden, green and blue;*
> *Striped like a zebra, freckled like a pard,*
> *Eyed like a peacock, and all crimson barr'd;*
> *And full of silver moons, that, as she breathed,*
> *Dissolv'd, or brighter shone, or interwreathed*
> *Their lustres with the gloomier tapestries –*
> *So rainbow-sided, touch'd with miseries,*
> *She seem'd, at once, some penanced lady elf,*
> *Some demon's mistress, or the demon's self.*
> *Upon her crest she wore a wannish fire*
> [*Sprinkled with stars, like Ariadne's tiar:*]
> *Her head was serpent, but ah, bitter-sweet!*
> *She had a woman's mouth with all its pearls complete:*
> *And for her eyes: what could such eyes do there*
> *But weep, and weep, that they were born so fair?*
> *As Proserpine still weeps for her Sicilian air.*
> *Her throat was serpent, but the words she spake*
> *Came, as through bubbling honey, for Love's sake.*[28]

This poem tells of the dissolution of the woman-serpent Lamia before the 'brow-beating stare' of the philosopher Apollonius:

> *Do not all charms fly*
> *At the mere touch of cold philosophy?*

The superimposition of the Lamia image upon Rossetti's morbid effusion results in a picture which

64

testifies to Lethaby's interest in symbolism at this stage of his development. More powerfully, it suggests hidden terrors about the nature of which we can only speculate.

The designs and drawings discussed here, however interesting and successful, could be seen as purely exotic adventures, attempts to introduce some 'strangeness in the proportion', were it not for the intimations of a search for something beyond the expression of wilful individualism and formal fireworks. The importance given to symbolism suggests that they are also conscious attempts at the creation of a modern style with a profounder meaning than that endless combining and recombining of elements from the art of the past which formed the basis of so much contemporary art.

This survey of Lethaby's independent work has shown him reaching out into a world of thought and expression beyond the scope of his tasks as an assistant. It has also, however, provided sufficient evidence that Lethaby's enthusiasm for neo-classicism probably predated Shaw's own; it is therefore likely to have been Lethaby who led Shaw further into neo-classicism, rather than the reverse. By the mid-1880s he was designing much of the classical detail for Shaw's houses; and that must explain in part why he made so many studies of Georgian London in the search for source material, for accurate Renaissance source books were rare before the 1890s.[29] There can in any case have been few disagreements between the two. All the evidence we have speaks of harmony, of confidence and affection. Insofar as the actual quality of Shaw's buildings is concerned, we are on surer ground, as is proved by Lethaby's drawings and watercolour office details, which suggest that he had more feeling for that quality of colour and texture which comes from the sensitive selection and shaping of materials than had his principal. Thus the final particularity of Shaw's buildings must owe a great deal to Lethaby, for it is notable how much the standard of the detailing declined after he left.

The relationship between Lethaby and Shaw is of great interest. Though it never deepened into intimacy it was founded on mutual respect and admiration, and there is no doubt that for many years Lethaby was his principal's most devoted henchman. In work, their collaboration was so close that it is often impossible to tell their perspective drawings one from the other. Lethaby's respect was for 'not only a man of high gifts, but . . . also a most delightful person'.[30] In later years he was to reject many of Shaw's ideas, but to the man he remained loyalty itself. 'His respect for Shaw', wrote a colleague, 'was unbounded, but he would never discuss him with anyone, and if the subject was ever mentioned, he adroitly changed it.'[31] For his part, Shaw, though he trusted the younger man implicitly, 'had been known to say that he never pierced to the heart of Lethaby! At the end of twenty years he was no nearer knowing him than at the beginning.'[32] Characteristically generous, Shaw was ready to say that Lethaby knew more of building, ancient and modern, all over the world, than any man he had ever met, and to admit that on occasions he had been Lethaby's pupil.[33]

Though Shaw confessed that he did not understand Lethaby, their ideas about architecture, at least in those early days, must have been sufficiently alike, as also was their view of the architect as an isolated genius and creator of masterpieces. Lethaby recalled:

When first I had to do with the building trade . . . I thought of 'designing' as a mysterious 'gift', and awesomely hoped I had 'got it' or that it would come, for it was of the nature of inspiration. One had to know something of disagreeable building facts, and the employer's horrid requirements, but 'design' itself was the embodiment of vision by genius.[34]

It is this view which makes credible Lethaby's response, presumably to a client of Shaw's, who had complained, 'I cannot see, Mr Lethaby, that you have done a single thing that I asked you to do.' To this he replied, 'Well, you see, my first duty as an artist is to please myself.'[35]

During this period, the young architect was eagerly absorbing a great diversity of influences: from practice, from friendships and, not least, from travel. For his summer holiday after the first year in London, Lethaby crossed the Channel and, embarking on his initial Soane tour, set foot in France for the first time. From Dieppe he travelled through north-west Normandy and may have got as far as Mont-Saint-Michel before turning back. A year later, a vigorous watercolour from this expedition was shown at the Royal Academy.[36] The second visit, which he had to make in order to fulfil the requirements of the Soane prize, was put off for a year because, in 1881, he had won the Pugin Travelling Scholarship. In August, therefore, he set out for the west country, studying, as had been demanded by the scholarship, English mediaeval architecture and 'buildings designed on mediaeval principles' (a caveat he had cunningly written into his acceptance of the award, thus providing himself with a justification for his investigations of early Renaissance architecture)[37] (Plate 39). The following summer he was back in France, and the purpose of this trip, to study the Loire châteaux, was quite clear. The large number of drawings which survive enables his route to be traced in detail; as well as visiting Beauvais, Paris and Chartres, he went through Chambord, Blois, Amboise, Chenonceau, Tours, Azay-le-Rideau, Langeais, Saumur and Anger (Plates 40, 41).

Another influence, albeit of secondary significance, was that of formal study. Shaw, a great supporter of the Royal Academy and its Architectural Schools, expected his clerks to do their stint, and Lethaby was accordingly enrolled as a probationary student. Apart from producing some new and ultimately important friendships, it is unlikely that his time there influenced him much, except perhaps to focus his attention even more on the perenially insistent question of what style was most fitting for a modern architecture. It certainly convinced him, however, of the inadequacies of the education available for young architects.

Friendships then and later played a large and very important part both in the development of Lethaby's own personality and in the initiation of movements with which he was closely concerned. His first friends came from the group of Shaw's brilliant, idealistic young men who were known as 'the family',

PLATE 39.   Montacute House, Somerset, executed during Lethaby's Pugin Scholarship tour in 1881.
Watercolour.

PLATE 40.   Chartres, 1882. Soane tour in France. Pencil.

PLATE 41.   Blois, 1882. Soane tour in France. Watercolour.

and who joined in many activities outside office hours in those 'days of old Bloomsbury and horse buses'.[38] Others were to come his way soon, forming part of that 'advance guard of the young men of movement' the progressiveness of which, according to Reginald Blomfield, 'was largely due to Lethaby's influence, and the regard we all had for his personality'.[39] Besides Blomfield, this expanding group included, among the younger generation, Walter Maitland, Alfred Powell, the Barnsley brothers, Ernest Gimson, Sidney Cockerell and Detmar Blow; among the older were Sedding, Spiers and Webb.

No friends, it seems, were made outside the profession, and even meetings with professional friends

69

were occasioned by their desire to work together. But many of the friendships formed in this way were important and lasting, and one of the most valuable was that with Beresford Pite. One evening Attwood Slater, a fellow R.A. student, introduced Lethaby to Pite in the South Kensington Museum's Green Dining Room that had been decorated by Morris & Co. Walking back to their Bloomsbury lodgings they decided to form a sketch club and work together; the arrangement proved rewarding for both.[40] Another very valuable friendship was with John Sedding whose personality as much as his architectural style appealed to Lethaby. He was 'a most friendly and sympathetic man, with moods easily falling into seriousness or gaiety – one could talk with Sedding from the heart about realities'.[41]

Lethaby did not meet Ernest Gimson, who was, of all the men of his generation, to influence him the most, until one evening early in 1889, when Alfred Powell brought him round to Lethaby's lodgings for tea. From that time they were often together, studying, arguing over socialism and over Auberon Herbert's philosophy of individualism, known as Voluntaryism, that attracted Gimson; and looking at old and new buildings, including Webb's Joldwyns. Gimson drew his friend's interests away from the exotic and from the fascination of Europe's great buildings to the modest and commonplace habitations of England, which, a direct expression of tools and material, were unconscious of style.

One day when out walking in Knole Park, where no doubt they had gone to look at the plasterwork decoration in the Prior's House, Gimson and Lethaby ran into Sidney and Leslie Cockerell, Thomas Rooke the painter, and Detmar Blow.[42] This was Lethaby's first meeting with Sidney Cockerell; though they did not become intimates until the latter moved, two years after, to Gray's Inn, it then became one of the firmest friendships, broken only by Lethaby's death forty years later. The son of a coal merchant, Cockerell was then still in the family business, but shortly afterwards he went to work for William Morris, becoming in due course the secretary of the Kelmscott Press.

A subject certainly discussed on the walk in Knole Park is described in an extract from one of Gimson's letters:

> Lethaby, Blow and I are joining together in a little business. We are going to take a shop in Bloomsbury for the sale of furniture of our own design and make, besides other things, such as plaster friezes, leadwork, needlework, etc. etc. We are all to have bedrooms and offices in the same building and to share expenses.[43]

By the end of July they had got as far as having 'two shops in view',[44] but this scheme was soon abandoned for the relatively less ambitious one which got under way in October in the form of the joint concern known as 'Kenton & Co.'.

Though Lethaby had set up for himself in May 1889, he continued to work for Shaw three days a week;[45] but the hour was rapidly approaching when he must have realized the inconsistencies of what he was doing – with one hand designing in an historic style for his ex-principal and the other searching out a 'modern' style without such reference. Although his own account of this first 'little business' was written many years later, it does suggest that at the time he was aware of the conflicting practices, for he describes how they were to join 'in a sort of architects' shop, something outside the deadly dreariness of the respectable offices, with framed perspectives on the walls and clerks slaving away in the background'.[46]

In May 1883 some young architects from Shaw's office gathered at Ernest Newton's offices at 14 Hart Street, WC1, for the purpose of founding a society to hold monthly discussions on art and architecture. They decided, half in fun, to call it the St George's Art Society [47] after Hawksmoor's church on the other side of the street. The Society had at most a dozen members who, though they conducted its proceedings with much mock formality, discussed with great seriousness every aspect of architecture. It lasted for about three years; its chief importance lies in the fact that, during this period, it founded the Architectural Illustration Society and was the prime mover in the founding of the Art-Workers' Guild.

The Architectural Illustration Society grew out of members' dissatisfaction with the poor and unrepresentative quality of the illustrations to be found in the building press. At their fourth meeting, they decided to publish a sketch book, to be edited by Lethaby. According to Weir, 'This not having been found feasible, they formed a small group they called *The Architectural Illustration Society*, which arranged with one of the weekly journals, *The Architect*, to publish selected works.'[48] What little evidence there is suggests that this Society was run by Horsley, Macartney and Lethaby.[49] Throughout its existence – from 1886 to 1893 – it published some 600 drawings and photographs of old and new work, and topographical studies, though ordinary commercial buildings were excluded. As an unofficial platform for the architects of the Art-Workers' Guild it carried on a remarkable campaign for better architecture, for the work published – much of it by Guildsmen – was in the main modern vernacular building of high quality.

Horsley and Macartney did most to launch, in 1884, the Art-Workers' Guild, which had started with a discussion on whether

the aims of [the St George's Art Society] might not have a wider field. Art and Architecture were drifting asunder. Was it possible to bring them together again? Close connection had been historically necessary to both. Was this now to be accepted as mere ancient history? To all seeming the Societies which had the right to foster the unity of the arts, had come to emphasize their distinctions. On the one hand was the Royal Academy, chartered for Architecture, Painting, and Sculpture alike, but now giving its favour almost entirely to oil-painting; allowing to architects a membership of five out of a total of seventy, and it would seem selecting these more often on the basis of culture or professional success, than in view of the merits of their art. On the other there was the Institute of British Architects, whose theory of architecture had driven from its doors most of those architects whose art was acknowledged; which had forbidden to Artists a personal interest in their handicrafts, and had opened its doors so widely to business that Surveyors had become the largest element of its body. Still the unity of Art, and the place of architecture therein, supplied the principle on which the most thorough artists worked. There were many such who were neither the oil-painters of the Academy nor the Surveyors of the Institute, but craftsmen in Architecture, Painting, Sculpture, and the kindred Arts, and on the basis of a principle they could be brought together. Such an Association would be the body of the Art of the time, and would hand on its tradition to another age.[50]

Most of its founders had had high hopes that it would play a public rôle but, despite its becoming the first organized group of designers and the most important source of arts and crafts teachers, this was not to be. After the early days there was little public action, even on important questions connected with the arts where its voice should have been heard. While this may have been due to apathy,[51] it is also possible that the impotence resulted from the widely different political views of the Guildsmen. Lethaby did a great deal of the preliminary committee work that went into founding the Guild, putting forward a proposal of what he hoped the Guild might become; and finally, in 1911, he became its Master. Had Lethaby's proposals been implemented it would have been a very different body from the exclusive club that it became. It should be, wrote Lethaby,

> an Associated Art-Society of Painters, Sculptors, Architects, Designers, and actual workers in the minor arts, with the object (1) of promoting association and forwarding the cause of Art, (2) of helping Decorative Art, and especially restoring certain art handiworks now almost lost or entirely forgotten, (3) of spreading a knowledge of principles among the several trades and the public. And this, in the interest of the Society itself, to an understanding of one another's Arts by the Members of it, and secondly, in the interest of Monumental Art, as arousing public opinion, especially in the matter of architecture; and also in the matter of the institution of a National Gallery of Representative Modern Painting and Sculpture. The Society should discuss current Art; permanent collections should be formed by it; each craft should arrange for lectures on its own methods and have loan exhibitions of its works; and finally, the instruction of the public should be attempted by tracts, pamphlets, letters and articles.[52]

Had the Guild realized the hopes of its more progressive members it is unlikely that they would have founded the Arts and Crafts Exhibition Society in 1888. Although it was primarily committed to mounting exhibitions, the members of this Society, who sought recognition not as artists or architects but as designers, made it the most important organization in shaping the Arts and Crafts movement. More outspoken and militant than the Guild, in which designers – a new profession – were in the minority, it expressed in its lectures and publications a progressive and often socialist point of view. Lethaby, who eventually became its president, devoted much of his time to its well-being and undoubtedly did much to shape its policies, at least in the early days.

One of the important friendships already mentioned was that with the architect J. D. Sedding, whom Lethaby first met during the discussions which led to the founding of the Art-Workers' Guild. John Sedding, a passionate admirer of Ruskin, was humble and unworldly, with a great love of nature and an understanding of old buildings, particularly those of his native west country. Both his personality and the free and original Gothic style of his architecture appealed to the young men of the Guild, many of whom – including, at the time, Lethaby – felt that this style indicated a way forward. Henry Wilson, a man then close to Lethaby and a sharer of many of his enthusiasms, wrote:

> The best work of John Sedding will, I think, never be fully known . . . It was not what he did . . . but what he made others do. His claim . . . does not rest . . . on the invention of a new style [but] on his personal influence, on his inspiring enthusiasm, on the intellectual stimulus he provided. Certain natures flash like luminaries across the mental sky, warming us in their passage, lighting our way. Their path shines with borrowed radiance long after the source has gone. Sedding was one of these. He was a radiant centre of artistic activity; a focus of creative fire; a node of magnetic force. Enthusiasm streamed from him, and, like electric waves, vitalized the spiritual atmosphere and raised the mental temperature of those around him. The exponent in his time of personal art, his example taught all to care little for the grammarian of art, for the classifier, or the scholarly artists.[53]

Lethaby saw a great deal of Sedding between 1887 and 1890, for they had planned that he should illustrate Sedding's book on Saxon and Norman architecture; together they went to many places in search of material, spending their 1888 summer holiday visiting Northampton, Hexham and Carlisle. Though Lethaby did many drawings for the book, it was never published: Sedding probably did not complete the manuscript. The friendship lasted until Sedding's early death in 1891.

The influence of this contact can be seen in Lethaby's essay, published in 1889, 'Of the "Motive" in Architectural Design'. With the single exception of the lecture on Renaissance architecture mentioned earlier, it marks the beginning of his long literary career, initially as historian and theorist, latterly as critic and propagandist for a more rational architecture and society. The essay discusses, rather incoherently, questions that he, and no doubt other members of the Guild, found absorbing. Architectural education was, he wrote, limited in that it included no critical examination of theories of design. The only such theory indeed ever propounded was 'that old dogma of utilitarianism, of which Pugin was the exponent'. To this was added an account of the past styles of architecture. Training consisted of learning to design a convenient plan and then to select an appropriate style for the elevation. This, he argued, was nonsense. Architecture defined thus was both dreary and dead: it was not a question of styles but of Style. The principle of real design was selection and an

> expression of our instinct for order and beauty, life, and right, which no formula will make clear

– but once seen, we feel there is a common instinct for its enjoyment, and call it 'art' or 'style' – it is this alone which, expressed in building, is Architecture. And the end to set before ourselves is this sensitiveness to beauty.[54]

The principle, said Lethaby, could be understood through an ever-increasing experience of the practical conditions of building construction and an intense study of the past; thus could be understood 'the compromise between the thought and its realization'.

> It is, however, the power to embody the old principle to the ever-new conditions . . . distinguishing and setting aside that which does not form part of the living thought of the time, which is the true objective of the true architect.

> Yes, but how should an architect really design? I fancy it must be in the way the painter told Mr Ruskin he composed his picture – he knew what he wanted to do, and did it. An architect wants to try something which he sees, foresees, *invents,* in a mental picture. Form, expression, colour; he has a problem to work out – a motive.[55]

In 1889 Lethaby published two delightful essays entitled 'Some Northamptonshire steeples' which were written as a commentary on a set of drawings by Raffles Davison. In them he attacks the social exclusiveness of art since the Renaissance and states the folly of restoration. A Gothic building, he says, is itself history. It is not like a history book *about* the Middle Ages, it *is* the Middle Ages.

> Does the learning, sometimes crude, and the caprice, often vulgar, of our Renaissance, the Elizabethan age, compare with the work, perfectly modest and yet full of gaiety, the Art, unconscious but not unthoughtful, of the thirteenth and the fourteenth centuries, and the fifteenth, less perfect, but more human and humoursome . . . ?[56]

> In the sixteenth century the Renaissance changes the whole object and temper of Art, substituting the trained skill of scholars for the traditional methods of the trades, an Art addressed to the cultured and not for the people – of rules instead of feeling. Yet withal the change had to come, and its method must be ours yet awhile; an Art of culture, individual and arbitrary, but, if earnestly thought, not without avail.[57]

His own desire was for an art which should have, in its own contemporary terms, that quality of being 'unconscious but not unthoughtful' which he had admired in the art of the Middle Ages. This desire finds expression in the quotation with which the second essay ends: 'Poesy is more ancient than the *artificiale* of the Greeks and Latines, coming by instinct of nature, and used by the savage and uncivall, who were before all science and civilitie.'[58]

The influence of William Morris, which is discussed elsewhere, and of John Ruskin is obvious in these essays. As to the latter Lethaby had by then clearly changed his mind about Ruskin whom he said he had discovered in his youth but had for many years read with 'an amused contempt'.[59] The process may well not have started until in 1888 he read, or possibly, under the guidance of Sedding, re-read that all-important essay 'The Nature of Gothic' from *The Stones of Venice* which Morris considered to be one of the 'very few necessary and inevitable utterances of the century'.

Seven years had passed between the publication of Lethaby's first lecture, in praise of the Renaissance, and the essays which have just been considered. It is obvious that in that period his ideas had greatly changed: once an advocate of neo-Elizabethan as an appropriate style for modern architecture, he now made such practices the main object of attack.

It was to this point that Lethaby had come at the end of his career as Shaw's assistant, a time of great personal development and change. More fundamental changes were yet to come.

CHAPTER THREE

ARCHITECT AND CRAFTSMAN: I

Workmanship in Theory
and Practice

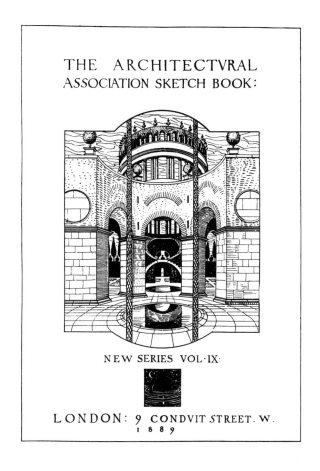

THE ARCHITECTVRAL
ASSOCIATION SKETCH BOOK:

NEW SERIES VOL·IX·

LONDON: 9 CONDVIT STREET. W.
1 8 8 9

PLATE 42.   Frontispiece from the *Architectural Association Sketch Book,* 1889. The design is influenced both by the illustrations in the *Hypnerotomachia* and, in its irrational space, by the descriptions of mysterious and imaginary places.

ON 30 MAY 1889 LETHABY LEFT SHAW'S OFFICE
TO START HIS OWN PRACTICE IN AN ATTIC OFFICE AT 9 HART STREET (NOW
BLOOMSBURY WAY).[1] HE WAS JUST ROUND THE CORNER FROM SHAW AND A
stone's throw from the offices of his friends Newton, Horsley and Macartney. For another two years he continued to work three days a week for his old principal. For the rest of the time, he was busy on a wide variety of tasks: work for friends, imaginative illustrations, articles for the architectural journals and the writing of two books, soon to be published: *Architecture, Mysticism, and Myth,* and *Leadwork.* He also produced designs for work in many media to be made by several firms for the Arts and Crafts exhibitions.

The work of John Ruskin and his later contemporary William Morris, fusing as it did the realms of art and politics, was profoundly significant for artists of the late nineteenth century. Lethaby was deeply indebted to both: to Ruskin for theory, to Morris for both theory and practice. He has left no record of his introduction to Socialism but soon after coming to London, in the days of the first Socialists, he attended meetings, addressed by Philip Webb, of the Labour Emancipation League – a group of Radical–Socialist workmen.[2] Presently he was taking an active part and recruiting others for the Cause, but how long his direct involvement lasted is unknown. In later life, although Morris's thought remained for him of the greatest political importance, his militancy was of a different kind. But undoubtedly his early involvement in Socialism was a strong factor in the all important stylistic break with the past.

The break came in February 1891, when Lethaby gave up both his office and his lodgings and moved to chambers at 2 Gray's Inn Square, WC1.[3] This move marked the parting of the ways with Shaw for, though they remained on the best of terms, Lethaby never again worked for his old principal. By joining the 'Square Circle', as he called it, he threw in his lot with Philip Webb, Sidney Barnsley and Gimson, all of whom lived at Gray's Inn Square. Webb became Lethaby's 'own particular prophet', for whom he felt the 'most uncritical admiration and reverence . . . and in his life I find a means of judging my own'.[4] Friends of both thought that they were 'exactly the same type, unselfseeking, far sighted, generous minded and righteous men'.[5] But there were great differences too. Though Webb had far less of that rational intellectual quality so notable in Lethaby, he was greatly admired for his force and imagination. 'I have found in myself sometimes the thought', wrote Lethaby, 'that Webb was a funny old buffer who somehow has a way of doing things in building . . . But his power of getting at greatness was his central self.'[6] They were neighbours during the 1890s, a decade which ended with Webb's retirement and in this close contact, through numerous conversations, Webb became the touchstone that enabled Lethaby to define his own more radical theories and interpret those of the older man, which he eventually set down in that splendid biography *Philip Webb and His Work.* More than anyone else, Webb changed Lethaby's

79

ideas about building, and perhaps about life too, though in the end he was to carry Webb's thought to a conclusion that even Webb hardly recognized.

At this point can be seen the emergence of another interest, which was to become a passion and a lifelong concern. In September 1891, proposed by William Morris and seconded by Ernest Gimson, Lethaby was elected a member of the Society for the Preservation of Ancient Buildings.[7] Within a short time he was on the committee, where he became as intimate with Morris as his shy nature would allow. He was to become one of the greatest authorities in the world on building conservation, and his long work on the fabric of Westminster Abbey must have contributed to the almost universal acceptance of the principle of conservation rather than restoration.

The nineties saw Lethaby's emergence as a writer. He had published his first article at the age of twenty-seven; but not until he left Shaw's office did he begin to produce the constant stream of work which showed him as one of the most prolific writers of his time on architecture and the allied arts. It is appropriate to consider some of these writings in this chapter since his writing is so closely linked with his work. His increasing impatience with the endless combining and recombining of elements of historic styles that was the mode of expression of contemporary architecture, coupled with the conviction that architectural form had to have a significance deeper than the aesthetics of style, led him to examine what other meanings architecture had had in the past. He dug into the myths and legends of sacred buildings – particularly those which regarded the temple as a microcosm – which he put together in his first book *Architecture, Mysticism, and Myth* (1891). This puzzling, inaccurate but ultimately influential work advanced for the first time the theory that ancient architecture symbolized in a variety of different ways man's conception of the universe. In the course of his research he stumbled across that curious and celebrated Italian Renaissance romance, the *Hypnerotomachia Poliphili*, principally famous for its woodcut illustrations. By the end of the 1880s these illustrations had already become the source for some of Lethaby's designs (Plates 42, 43 and 47).

In *Architecture, Mysticism, and Myth*, he sought to discover the reasons for certain architectural forms of the past, 'to set out from the architect's point of view the basis of certain ideas common in the architecture of many lands and religions, the purpose behind structure and form which may be called the esoteric principles of architecture'.[8] Its writing was inspired by a desire to enrich the sources of contemporary design, and thus the vocabulary of contemporary architects and designers, outside the restraints of historicism. He seems to have started collecting material at about the time he was working on the Symondsbury window, when he was studying Anna Jameson's *Sacred and Legendary Art*, a work which has certain parallels with his own. His interpretation of the evidence was inspired by Herbert Spencer's dictum that, on the basis of the data available to him, primitive man made essentially reasonable inferences about his world. The introduction states that the

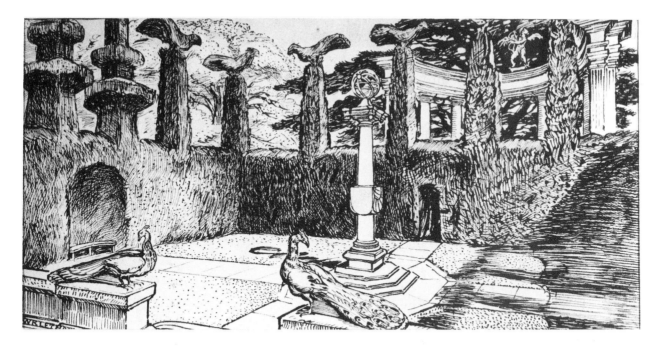

PLATE 43.   A garden enclosed, 1889. Pen and ink. Reproduced in J. Sedding, *Garden-Craft Old and New,*
Kegan Paul, Trench, Trübner & Co., 1892, plate 8.

history of architecture as usually written, with its theory of utilitarian origins . . . [and] the
adjustments of form to the conditions of local circumstances . . . is rather the history of
building: of 'Architecture' it may be, in the sense that we often use the word, but not that
Architecture which is the synthesis of the fine arts, the commune of all crafts.[9]

The real purpose of architecture, Lethaby argued, was on the contrary to satisfy the intellect by
embodying thought in forms, realized unconsciously by a desire for certain aesthetic qualities such as
symmetry, smoothness and sublimity, and consciously by a desire to embody metaphysical concepts in
comprehensible symbols. Symbolism, in other words, must play a vital part in any credible theory of
architecture. The 'ultimate facts behind all architecture' were:

Firstly the similar needs and desires of men; secondly on the side of structure, the necessities
imposed by materials, and the physical laws of their erection and combination; thirdly, on the
side of style, nature. It is of this last that I propose to write; the influence of the known and
imagined facts of the universe on architecture.[10]

81

He followed Vitruvius with his first two 'facts'; but his third was quite different: instead of 'Beauty' or 'Delight' he offered 'style', which he equated with 'nature'. And as an example of the workings of this third 'fact' he instanced the temple idea, which was to set up

> a local reduplication of the . . . World Temple itself – a sort of model to scale, its form governed by the science of the time, it was a heaven, an observatory and an almanack. Its foundation was a sacred ceremony, the time carefully chosen by augury, and its relation to the heaven defined by observation. Its place was exactly below the celestial prototype; like that it was sacred, like that it was strong, its foundations could not be moved, if they were placed four-square to the walls of the firmament.[11]

Thus the temple, in mirroring man's philosophical ideas, was an expression of the 'known or imagined facts of the Universe' and could therefore be taken, in Lethaby's reasoning, as defining 'nature' in a totally new way. It was a concept that was to have a great effect on contemporary thought and practice.

The introduction, a clear exposition of the socio-historical nature of symbolism, concluded with a demand that the symbolism of modern architecture be comprehensible, rational and egalitarian. There could be nothing esoteric about modernity. But the main text contradicted this noble sentiment. In it we find, for example, the author speaking with evident approval of Burges's design for 'a modern ceiling with a real feeling for mystery'.[12] At the same time his own designs, like that for the font cover for St John the Baptist, Low Bentham, which he described as being in a 'style for to-day',[13] are frequently composed of mysterious and hidden symbols. Thus, both by word and deed, he contradicts himself, speaking of a modernity which looked, Janus-like, two ways at once.

This confusion is then compounded by his equating, quite wrongly, mystery with mysticism – a mistake as common perhaps now as then. There was, as Lethaby later admitted, nothing whatever about mysticism in the work.[14] Nevertheless, however distant, there are affinities with the contemporary Symbolist movement, but Lethaby's intentions were the reverse of Oscar Wilde's who wrote in *The Picture of Dorian Gray* (published in the same year as *Architecture, Mysticism, and Myth*): 'Those who go beneath the symbol do so at their peril. Those who read the symbol do so at their peril.'[15] But, while Lethaby's attempt to formulate a rational theory of symbolism was perfectly successful, he could not escape the influence of the contemporary *fin de siècle* climate, with its wide but superficial interest in mysticism, which affected his style. In his attempts to convey his enchantment with archaic secrets, his style became in some passages overcharged with imaginative phrases, and his meaning, perhaps half deliberately, obscured.

These contradictions make the book difficult to come to terms with. In fact, one cannot do so, at least not until it is realized that paradox was an essential part of Lethaby's complex personality. The book, however, holds a unique place in the history of architectural thought, which had until then concerned

PLATE 44. Design for a town mansion by J. A. Slater. Dedicated to Lethaby, it shows the influence of *Architecture, Mysticism, and Myth.*

itself almost exclusively either with theories of utility or with aesthetics, for it was the first to try to substantiate the then novel idea that the actual forms and decorations of buildings expressed philosophical and psychological ideas. It made little direct contribution to the objective study of symbolism, since the analysis of the evidence, which was itself a rag-bag of first- and second-hand authorities, was uncritical and inexpert. Had architects and designers been more learned, it might not have had the wide influence that it undoubtedly did have on Arts and Crafts decoration (Plates 44, 45, 46). This book is, however, much more than a work of faulty scholarship, for to read it even today is to find there a quality of mystery and

83

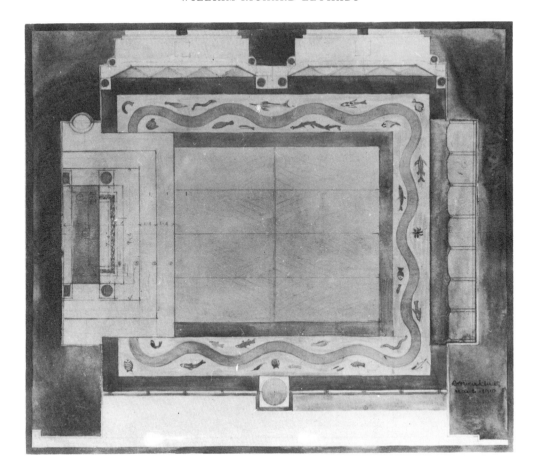

PLATE 45.   Design for the pavement of the Chapel of St Andrew, Westminster Cathedral, by R. Schultz Weir.
Pencil and watercolour.

romance which still conjures up a compelling vision of the transcendental Work Temple 'built without sound of hammer or tool of iron'.[16]

As soon as he was free of his assistant status, Lethaby launched into a bewildering variety of designs in the most adventurous and experimental styles which must have been the work of lengthy gestation. Though some of the sources (for example, Hellenism or English seventeenth-century furniture) are the familiar ones, others are quite new. Some arise from the researches he made for his first book, others are probably the result of the influence of Sedding, Morris and Ruskin. But each design was a conscious, even wilful attempt to be modern – to break away from the constraints of contemporary fashion. The various

PLATE 46. Wall-hanging, with its principal motif the tree of life, designed and embroidered by May Morris (after the influence of *Architecture, Mysticism, and Myth*) for Theodosia Middlemore, 1894. Formerly in Melsetter House, now in the V&A.

threads from which they were woven can be picked out by analysing the following: a font and font cover (Plate 47), a fanciful reconstruction of The Chrysotriclinium at Constantinople (Plate 48), a stained glass window, 'Spring' (Plate 49), a walnut cabinet (Plate 50) and a design for a cast-iron fire grate (Plate 51), all produced between 1888 and 1890.

The font and font cover were for the church at Low Bentham, Yorkshire, and the commission was probably passed on by Shaw, who had restored the church the year before. The source for Lethaby's astonishing design was the *Hypnerotomachia Poliphili* which he describes as a 'collection of all the architectural wonders of the world'.[17] Like *Le Roman de la Rose*, this book is a gothic tale of allegory and adventure, but written in the dawn of Renaissance Italy; the romance of a dream world, full of the monumental ruins of the classical world, through which a lover seeks his love. Probably no other book could have been better calculated to excite him, a man with his head already stuffed with architectural myths and legends, but at the same time aware of the conflict between the poetry of the past and his prosaic present and just the same kind of conflict that Keats had imagined in *Lamia*.

The font itself is a monolithic basin, unembellished save for an incised aquatic plant scroll round the top, which makes a studied contrast to the lightness and complexity of its cover. This has six fretted brackets decorated alternatively with wild roses and honeysuckle which support a canopy of two hexagonal shapes, one above the other. The larger of these carries two tiers of pinnacles supporting gilded, half-opened pomegranates; the other is a spiret topped with a gilded armillary sphere. Though in general it resembles a free rendering of a sixteenth-century form, its actual inspiration was an illustration in the *Hypnerotomachia* (Plate 52), of a hexagonal building which is described as standing on a monolithic base of the same configuration; with six columns that support an architrave, frieze and cornice with neither ornament or moulding, all being very simple. Above them is a cupola which terminates in a chimney so grooved as to permit daylight to fall directly into the round vault at the centre of the base.[18] There is no such exact source for the armillary sphere and spiret, but the book is full of such devices. It could be argued, however, that the two are no more than an imaginative representation of the sun's rays falling into the font – a typical Lethaby touch! But for a suitable *symbol* he went back to Mrs Jameson, who had explained that the 'pomegranate' bursting open, the seeds visible, was an emblem for the future – of hope in immortality (Plate 53).[19]

'The Entrance to the Chrysotriclinium' is a fanciful representation of the sanctuary of the Imperial cult in Constantine's palace and in its suggestion of poetry, mystery and awful might is no more fantastic than the verbal descriptions of the building. Like the font he designed for Shaw's All Saints' church, Leek (Plate 54), it foreshadows the coming popularity of the neo-Byzantine style that Lethaby helped, unwittingly, to bring about. 'Spring' is the title of a sash window design in grisaille glass: in the centre of the lower window, within an oval, a Pre-Raphaelite girl kneels on the flower-strewn grass gazing down into

PLATE 47. Font and canopy, St John the Baptist, Low Bentham, Yorkshire, 1890. The bowl is alabaster, the cover walnut. Lethaby's intention in the design of the canopy, which was strongly influenced by the illustration in the *Hypnerotomachia* (see Plate 52), was 'to bring the cord of suspension down to the actual cover, the very light upper woodwork encircling this cord, so that it should not be (as is usual) a sort of spire hung up by the finial. As to style, it was hoped that it might be of today.'

PLATE 48.   'The Entrance to The Chrysotriclinium', 1889.

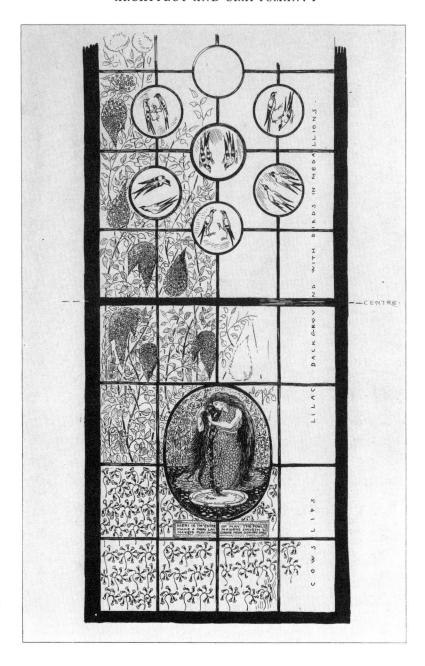

PLATE 49.   'Spring'. Design for a sash window in grisaille glass for a house in Bromley, Kent, 1890. 'A modern window for a modern house', wrote Lethaby.

PLATE 50. A corner in the Third Arts and Crafts Exhibition, 1890. (From left to right) Green-stained chest of drawers, designed by Ford Madox Brown; rosewood occasional table, by Lethaby; corner cabinet, by Blomfield; oak cabinet, by Gimson; walnut cabinet, by Lethaby, with his rosewood china stand upon it. Lethaby's pieces were made by Marsh, Jones and Cribb of Leeds.

PLATE 51.   Cast-iron fireplace, with reliefs representing indoor and outdoor life, modelled by Emmaline Halse. Manufactured by the Coalbrookedale Iron Company and exhibited at the Third Arts and Crafts Exhibition, 1890.

PLATE 52.   A wood-cut illustration from Francesco Colonna's
Hypnerotomachia Poliphili, printed by
Aldus Manutius, Venice, 1499.

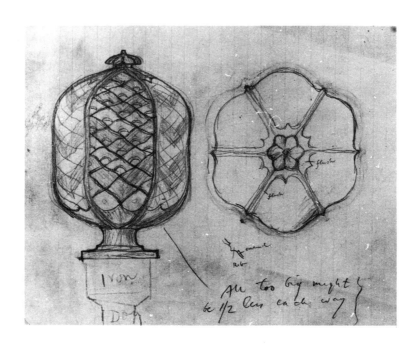

PLATE 53.   Design for a pomegranate for the font canopy of St John the Baptist, Low Bentham, Yorkshire.

PLATE 54.   Font designed for Shaw's All Saints' church, Leek, Staffordshire, *c.* 1886.

a pond. Beneath is a quotation from the *Romance of Merlin*. The panes below the oval are painted with cowslips and those above with flowering lilacs that extend up into the upper window, where paired birds are placed in clear medallions. Design and decoration are such that the birds appear among the flowers when the window is opened. Here the source for both flora and fauna is Nature herself. It was probably the first design Lethaby ever made that went to the 'essence of all things'.

The piece of furniture which best exemplifies his work in this period is a superb cabinet in walnut veneer, with straight sides and heavy moulding at top and bottom; it stands on bun feet and complex curvilinear mouldings are fixed to its four doors (Plate 50). Its sober elegance and general form look back to the English seventeenth century, but the decorative forms – the mouldings and crossbanding – are applied in a way that gives the piece a decidedly novel look.

Finally comes the cast-iron fireplace. As with the previous piece, the intention was to build on an earlier tradition and be modern, without noticeable reference to the past, but again the inspiration is from nature and, in this case, from the eighteenth century.

All these examples are the outcome of some thoughts which, at about the time, he set down:

Directly we think of design, a crowd of questions appeal for answers, questions probably enough that have no answer or answers as many as those who enquire . . . the following interest me as matters to enquire into:

1. The 'motive', or central thought in design.
2. What is that dignity in the realization we speak of as largeness, breadth, style?
3. The use and limits of a study of past art.
4. The reference to nature.[20]

This debate particularly on his third point was, of course, not restricted to Lethaby and to his own generation. To what degree, it was asked, was the revival of the forms of past art a legitimate activity and should not an attempt be made to find new forms appropriate to the new (a word that was then becoming increasingly popular) age. Among the architects of the older generation Sedding was rare in thinking so too. He wrote:

We shall have designs *by* living men *for* living men – something that expresses fresh realizations of sacred facts, personal broodings, skill, joy in Nature – in grace of form and gladness of colour . . . We must clothe modern ideas in modern dress; adorn our design with living fancy . . . There is hope in honest error; none in the perfections of the mere stylist.[21]

To talk in these terms was easy enough but the actual creation of modern artifacts was another matter. A more profound understanding of the relationship of art to life was needed and that had been supplied by Ruskin in the marvellous essay 'The Nature of Gothic'. But it seems that the implications of his words for contemporary society were perhaps not clearly understood until Morris pointed them out: 'The essence of what Ruskin then taught us was simple enough, like all great discoveries. It was really nothing more recondite than this, that the art of any epoch must of necessity be the expression of its social life'. Ruskin's key passage, which Lethaby was to quote, argued that 'the great leading error of modern times' was founded on two mistaken suppositions:

the first, that one man's thoughts can be, or ought to be, executed by another man's hands; the second, that manual labour is a degradation when it is governed by intellect . . . We are always in these days endeavouring to separate the two, we want one man to be always thinking and another to be always working. Now it is only by labour that thought can be made healthy, and only by thought that labour can be made happy; and the two cannot be separated with impunity.[22]

The moral spanner which Ruskin had thrown into the works – the debate on aesthetics – meant that it could never again be the same. Morris was profoundly affected by Ruskin's essay which, when he reprinted it at the Kelmscott Press, he introduced in the following way:

It is one of the most important things written by the author and in future days will be considered as one of the very few necessary and inevitable utterances of the century. To some of us . . . it seemed to point out a new road on which the world should travel [as there is] no other way out of the folly and degradation of Civilisation. For the lesson which Ruskin here teaches us is that art is the expression of man's pleasure in labour, that it is possible for man to rejoice in his work, for strange as it may seem to us today, there have been times when he did rejoice in it, and lastly, that unless man's work once again becomes a pleasure to him, the token of which change will be that beauty is once again a natural and necessary accompaniment of productive labour, all but the worthless must toil in pain and therefore live in pain.[23]

The lesson of Ruskin's words was clear enough to Morris who threw himself into the political struggle for a revolutionary change in society. Clear to him, by implication too, was the proposition that there could be neither a living art nor architecture until capitalism was replaced by socialism. Morris, in other words, moved the debate on to another plane, giving scant consideration to the question of a contemporary style. It was not that he thought such questions to be irrelevant; they were, under present social conditions, unanswerable.

But other comrades – Lethaby was one – were not so sure. For him, with his fundamentalist background, who had drunk deeply of Ruskin, it was primarily an ethical question urgently demanding an answer. To understand how he resolved it, as far as was then possible, we must turn to a comparison between his words and his work. By 1890 he had two propositions in mind: first, that since style was socially determined it was not possible honestly to continue to borrow forms from the past; second, that as far as he personally was concerned the division of labour manifest in his own work was morally indefensible.

Action on the first proposition did not, however, mean a complete break with the past – quite the contrary in fact. But a separation had to be made between a slavish subjugation to forms of past art and an acceptance and understanding of continuing tradition manifest in these forms. When speaking on the subject of cast iron he made this distinction perfectly clear:

> The fire grates . . . that came into use about the middle of the last century, are decorated all over the field with tiny flutings, beads and leaf mouldings, sometimes even with little figure medallions, and carry delicacy to its limit. The best examples are entirely successful, both in form and in ornamentation, which, adapted to this new purpose, does no more than gracefully acknowledge its debt to the past, just as the best ornament at all times is neither original nor copies: it must recognize tradition and add something which shall be tradition for the future.[24]

In his attempts consciously to produce a 'style for today' Lethaby had already achieved some notable successes, not least with the walnut cabinet (Plate 50), first acclaimed at the Third Arts and Crafts Exhibition in 1890. Writing twenty years later, Lawrence Weaver could still say that it was one of the most important pieces of modern furniture designed in England. He continued, 'it stands as an exemplar of the right direction for furniture designers to take if they would found a school and leave behind household equipment that may be afterwards recognized as twentieth century and as bearing comparison with that of the preceding centuries'.[25]

There is, however, evidence of a change of direction in Lethaby's thought at this time in a lecture given at the Third Arts and Crafts Exhibition, in which he spoke of carpenters' furniture as representing an ideal, which could be identified and fostered by gathering up that furniture that had not been 'bought to look expensively useless in a boudoir, but serves everyday and commonplace need, such as must always be the wont, where most men work, and exchange in some sort life for life'. After proposing models that were drawn from the Middle Ages, he continued:

> Things as simply made as a kitchen table, mere carpenter's framings, were decorated to the utmost stretch of the imagination, by means simple and rude as their construction. Design, indeed, really fresh and penetrating, co-exists it seems only with the simplest conditions.
>
> Simple, serviceable movables fall into few kinds: the box, cupboard and table, the stool, bench and chair.[26]

To speak with such enthusiasm for this work, which was both designed and made by the same hand, must imply a rejection of his own then on show at the Exhibition, which had been made by the cabinet-making firm of Marsh, Jones and Cribb and was therefore the product of divided labour.

There seemed to be two answers to the question as to how labour could again be united. One, of the present day, was imperfect; the other, less limited, was located in the future. First, the designer and maker could become one – a notion that provided much of the philosophical justification for the Arts and Crafts movement. Second, and necessarily in the future, society could be so changed that the division of labour inherent in the capitalist system would disappear.

Like everything of Lethaby's, his answer was an intensely personal one, but it is possible to pick out the sources which were to inspire his new work. In carpenters' furniture Lethaby had found a new ideal; he found it too in the work, first of his friend Ernest Gimson and second of Ford Madox Brown. Gimson, he later said, had taught him more than any other of his own generation and he had found his furniture 'one kind of "perfect", that is, it was useful and right, pleasantly shaped and finished, good enough, but not too good for ordinary use'.[27]

The evidence for the influence of Brown is less direct and is based on the selection of his 'Chest of Drawers designed for working men' (Plate 50), by the Furniture Committee (Lethaby was a member) of the Arts and Crafts Society for inclusion in its Third Exhibition. Its inclusion must be counted as the result of 'gathering up' furniture 'that serves everyday and commonplace need' and its exhibition there, some thirty years after it was first designed, must have had such an exemplary purpose. It was in these three sources that Lethaby found the inspiration for his future designs for furniture but their philosophical justification was probably and unexpectedly in 'The Nature of Gothic' where Ruskin wrote:

On a large scale and in work determined by line and rule it is possible and necessary that the thoughts of one man should be carried out by the labour of others. But on a smaller scale, and in a design which cannot be mathematically defined, one man's thoughts can never be expressed by another.[28]

Lethaby may well have argued that the converse was equally true; that is to say, on a small scale in a design that *can* be mathematically determined one man's thought could be expressed by another. It would certainly have provided the outline of his working programme for his next venture – the founding in October 1890, with some friends, of the furniture making cooperative Kenton & Co. The group consisted of Sidney Barnsley, Blomfield, Lethaby, Gimson, who was 'the most active spirit',[29] Macartney and his friend Colonel Mallet, 'who had taste and knew people'.[30] A workshop over some stables was rented at 29 Brownlow Mews, WC1, a stone's throw from Lethaby's lodgings in Calthorpe Street, and four or five first-rate craftsmen were employed to work there. Lethaby was 'our fount of inspiration' wrote Blomfield who continued: 'We used to meet in each other's rooms, undertake designs of our own choice and invention more or less in turn . . . Each man was solely responsible for his own design and its execution.'[31] (Plates 55, 56, 57 and 58.)

In December 1891 the firm held an exhibition in Barnard's Inn, then the home of the Art-Workers' Guild which was a success, despite some unfavourable criticism of its avant-garde nature: 'the new school

PLATE 55.   Kenton & Co. exhibition in December 1891 in the little hall of Barnard's Inn. The bookcase, desk (at rear) and walnut chair are by Macartney, the cabinet by Blomfield, the table by Barnsley and the work box by Lethaby.

of designers appear to be losing the sense of style, and the dignity of design which accompanies it, altogether. The object now seems to be to make a thing as square, as plain, as devoid of any beauty of line as is possible and call this art.'[32]

Describing the firm, which was probably wound up towards the end of 1892, Lethaby wrote: 'We enjoyed ourselves greatly for about two years, making many pieces of furniture, selling some at little over cost price – nothing being included for design or for the time expended by the proprietors.'[33]

In the same year he published 'Cabinet making' which, significantly, was addressed not to the designer as such but to the man who wished both to design and make his own furniture. It describes the construction of the sort of work he had praised in his 'Carpenters' furniture' lecture where he had said:

Design comes by designing. On the one hand tradition carefully shapes the object to fill its use, on the other spontaneous and eager excursions are made into the limitless field of beautiful device. Where construction and form are thus the result of long tradition undisturbed by

PLATE 56.   Arm chairs in oak made by Kenton & Co. The first of these two chairs is now in St John the Baptist church, Aldenham, Herts; the other, which is illustrated in Lethaby's pamphlet 'Plain Furniture', is in the Art-Workers' Guild. Both were made *c.* 1891.

fashion, they are always absolutely right as to use and distinctive as to beauty, the construction being not only visible, but at one with the decoration.

　　All art is sentiment embodied in form. To find beauty we must consider what really gives us pleasure – pleasure, not pride – and show our unashamed delight in it – and so when we have the leisure to be happy and the strength to be simple we shall find Art again – the art of the workman.[34]

Lethaby states in 'Cabinet making' that true design was the outcome of an analysis of purpose, a thorough knowledge of construction and the choice of sound and appropriate materials. It could be

99

PLATE 57. Oak ship chest, Kenton & Co.

PLATE 58. Inlaid oak cabinet, Kenton & Co., *c.* 1891. Now lost, it was once owned by Heywood Sumner.

beautiful even when most plain . . . do not pretend to cleverness nor originality – what is the good: consider place, use, size, strains and other conditions of make, shape and service. For, by putting your work together in the best practical way, by smoothing a surface or rounding an edge as thought will suggest, you will have a sensible form.[35]

However, between the idea of bringing divided labour together and putting it into practice there was, as there still is, a hiatus, and one made worse because it went unrecognized by many architects. It is principally the resolution of this problem that Lethaby talked about in an AA Symposium on 'The Problem of Modern Architecture'. The ensuing discussion, which sheds a unique light on Lethaby's own thinking, came about when *The Builder* argued that his words were at odds with his actions, for he seemed on the one hand to be saying that the making of drawings of designs was a useless and superfluous operation, but on the other to be exhibiting work at the current Arts and Crafts exhibition which was catalogued as 'designed by Lethaby'. The editor went on to ask what had been the relationship between designer and artisan and how had the idea of the design been conveyed from one to the other if not by means of a drawing. If that then was the case was he not in 'the same condemnation' as the 'designing architects' to whom he objected? The gulf between idea and reality in Lethaby's work is precisely delineated in his reply:

There is no 'condemnation'. I had no intention of beating the breasts of others . . . So far as the design is a diagram or memorandum fixing the thought of one well conversant with work and materials, it may evidently be a helpful means to an end. Of knowledge of work and materials there are, of course, degrees; but only vital fresh knowledge comes of actual handling, as by a Greek sculptor, a mediaeval mason or a modern painter. Failing [this] living first-hand knowledge of work, fall back on such simple things as can best be carried out by the mechanical means available, leaving ornamental work to independent artists.

In speaking of a large subject, I have never felt it necessary to chain my *thought* within the limits of my practice. I feel a certain absurdity in explaining what I *do* . . . I 'design' with drawings from sketches to full sizes. It is for this reason that there is no attempt in the things referred to beyond that 'extreme simplicity' and 'mere putting together of material' which you notice on your front page.[36]

Now that one aspect of Lethaby's new found philosophy and the change in his work methods has been stated we can see what they were by comparing two pieces of furniture – the walnut cabinet exhibited in 1890 at the Third Arts and Crafts Exhibition (Plate 50) and an oak chest made by Kenton & Co. (Plate 57) about a year later. In the first case the skin of walnut veneer concealed both carcass and construction; furthermore the decoration, those complex curvilinear mouldings applied to the doors, was designed on paper by one man and carried out by another, albeit a skilled carver. Thus not only was it a product of divided labour but its decoration was unrelated to its construction. The chest, on the other hand, was entirely different. Made from solid oak it could almost have been one decribed in 'Carpenters' furniture' for it had 'purlins at the edges formed by ingeniously elaborate dovetails fitting together like an inlay', thus its 'construction [was] not only visible but at one with the decoration'. But more importantly, the design arose from 'the mere putting together of material' and did not involve the carving of mechanical decoration. Here, then, Lethaby must have believed he had come close to reconciling his practice with

PLATE 59.   Inlaid oak sideboard, c. 1900. Designed and made for Thomas Middlemore at Melsetter House.
V&A.

PLATE 60. (*left*)   Design for the panels of inlay for the
Melsetter sideboard.

PLATE 61. (*above*)   Marble chimney-piece, made by Farmer &
Brindley, 1889. Exhibited at the Second Arts & Crafts Exhibition, 1889.

Ruskin's precondition. That is to say that when a design *was* mathematically defined it could be 'expressed by another'. All his future designs, when carried out by others, were to come from such simple mathematical arrangement of materials, even when the materials themselves were costly (Plates 59, 60, 61 and 62).

PLATE 62. The Fifth Arts & Crafts Exhibition, 1896. Lethaby designed the chimney-piece, executed by Farmer and Brindley, in marble and onyx; the enamelled fire irons and probably candle-sticks executed by Longden & Co; grate executed by T. Elsley & Co.

104

In this chapter we have begun to see the thread of ideas that runs through Lethaby's work as designer and thinker. To this we should link the innate feeling and intuition which, as well as rational problem-solving, played such a significant part in his development.

To the modern reader and to some of Lethaby's contemporaries the distinction between the artisan who carved the decoration for the cabinet and the one who made the chest might not seem very great. Indeed his behaviour must seem quite quixotic to some, while others will argue that his attempt to resolve the dilemma presented by the division of labour only weakened the political struggle for a change in society. But this is to ignore two facts which informed Lethaby's actions. In the first place we are not confronted as he was by that characteristic product of Victorian society – vast quantities of ill-conceived, mechanical and inappropriate decoration, which must have had parallels, however remote, with his own work – and in the second, Lethaby's behaviour was invariably directed by a strong and very personal morality.

ARCHITECT AND CRAFTSMAN: II

Buildings

PLATE 63. Stanmore Hall, Middlesex, 1891. The entrance hall.
The table was probably designed by Lethaby and made by Kenton & Co.

108

FOR ALL HIS VERSATILITY, IN THIS PERIOD

LETHABY WAS PRIMARILY AN ARCHITECT. IN HIS FIRST YEAR OF INDEPENDENT PRACTICE HE BUILT A STUDIO FOR HIS FRIEND HEYWOOD SUMNER on top of a house in Nottinghill Square (now Campden Hill Square)[1] and worked for Macartney on his commission for the Guinness Trust Artisans' dwellings in Marlborough Road (now Draycott Avenue), London.[2]

STANMORE HALL, STANMORE, MIDDLESEX 1891 (Plates 63–66)

A year or so later, and probably after he had received the commission for Avon Tyrrell, he was employed by Morris & Co. on the partial redecoration of Stanmore Hall in Middlesex, which had recently been bought by the Australian millionaire William Knox D'Arcy, who had commissioned an Ipswich architect, Brightwen Binyon, to alter the house. These alterations had produced an entrance hall and a suite of rooms along the garden front: the library, the vestibule or octagon room, the large and small drawing rooms and the dining room. This last, which seems to have been the only structural addition, was destined to house the specially commissioned Burne-Jones *San Graal* tapestries. This 1890 letter from Morris shows that he disliked the house as much as its architect:

> [It is] a house of a very rich man – and such a wretched uncomfortable place: a sham Gothic house of fifty years ago now being added to by a young architect of the commercial type – men who are very bad. Fancy! in one of the rooms there was not one pane of glass that opened![3]

Lethaby designed the five new chimney-pieces, all the woodwork including the panelling, cupboards, doors, the dog-leg staircase to the first floor and some built-in and free-standing furniture. The chimney-pieces are as uncompromising as one would expect from his new philosophy, but some of the woodwork is less so, particularly in the small drawing room, which harks back to his earlier manner. This inconsistency may have come from the demands of the commission. Those demands may account too for the fact that some of the furniture he designed was not made. It was probably thought too austere.

Though badly damaged, much of the decorative scheme survives and it is enormously interesting to see the work of the two men who, a generation apart, made the most important contributions to the Arts and Crafts movement; to compare Lethaby's cool precursor of a twentieth-century style with the richness and flamboyance of Morris's richly painted work.

PLATE 64. Stanmore Hall. The staircase hall.

PLATE 65.   Stanmore Hall. The dining room, with built-in sideboard by Lethaby, carving table probably by
George Jack.

AVON TYRRELL, CHRISTCHURCH, HAMPSHIRE 1891 (Plates 67–73)

The design and construction of Avon Tyrrell in 1890, the new country house for Lord Manners that was to
be built on high ground overlooking Christchurch and the Avon Valley in Hampshire, coincided with the
great period of change in Lethaby's life and thought. It is not surprising, therefore, to discover that this
transition is reflected in the house itself. Thus, the plan and general structure owe a debt to Shaw, but a

III

PLATE 66.   Stanmore Hall. Chimney-piece in the large drawing room,
probably executed by Farmer and Brindley.

new and different influence – that of the burgeoning Arts and Crafts movement – is obvious in the fittings and decoration. Nonetheless it is an intensely personal house, clearly expressing its creator's individuality, and the work is handled with great sensitivity.

Francis Henry, the first Lord Manners, was said to be singularly modest and unassuming, so much so that few people realized how original and unconventional his mind was, nor credited him with much sensitivity or imagination. Perhaps he saw some of these qualities in Lethaby, for he employed him rather than Macartney or Newton, both of whom were considered. Planning began in mid-1890 and went on until the following August when the contract was signed. Although nothing is known of the first discussions between the two men, Lethaby had recently made his own ideas fairly clear in an article attacking the contemporary architectural practice of first making the most convenient plan and then tacking the elevations to it. It appears nevertheless, from letters between Lethaby and Manners, that in this case not only did the plan come first but the two spent a good deal of time poring over it before getting it right. The first surviving letter to Manners dated 26 August reads, in part:

I have thought that considering the magnificent prospect from the windows of the garden front, that it would be well to keep that front generally without wings projecting enough to hide the view from some of the windows; but instead to put a series of Bay windows which would both catch the morning sun and command the view.

By this same arrangement we are able to obtain a terrace in the front sufficiently long & this I have stopped at one end by a Summer House or Tea room and at the other it would lead down some steps into the formal old-fashioned garden that I think might be most suitably formed at this point.

I have also thought over the placing of the stables and still think that instead of hiding them away it would be well to make use of them in 'furnishing' the site. They would thus give a character to one of the roads of approach in distinction to the other; but I should quite agree with your view that they should be quite plain, sufficient interest being given to them by mere grouping of the roofs. I have shown this generally in the block plan to a small scale.

In the ground plan of the house, availing myself of your suggestion to take the Hall through from front to back I have planned a long and somewhat narrow hall, the part where you enter being cut off from the rest by a screen like an old hall.[4]

It is not until October that the first mention of the elevations occurs: 'I have been working on the elevations but they will need more time and thought before I can show them to you.'[5] When Manners wanted changes Lethaby usually respected his wishes, provided that they did not conflict with his principles. If, however, he was set, as here, on a certain effect, he usually managed to find some good reason for making only the smallest alterations.

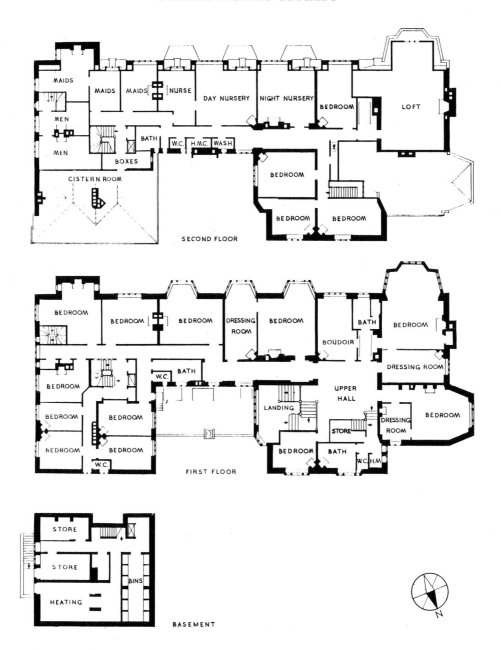

PLATE 67.   Avon Tyrrell, Christchurch, Hants, 1891.
Plans, redrawn by John Brandon-Jones.

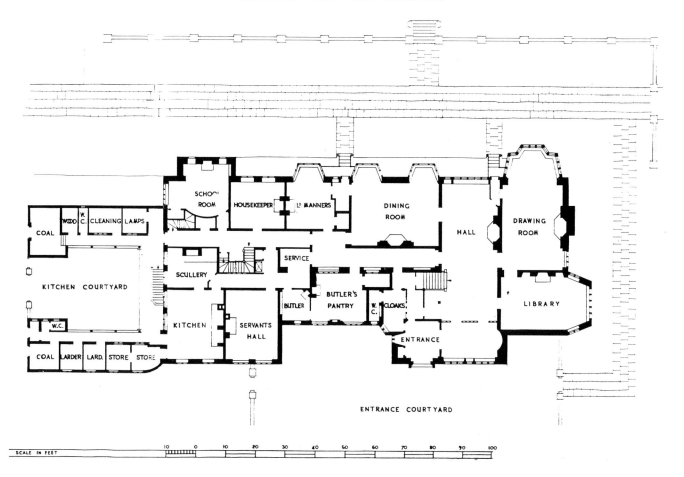

The Schoolroom chimney might well be brought out further, anything I think up to two feet as far as the outside goes, but as you say it is a loss to the sunlight of the rooms in the morning, not only to those on the Ground floor but the *Bedrooms* also.

The smaller chimneys look small on the drawings in contrast to the large ones which are really very bulky *where the walls* beneath are sufficient to take them, I will go over them however and see where by adding a little below they may, some of them, be enlarged.[6]

He had quite decided ideas about where the nurseries should have been placed; and Lady Manners 'had the greatest difficulty in persuading him to put [them] on the second floor and behind a green baize door, in the usual fashion'.[7]

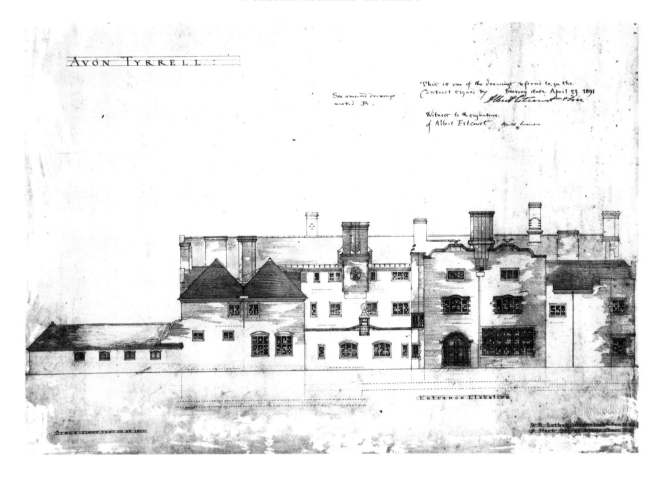

PLATE 68.   Avon Tyrrell. Entrance façade. Contract drawing dated 23.IV.1891.

When there was a possibility that the setting for the house might not be as he had planned, Lethaby wrote immediately to Manners. He was, for example, anxious about the activities of a Mr Milner who, it seemed, was responsible for the layout of the grounds:

I want to see the plan of the arrangement as a whole on the North-side if Mr Milner will be kind enough to send it to me, he tells me that it is 'based on my sketch'. However simple it is – & the simpler the better – I do not think modification should be made by him without my seeing it: given the conditions of large or small &c it is the exact placing of the lines as a composition with the house that I am anxious about.[8]

116

PLATE 69.   Avon Tyrrell. Entrance façade from the north. The clock seen in the contract
drawing has been substituted for the peacock (the Manners family device) on the chimney breast.

Even after this he was not convinced that Milner would arrange things on the north side of the house as he
wanted, and after drawing out a new plan was soon writing again:

Would you kindly look it over making any observations that may occur to you & I could then
finally modify the plan as required & again send it to Mr Milner.

I do not intrude as far as Mr Milner is concerned for it was plainly understood from the day I
first met him on site that the arrangement immediately about the house would necessarily have
to be considered by me in regard to the lines of the house. It is only just that while this is
understood that my plan should not be taken and omissions & alterations made without letting

117

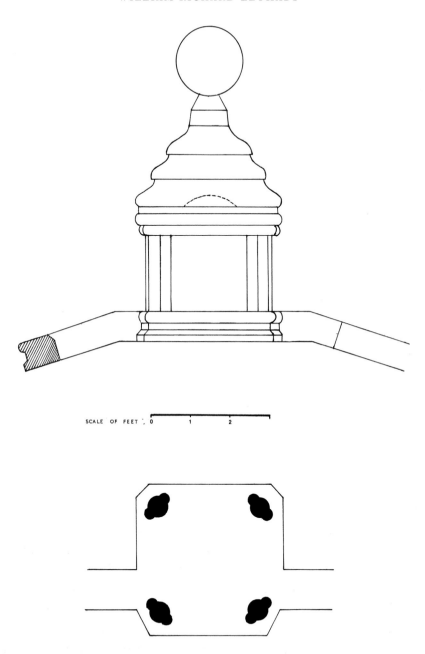

SCALE OF FEET : 0   1   2

PLATE 70.   Avon Tyrrell. The bellcote, a recreation of the perfect temple described in *Architecture, Mysticism, and Myth*. Redrawn by the author.

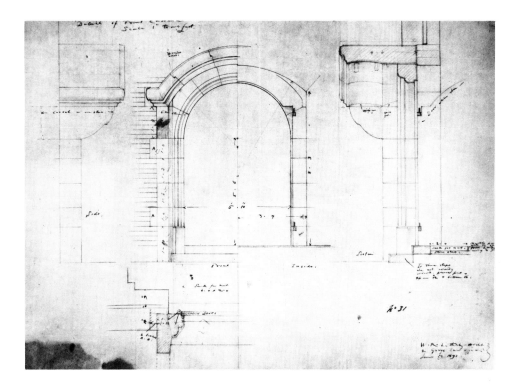

PLATE 71.   Avon Tyrrell. Detail of the front entrance.

me know as was the case in the front gardens; for I am fully prepared to meet any suggestions. If this is not done I must clearly withdraw my advice in the matter altogether.[9]

The plan of Avon Tyrrell makes no radical departure from the Shavian country house type, except for its greater economy, achieved by packing the essentials of a great house under one enormous roof, modified only as dictated by necessity or composition. On the ground floor the main corridor divides the house along its major axis, with the principal rooms on the south side overlooking the garden. Immediately above it are the corridors of the first and second floors which, because the house is less wide above the ground floor, are on the north side. Through the hall, extending from front to back of the house, runs the minor axis, which points away to the south and the church tower of Christchurch. The composition of the north and entrance façade, the relationship of the elements one to another and the way that the five units – the vertical divisions of the building – build up to a crescendo is masterly. It is strikingly different from the garden side of the house, where the long façade, with its regular line of six dormers, is more symmetrical

PLATE 72.   Avon Tyrrell. The hall, looking north. The table was designed by Lethaby and
probably made by Kenton & Co., plaster work designed and executed by Ernest Gimson.

than it appears at first sight to be. At the west end the first dormer is prolonged to become the roof of the
drawing room bay and the last, at the other end, is also lengthened, but is hidden behind the massive
chimney breast. The treatment too is simpler and, as it should be, more intimate than the bold
orchestration of the entrance.

The contract for building the house went to Albert Escourt & Sons, the old established Gloucester
firm; and the architect, leaving nothing to chance, controlled the construction with meticulous care, as is
shown by the two hundred or more surviving drawings of every detail. He was equally conscientious over
costs; for the house was finished within the estimate and without subsequent complaints from the client.
Built of brick, with stone trims and dressings, the composition, with its sheer walls, bulky chimneys and
lack of ornament, is massive, austere and conservative: there are, for example, no fashionable sash
windows. The three sill areas between the ground and first floors of the bays on the garden side were
pargetted by Gimson; they bore the initials of John and Constance Manners and the family's heraldic

PLATE 73. Avon Tyrrell. The garden front, from the north.

devices. These areas are now tile hung. Gimson was also responsible for the delightful plaster work with which part of the interior is decorated. It seems certain that the decoration on the main staircase window was done by Lethaby; in a letter dated 26 February 1892 he wrote: 'I had thought that some writing would be nice on the lower tier of the lights in this . . . window and was going to suggest your and your children's names (or initials) some dates and a little device in each centre pane, so as to give a touch of personal interest in aftertime.'[10] In Lady Manners's room on the first floor there is a wooden panel of decorative inlay, similar to the ship chest previously discussed, which was presumably made by Lethaby at the Kenton shop.

Avon Tyrrell was a transitional house for it shows, on the one hand, Lethaby pursuing conventional practice in that the enrichment of the house was tightly controlled by many drawings of details – mouldings and so forth – in the old way, yet, on the other putting into practice his new ideas of 'leaving ornamental work to independent artists', namely himself and Gimson.

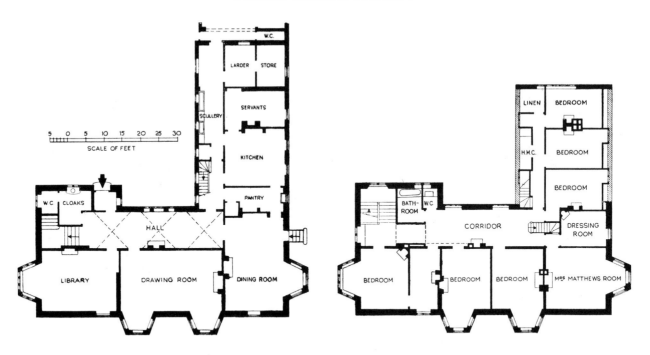

SCALE OF FEET

PLATE 74. The Hurst, Sutton Coldfield, Warwickshire, 1894. Plan.

THE HURST, SUTTON COLDFIELD, WARWICKSHIRE 1894 (Plates 74–80)

The Hurst, a medium-sized country house and stables was designed in 1893 for Charles Edward Mathews, a well-known Birmingham solicitor, local philanthropist and politician. The commission probably came through a friend of his wife, Theodosia Middlemore, herself the wife of Thomas Middlemore, for whom Lethaby was later to do a great deal of work in the Orkneys. Theodosia was a keen embroideress who exhibited at the Arts and Crafts exhibitions and was friendly with May Morris. The Hurst, standing on the lower side of a wood overlooking Four Oaks Park at Sutton Coldfield, was probably intended for Mathews's retirement. It was built of thin red Leicester sand stock bricks with stone copings and roofed with hand-made Hartshill tiles. However, the stables, which were subsequently whitewashed, were of a local stock brick. Such exterior decoration as existed was limited to a few simple stone and terracotta forms which, in a manner reminiscent of the inlay of Lethaby's furniture, were let into the brickwork. But the interior was given a richer yet equally simple character by his fireplaces, chimney-pieces and plaster work.[11]

PLATE 75.   The Hurst. The entrance façade, *c.* 1894.

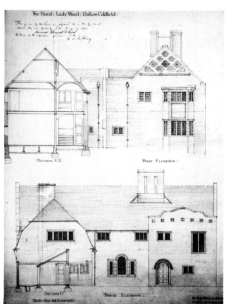

PLATE 76.   The Hurst. North and west elevations.
Contract drawings dated 29.v.1893.

123

PLATE 77. The Hurst. Rear view from the south-east.

There were certain similarities between the appearance of Avon Tyrrell and The Hurst but they were superficial: where the elevations of the former were largely dominated by aesthetic considerations which only reflect the plan in a general way, those in the latter were a direct expression of it. They had, *The Architectural Review* thought, 'that peculiar interest and dignity which is attainable in no other way'.[12]

The architecture of the house had more to it than mere aesthetics. In its realization Lethaby sought not just to represent but to symbolize the functions of the various parts, so that it became Expressionist architecture in the manner that he defined Expressionism – i.e. as buildings expressing their functions (see p. 206) – in a lecture on Modern Building Design a year or so later. In the north facing entrance front for example, this 'houseness' was expressed in three distinct zones; the main block, the servants' wing and the entrance bay. The main section under a massive pitched roof and a bulky chimney contained the principal

PLATE 78. The Hurst. The hall. The two doors on the left are to the drawing room and library.

rooms, was pierced at its centre by an impressive Serlian window and overshadowed the servants' wing. The wing, distinguished by its low Mansard roof and dormer windows, extended an arm towards the visitor at one side of the entrance court. Access was through the third section containing the front door, principal staircase, bathroom and WCs. Its projection and termination in a gable were enough to give this composition just the hint of a staircase tower. The Serlian window was given a meaning that its originator would hardly have recognized, for it was employed to express, on the exterior of the house, the median section of the groin vault of the hall within. It is further arguable that this type of vault had a special significance for Lethaby – perhaps it too symbolized 'houseness'; for not only did the family home in Barnstaple have such a vaulted entrance (Plate 81) but he gave to each of his own houses a similar one. The rest of the fenestration was equally descriptive of the plan and in marked contrast to that at Avon Tyrrell,

125

PLATE 79.   The Hurst. The drawing room. The chimney-piece was exhibited at
the Fourth Arts & Crafts Exhibition, 1893, executed by Farmer and Brindley.
Lethaby modelled the plaster work and designed the cast-iron grate,
made by H. Longden & Co.

PLATE 80.   The Hurst. Stables.

where in at least one place it is determined by aesthetic considerations alone: in a prominent position on the entrance façade there was a modified Serlian window which illuminated not, as might be supposed, one room but two; for what appeared to be one of its mullions was in reality the end of the wall that divided the rooms (see first floor plan, Plate 67).

The Hurst had an ageless quality achieved by economy, neatness of plan and the simplicity of its virtually undecorated elevations. It was a sad loss when, a few years ago, this remarkable Victorian house was so wantonly destroyed.

127

PLATE 81.   The porch at 2 Ebberley Lawn.
In the houses designed by Lethaby, all the vestibules
have groin vaults.

128

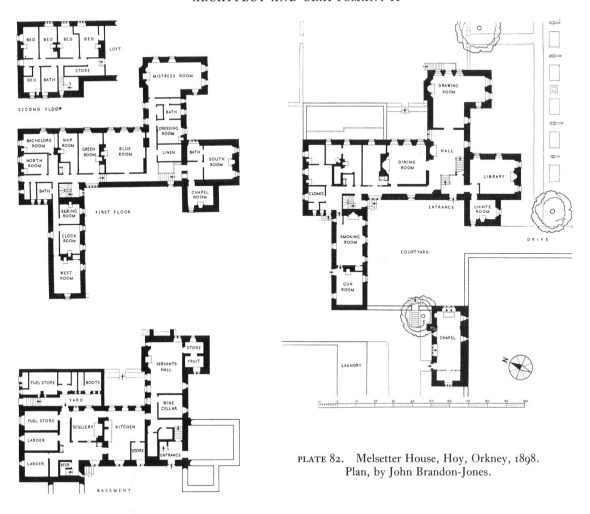

PLATE 82. Melsetter House, Hoy, Orkney, 1898.
Plan, by John Brandon-Jones.

MELSETTER HOUSE, HOY, ORKNEY 1898 (Plates 82–93)

Thomas Middlemore, a Birmingham businessman, inherited the family business (manufacturing bicycle saddles) and a large fortune; by his fifties he had so successfully increased the fortune that he was able to sell the business and retire to Rousay, in the Orkneys. There he bought Melsetter, then a laird's house, and an estate of some 40,000 acres, comprising the southern part of the island of Hoy, part of Walls Island and the smaller islands of Rysa and Fara. Even before he bought the estate he appears to have commissioned Lethaby to design his house.[13]

PLATE 83. Melsetter House. The original house before alteration, from the south.

PLATE 84. Melsetter House. The view after reconstruction, from the south.

PLATE 85.   Melsetter House. Aerial view.

Once Lethaby had visited Melsetter and seen the site at the southern end of Hoy, where he found a steading and several ranges of substantial outbuildings besides the big house, he told Middlemore that his design would not do at all.[14] Despite Middlemore's objections he produced another plan which incorporated the original house. Besides this reconstruction, Lethaby carried out a good deal of work on the estate, which included a new steading, two shooting lodges at Rysa and Orgill, several cottages and other buildings. (According to local tradition, it also included the local hotel but, judging from its appearance, this seems most unlikely.)

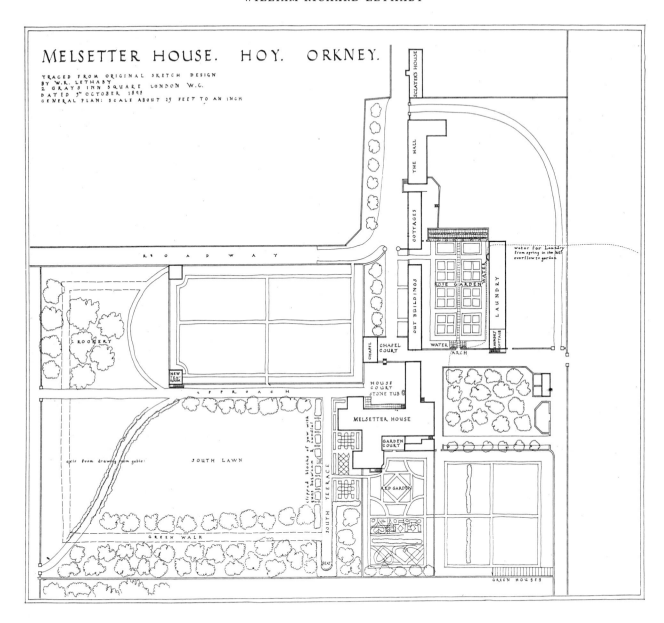

MELSETTER HOUSE. HOY. ORKNEY.

TRACED FROM ORIGINAL SKETCH DESIGN
BY W.R. LETHABY.
2 GRAYS INN SQUARE LONDON W.C.
DATED 3rd OCTOBER 1898
GENERAL PLAN: SCALE ABOUT 25 FEET TO AN INCH

PLATE 86.   Melsetter House.
Plan showing planting of gardens.
Redrawn by John Brandon-Jones after Lethaby.

PLATE 87. Melsetter House. The east front under construction.

The largest single work was, of course, the sensitive transformation of the old house, steading and numerous outbuildings, by a brilliant piece of imaginative planning, into a large, informal, but coherently organized country house, dependencies and a chapel, in a system which would as far as possible preserve the original structures (cf. plans of original house, and Lethaby's new designs, Plates 82 and 91). The new work, though of a better standard than the old, was constructed in the traditional way of harled and whitened sandstone rubble. At the corners the harling stops a few inches short of the arrises, leaving them sharp and clean. The new trims are, like Lethaby's massive chimneys and corbie-step gables, constructed of exposed ashlar.

133

PLATE 88. Melsetter House. Reconstruction in progress on the north side of the courtyard.

PLATE 89. (*right*) Melsetter House. North side of the courtyard after reconstruction. The position of the original end wall of the range is marked by the rainwater downpipe. The form of the door, now a window, has been preserved by Lethaby's triple roll moulding. The original windows can be distinguished from the new by their simpler trims.

The original steading was turned into a walled rose garden and the buildings on its northern side converted into a laundry and laundry cottage. Those to the east, however, were partially demolished, leaving a single wall pierced by a re-erected stone doorway, bordered by the traditional Orcadian single roll moulding. Above it a bracket with a carved scroll is set in the wall and must have come, like the doorway, from one of the demolished buildings.

To the east, the row of buildings lining the road to the new steading, also designed by Lethaby, were put to a number of uses, and that part which had been the south side of the old steading became a packing room, a museum, a spinning room (Plate 94) and a manservant's room. The next building, to the west, became a hall, followed by the house for the agent (Plate 95) which was extensively rebuilt, receiving new fenestration and a deep porch.

PLATE 90. (*right*) Melsetter House.
The rose garden, *c.* 1911.

PLATE 91. Melsetter House. Plan before 1898.
1. Courtyard; 2. Steading; 3. Site of chapel;
4. Site of garden house; 5. Agent's house;
6. Road to site of new steading; 7. Lodge.

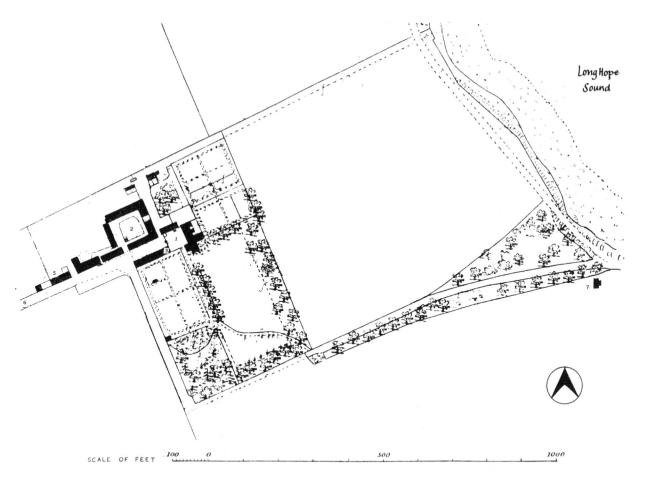

SCALE OF FEET   100   0   500   1000

PLATE 92.   Melsetter House. The hall.

The old walled garden to the south of the house court received a minor but significant change when Lethaby built a tea house at its southwest corner, similar in form to an already existing chamber in the opposite corner. Thus reconstructed, it is not unlike the walled garden at Montacute, Somerset, which had impressed the young Lethaby twenty years earlier.

Facing the house court and opposite the former steading had stood another range of buildings; this Lethaby partly demolished, leaving the back wall and a section of the courtyard wall to the east. After

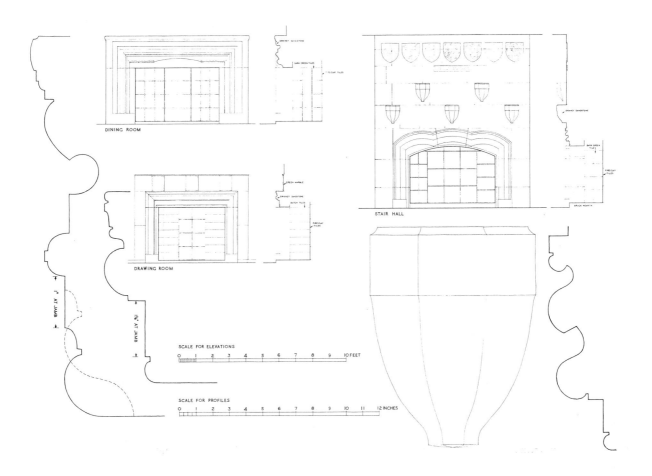

DINING ROOM

DRAWING ROOM

STAIR HALL

SCALE FOR ELEVATIONS
0 1 2 3 4 5 6 7 8 9 10 FEET

SCALE FOR PROFILES
0 1 2 3 4 5 6 7 8 9 10 11 12 INCHES

PLATE 93.   Melsetter House. Principal fireplaces.
Drawings by John Brandon-Jones.

strengthening, these walls formed part of the new chapel, which was dedicated to SS Colm and Margaret and consecrated in June 1900 by Bishop Douglas.[15] The chapel of SS Colm and Margaret is particularly relevant when considered with Lethaby's design for All Saints', Brockhampton, and his entry for the Liverpool Cathedral competition. Accordingly, they are considered together in more detail on pp. 148–53.

PLATE 94.   May Morris spinning at Melsetter House, 1902. Much taken with the house, she described it as 'a sort of fairy palace on the edge of the great northern seas . . . full of homeliness and the spirit of welcome'.

PLATE 95.   House for Middlemore's agent, Sclatter, seen here under construction from earlier buildings.

RYSA LODGE, HOY *c.*1900 (Plates 96 and 97)

Among the various other jobs that Lethaby did for Middlemore, Rysa Lodge was the largest and its L-shaped plan resulted from adding a two-storey block at right angles to an existing smaller croft. The Lodge, used, it seems, mainly as an overflow guest house, has a virtually undecorated interior save for some of Lethaby's plaster work cast from moulds previously used at Melsetter. Lethaby also worked on Orgill Lodge in the north of the island, but it has not yet proved possible to determine what exactly he did there.

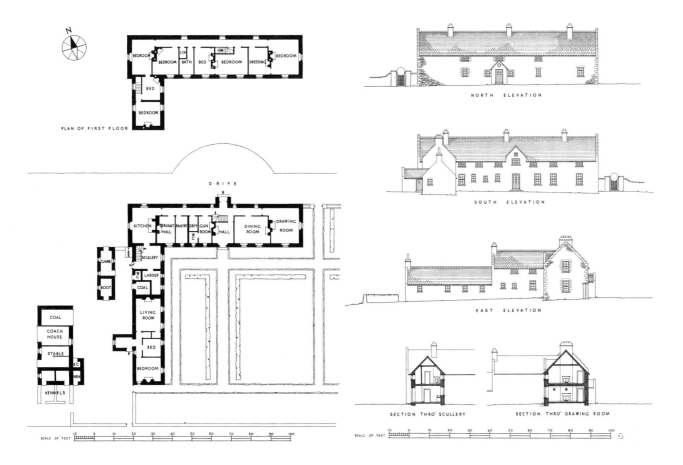

PLATES 96 AND 97. Rysa Lodge, Hoy, Orkney, *c.* 1900. Plan and elevations. The self-contained quarters for the caretaker facing the stables are the original croft to which Lethaby added the rest of the building. Drawings by John Brandon-Jones.

Nowhere better than in these houses, especially Melsetter, were the principles of the Society for the Protection of Ancient Buildings, and Lethaby's own convictions of the sanctity of human labour, expressed. It is an inspiration to see how he has preserved the work of the nameless Orcadian builders of the past, and quietly though distinctly separated his own from theirs.

THE EAGLE INSURANCE BUILDINGS, COLMORE ROW, BIRMINGHAM 1900
(Plates 98–105)

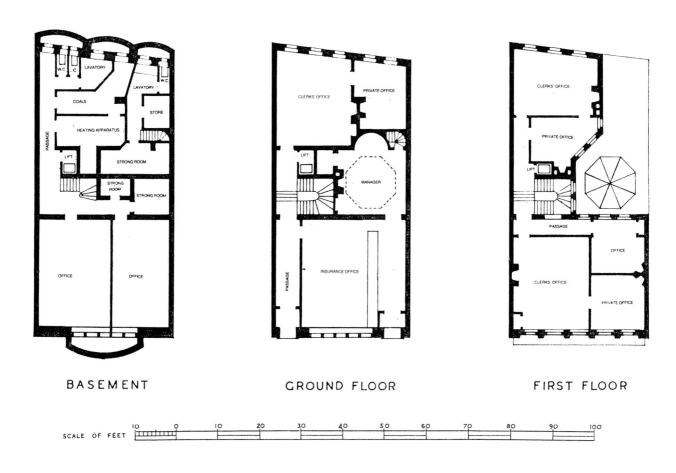

BASEMENT   GROUND FLOOR   FIRST FLOOR

SCALE OF FEET

PLATE 98. The Eagle Insurance Buildings, Colmore Row, Birmingham, 1900. Plan. J. Brandon-Jones.

Lethaby received the commission for the Eagle office block at about the same time as he was working on Melsetter. He chose to collaborate with Joseph Ball, a local man and the future director of the Birmingham School of Architecture. There can be little doubt that Lethaby designed the building, which was then carried out by Ball. All the preliminary drawings are in his hand, and the choice of building materials, coupled with the way they were worked, is equally characteristic. Furthermore, a comparison between the Eagle buildings and Ball's markedly different contemporary work makes this conclusion inescapable. The floors and roof are constructed of reinforced concrete and the fenestration of the façade is carried on steel joists with load-bearing walls, which give it structural parallels with Parr's Bank, a contemporary work by Norman Shaw in Liverpool. But where Shaw has disguised the construction under the clothes of an earlier style, Lethaby's composition has boldly *expressed* it.

PLATE 99.   The Eagle Insurance Buildings. Preliminary design. RIBA.

PLATE 100.   The Eagle Insurance Buildings.
Colmore Row façade.

PLATE 101.   19 Lincoln's Inn Fields. An influential
office block designed by Philip Webb for Valpy
and Leadsam. W. Curtis Green.

PLATE 102.   The essentials of Roman, Greek and Gothic architecture, from 'The Nature of Gothic'.

In the composition of the façade three influences of varying degrees of subtlety may be detected. The first was perhaps Philip Webb's office block at 19 Lincoln's Inn Fields for Valpy and Leadsam of 1868 (Plate 101) which, with its frontispiece of a four-storey stone bay with attached columns, was the most obvious starting point for Lethaby's design. His chevron moulding above the first floor windows was perhaps one of the sources for the continuous arched moulding that traverses the façade of the Eagle building above the windows of the top floor; yet it differs so markedly in its depth and placing from Webb's work that inspiration may in fact have come from something quite different.

PLATE 103.   The Eagle Insurance Buildings.
Main office, ground floor.

PLATE 104.   The Eagle Insurance Buildings.
Manager's office.

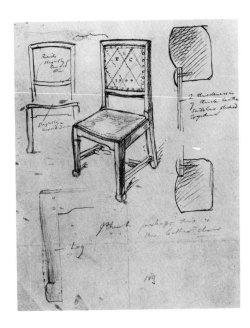

PLATE 105.   Eagle Insurance Company. Design for a chair, part of which may be seen in previous plate.

As usual, however, he did not go to some past art form for a model to bridge the columns, but turned back to Ruskin, who, in 'The Nature of Gothic', stated that there could be only three forms of architecture in the world and no more; he illustrated his theory with three structural diagrams entitled: 'Greek: Architecture of the Lintel; Romanesque: Architecture of the Round Arch; and Gothic: Architecture of the Gable'.[16] Lethaby took these dry little figures and transformed them into a superb decorative motif that, set in the parapet, spans the façade. We can only speculate on why Lethaby chose this decoration to bridge the columns which, unlike the heavy string columns, says nothing about the steel joists beneath. The most likely explanation must be that it provided a new way of linking columns without imitating past styles, bearing with it a typical touch of Lethaby's humour. In Lethaby's own words, this decoration 'does no more than gratefully acknowledge its debt to the past, just as the best ornament is neither original nor copied. It must recognize tradition and add something that shall be the tradition for the future.'

However, behind the direct visual simplicity of the composition of the façade there is a third source for its design and layers of meaning that relate it to the whole tradition of Western architecture and to Near Eastern sun temples. This is a curious claim for a building which has frequently been labelled a harbinger of modern architecture,[17] but one which will nonetheless be substantiated.

144

HIGH COXLEASE, LYNDHURST, HAMPSHIRE 1900 (Plates 106–109)

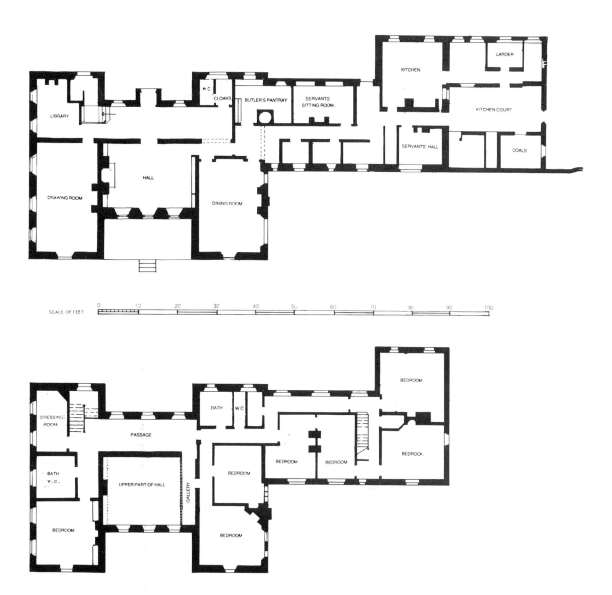

PLATE 106. High Coxlease, Lyndhurst, Hampshire, 1900. Reconstructed plan of ground floor and first floor. The form of the rooms behind the gallery may not be entirely accurate. G. Rubens.

PLATE 107.   High Coxlease. The garden façade.

Lethaby's next job was for Eustàce Smith, the wealthy son of the prosperous and extravagant founder of Smith's Docks, a ship-repairing business on Tyneside. The family had been implicated in the Dilke divorce case – one of the most notorious of the eighties – in which both Eustace Smith's mother and his sister were cited. The scandal not only ruined Sir Charles Dilke but drove Eustace Smith and his wife abroad to live in Algeria where they built a house and Mary Smith became an accomplished gardener. They did not return to England until the turn of the century, whereupon they decided to build a new house on a secluded New Forest site already well known for its gardens. High Coxlease is built of brick enlivened by inlaid brick patterns reminiscent of Melsetter's corbie steps, with a roof of dark red pantiles. The regularity of the long, low design is broken up by variations in roof height and the tall stacks made

PLATE 108.   High Coxlease. The entrance.

necessary by the surrounding trees, which further soften the outline, but it was both more formal and even simpler than anything Lethaby had previously built. Edith Lethaby, describing a visit to the Smiths shortly after the house had been finished, wrote of it:

It is such a pretty house and they are enthusiastic about it. The corridors are all to the north of the house & the rooms to the south overlooking a beautiful part of the Forest – A fine vaulted dining room with yellow walls and white wood trimming opens out upon the terraced garden – with library on one side, and drawing room on the other – there are some beautiful plaster decorations modelled by Richard – one notices them at once, they are so different from ordinary plaster work. Everything is a very happy combination of the artistic and

147

PLATE 109.   High Coxlease.
The hall, destroyed when the rear of the building was heightened and a floor added.

the practical – his fireplaces keep the house delightfully warm & one is struck with the convenience of arrangement.[18]

The related designs of SS Colm and Margaret, Melsetter, All Saints' church, Brockhampton, and Liverpool Cathedral were all made within three years of each other (1900–1903). They show a consistent development in Lethaby's ideas for the construction of churches and cathedrals in mass concrete.

SS COLM AND MARGARET, MELSETTER, HOY 1900 (Plates 110–116)

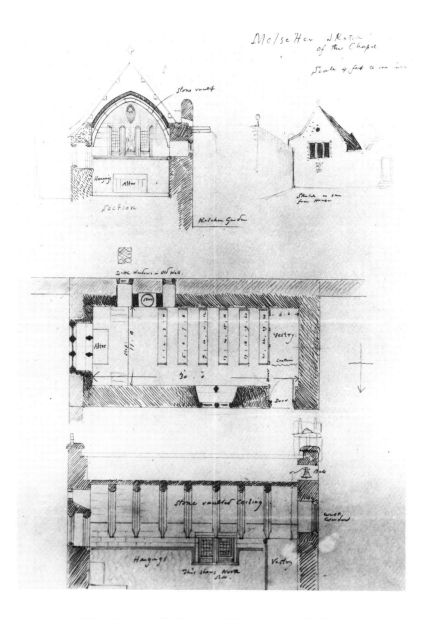

PLATE 110.   The Chapel of SS Colm and Margaret, 1900. Preliminary design.

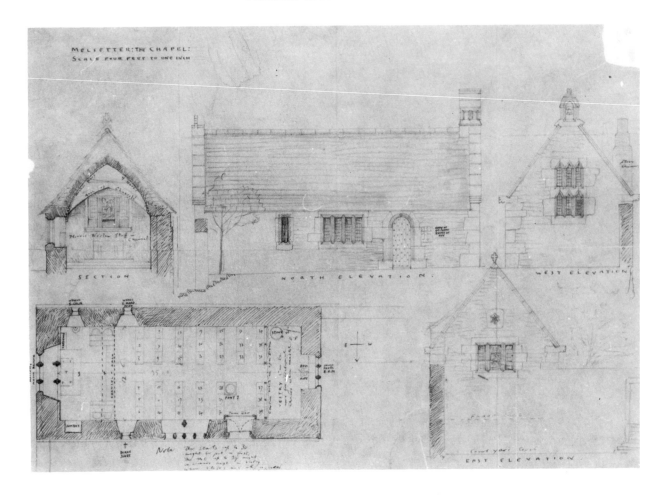

PLATE III.   SS Colm and Margaret. Design as executed except for concrete vault.

In the alterations for Melsetter, Lethaby had been chiefly concerned to construct a sound dwelling –
warm, light, convenient – but in his design for the chapel he was obviously after something else, a quite
different building more powerful and more primitive, which sought perhaps to express something of
much earlier wayside chapels of the north. His first design (Plate 110) had a vault supported on closely
spaced chamfered stone arches of unconventional form rising straight from the walls and unbroken by
capitals or abaci. This scheme was abandoned presumably because, with only twenty-four seatings, it was
thought to be too small to be replaced by another, which was built, for a larger vessel with seating for

PLATE 112.   SS Colm and Margaret. North façade.

thirty-nine and room for a vestry at the west end (Plate 111). Easily distinguishable from the other buildings by its construction of massive random rubble and roughly dressed quoins, it had no harling and was roofed, like the house, with large Caithness stone slates. The interior is both simpler and more personal than in the first design, for the vault which rises from low walls has been formed of mass concrete over shuttering, and a single arch bridges the nave, separating it from the chancel.

Equally massive and simple are the font and the altar, which is a stone cube standing on a low plinth with a projecting mensa into which is set a reliquary stone carved with a cross of St Columba. The monolithic sandstone font is a tall cylinder with a circular basin scooped out of the top. The base, the decorative roll mouldings on the shaft and the outside of the basin, enriched with wavy bands to symbolize water, are all cut into its column-like form, achieving, with a great economy of mason's work, a most satisfying result. There are four stained-glass windows: two (SS Colm and Margaret) by Christopher Whall, a Crucifixion by Burne-Jones and a Nativity at the east end by Ford Madox Brown. The significance of the fenestration at this end is discussed below in relation to All Saints', Brockhampton, where a more complex version of it was used.

151

PLATE 113. SS Colm and Margaret. Interior, looking west.

Once Lethaby had understood the moral implications of Ruskin's thesis of the division of labour, it caused him to change his practice radically, in small things such as furniture as well as in larger works of building. Ruskin offered Lethaby more than mere philosophy. It can be argued, for instance, that 'The Nature of Gothic' is the source of the basic section of Lethaby's churches. For Ruskin had declared

 all good Gothic is nothing more than the development in various way . . . of the group formed
 by the pointed arch for the bearing line below, and gable for the protecting line above . . . one
 law and one expression will be found in all . . . the real character of the building . . . depends
 upon the single lines of the gable over the pointed arch.[19]

To illustrate this point of view, he provided a diagram of a gable over a pointed arch which in its simplicity was perhaps the source of the design for the vaults of Lethaby's churches, for it was these 'single lines' that precisely determine the section of the chapel's monolithic concrete vault (Plate 115). Ruskin argued further that, provided a building had such a form, it was still definable as Gothic, even if in small work it had windows constructed in the 'readiest way' with flat stone lintels. This opinion he supported with another diagram of a rectangular three-light window, which bears a striking resemblance

PLATE 114. SS Colm and Margaret. Interior, looking east.

to much of the fenestration of Lethaby's churches of SS Colm and Margaret and All Saints' (Plate 116).

Ruskin also believed that certain qualities, of which the chief was the evidence of savagery or rudeness in execution, existed in the best Gothic architecture. This definition was accepted by Morris who extended it to mean something different, beyond style:

As to Morris's Gothicism I think [wrote Lethaby] he saw modernness primarily as a principle, some places it is expressed quite clearly, and he used the word 'Gothic' in a special sense, not only historically for the fourth century on, but also for now and the future in the sense of people's art and the organic building art.[20]

This was Webb's view too and explains why he could call Sancta Sophia, San Vitale and St Paul's Gothic buildings: he was referring, particularly in the case of St Paul's, to their structural innovations.[21]

Despite its qualities as a place of worship in the Western European tradition the chapel is not a Gothic Revival building, for no recognizable mediaeval form was employed. Yet – fresh, strong and savage – Gothic in Morris's sense it certainly is.

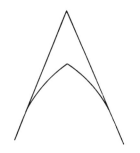

PLATE 115. Gothic section from 'The Nature of Gothic'.

PLATE 116. Diagram of windows from 'The Nature of Gothic'.

ALL SAINTS' CHURCH, BROCKHAMPTON, ROSS-ON-WYE 1902 (Plates 117–124)

When Alice Jordan, of Boston, U.S.A., married Arthur Foster of the Halifax mill-owning family, her parents paid for the rebuilding of Brockhampton Court as a wedding present, a reconstruction that transformed an eighteenth-century rectory into a full-blown neo-Tudor country house. After the death of her parents Alice Foster paid for the building of a new church in their memory.

Lethaby's commission came very probably through Mrs Johnston Foster, Arthur's aunt, who had employed Norman Shaw about a decade before to build All Saints' church, Richards Castle, Shropshire, in memory of her husband and must, therefore, have known Lethaby.

At first glance All Saints' church at Brockhampton, with its thatch and rubble masonry construction, appears to be a traditional Hereford building, but a closer look reveals the untypical precision of its massive strip buttresses, square-cut stone trims and sharp arrises. Inside it is even more astonishing, with a dramatic view down the aisleless nave from the entrance. Pevsner found it Expressionist in the sense in which central Europe designed churches around about 1920.[22] Three chamfered stone arches support the concrete tunnel vault deliberately 'formed over rough boards', which terminates at the more massive double-chamfered crossing arch. Beyond, the crossing is brightly lit by windows high up in the tower. The further crossing arch frames the darker chancel, which has a similar vault to the nave but is lower and unsupported. Originally the church was to have a conventional cover but in a repetition of events at Melsetter and at some short time between the approval of the contract drawings which showed this roof, and the drawing up of the specification of materials the decision was taken to use concrete and thatch instead. Undoubtedly the work at Melsetter, successfully completed less than a year before, had given

154

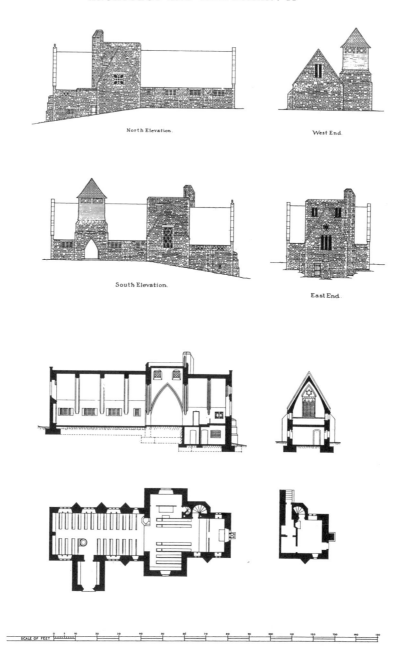

North Elevation.

West End.

South Elevation.

East End.

SCALE OF FEET

PLATE 117. All Saints' church, Brockhampton, Herefordshire, 1902. Plan and elevations. Redrawn by John Brandon-Jones from contract drawing.

155

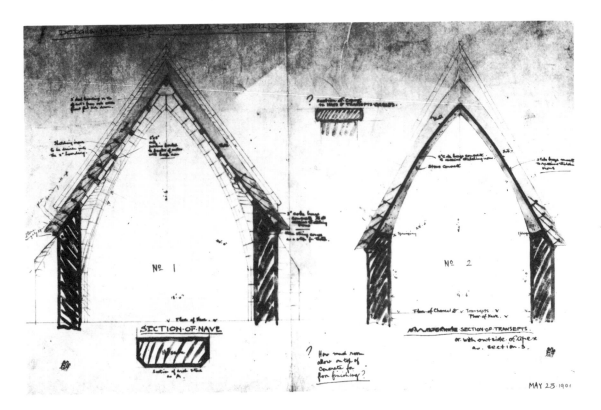

PLATE 118.   All Saints' church. Sections of nave and transepts.

Lethaby the confidence and technical experience needed for this far more ambitious scheme which was to be built by direct labour and not by a building contractor. Thatch was used to protect the concrete from weathering because it was not only cheaper and easier to use than slates but, being lighter, it exerted less pressure on the rather thin shell of the vault. It has proved an excellent if unconventional isolant for the concrete is still in excellent condition.

The All Saints' project was the occasion of an unhappy occurrence in Lethaby's life, one in which we can see how, in his case, the character of the man was inextricably interwoven with the profession of architect. It happened in this way. Like many other Arts and Crafts architects Lethaby believed that the way for architects to become real builders as in the past was to assume, where possible, the responsibilities of both building contractor and clerk of the works. Living on site, the architect was to buy the materials, hire the men and in the process of supervising the work be free to experiment and resolve problems as they

PLATES 119 AND 120.   All Saints' church, under construction.

PLATES 121 AND 122.   All Saints' church, from south-east (above) and north-east (below).

PLATE 123. All Saints' church. Interior, looking east, before removal of hanging lamps.

arose. But it was a doctrine fraught with difficulties when there was a demanding client who had no sympathy with such notions; difficulties made worse, as in this case, by the architect entrusting the work to another – Randall Wells, a bright though rather arrogant young man. But all seems to have gone well until Lethaby received a note from Arthur Foster demanding to know why he had not been informed about the collapse of an arch. Lethaby was obliged to ask Wells. He replied that he was 'putting it up again at once and had not thought it worthwhile to tell him – he had been trying some experiment in mortar which had not succeeded'.[23] Then without consulting his principle, Wells increased the height of the crossing tower by some ten feet. The Fosters, who clearly did not approve of Wells's experiments, were not at all pleased when the costs began to exceed the estimate. Worse was to follow. When the building was nearly finished it was discovered that the foundations did not rest, as had been supposed, entirely on rock and that a crack which appeared in the south transept wall might have been caused by their movement. Fearing that the wall would have to be underpinned and the foundations made safe, Lethaby called in an expert builder who gave his verdict that 'a sort of propping wedge of concrete'[24] at the east end below ground would be sufficient to arrest any movement.

The remedial measures taken were effective and there has been no subsequent movement in the structure. However, Lethaby took full responsibility for all and not only paid for the new work, but characteristically refused, because he believed he might have been negligent, even to take his fee.

159

PLATE 124.   All Saints' church. Font.

THE LIVERPOOL CATHEDRAL COMPETITION (Plates 125–129)

Lethaby's old friend Schultz Weir described how he, Lethaby and others came to enter for this competition. Lethaby, he said,

> had early come to the conclusion, based on his studies of mediaeval work, that no architect should bear the sole responsibility of an important building; so when the second competition for Liverpool Cathedral was announced in 1902, he thought it would be larks to have a shot at it, but only in collaboration with others; and he asked several of us to come together and discuss the matter.

160

Henry Wilson at that time had a large studio in Vicarage Gardens, and the result was that we agreed to meet there and thrash the matter out. The group consisted of Lethaby, Wilson, Ricardo, Troup, Stirling Lee, Whall and myself. Many jolly meetings we had and much argument, but it was Lethaby who was at the bottom of it all, and the design which was produced was largely his inspiration. Drawings were made and a model prepared, and these in due course were sent in, promptly to be relegated to the cellar! Shaw, who was one of the assessors, never I believe mentioned the subject to anyone. If he said anything to Lethaby, we never heard of it.[25]

There is no reason to doubt Lethaby's major share in the design. The earliest surviving sketch (Plate 125) which sets out the plan and the structural scheme in embryo is in his hand, as is much of the detailing in the finished competition drawings. It is only in the free-standing companile that it is possible to detect another hand – possibly that of Weir or even Wilson. Weir unfortunately says nothing about the material – concrete – from which the cathedral was to be built. This is very surprising for though it was being increasingly used by civil engineers and in the construction of commercial buildings which were hardly considered to be 'Architecture', the very notion of using it for one that was – that is to say a cathedral – was in itself shocking. English architects were then only just beginning, after a lapse of some two decades, to show an interest in concrete again. This lack of interest was partly due to its being seen as crude, characterless material and partly because to exploit it properly meant learning the technical skills of the engineer, something that few of them were prepared to do. But others – E. S. Prior, Ricardo and Lethaby among them – despite their insufficient grasp of engineering construction, maintained a lively interest and had some grasp of its potential. In the otherwise innovative design for the Liverpool Cathedral competition it was no doubt a desire to design in a modern material but within the knowledge and experience of the group that dictated the use of mass rather than reinforced concrete.

Moreover, there was a great deal of uncertainty about the durability of ferro-concrete; a fear which time has proved to be well founded, for a number of buildings constructed at about that time are showing increasing signs of failure where water penetration has damaged the reinforcement. It is most unlikely therefore that Lethaby and his friends would have taken such risks with the construction of a cathedral which would have to endure for generations. However, without the building specifications it is impossible to be certain, but judging by constructional forms it does seem unlikely. First, there was the corrugated form of the walls which, being self-buttressing, have great stability and need no reinforcement. Second, the nave vaults and spherical triangles of the roof of the chevet could have been built on the principles, which Lethaby well understood, of the pot domes of Byzantine architecture. The exterior of the cathedral was to be embellished with stone or terracotta figure sculpture and reliefs, presumably by Stirling Lee,

PLATE 125.   Liverpool Cathedral Competition, 1902.
Note from Lethaby to Weir setting out a preliminary design.

with stained-glass windows by Christopher Whall. Inside, Lethaby's drawings show that he had chosen some of the symbols from his first book as subjects for the murals.

As a design it invites comparison with a near contemporary, Anatole de Baudot's St Jean de Montmartre (1894–1902) in Paris. Although this is technically more advanced because the Cottancin system (not true ferro-concrete) was used in its construction, it expresses far less successfully the nature of the material than the Liverpool design would have done because its structure is very largely concealed and not expressed in the form of the building.

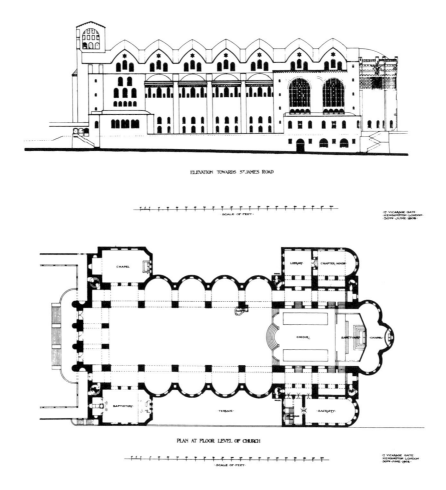

PLATE 126.   Liverpool Cathedral. Plan and elevation.

163

PLATE 127.   Liverpool Cathedral. Perspective view superimposed on a photograph.

In Lethaby's attempts to give his work symbolic meaning his thought ranged far and wide, and the results seem at first to be full of paradoxes similar to those presented in his first book, *Architecture, Mysticism, and Myth,* where the sentiments expressed in the introduction are, by implication, contradicted in the text. In short, though he demanded a 'positive', intelligible architecture, there is clear evidence of an important and fascinating esoteric element in several of his works, mostly occasioned by his researches for that book. Two motifs of this nature are part of the façade of Avon Tyrrell: the bellcote (Plate 70) (a 'world temple') and the principal chimney stack with its attendant birds. The position of the latter corresponds with his description of the Central Stone at Delphi (Plate 130):

two golden eagles were placed at the sides of the omphalos, the stone marking the sacred centre of the earth . . . We may see embodied in this myth of the centre stone the result of the general direction of thought; as each people were certainly 'the people' first born and best beloved of the gods, so their country occupied the centre of the world. It would be related how the oldest and most sacred city, or rather temple, was exactly on the navel. A story like this told of a temple would lead to the marking in the centre of its area the true middle point by

PLATE 128.   Liverpool Cathedral. Model.

a circular stone, a stone which would become most sacred and ceremonial in its import . . .

In the rites of Rome and Greece it was the hearth that signified, was specially identified with the omphalos and so . . . we have 'focus' and . . . 'Foyer' at once hearth and centre.[26]

A mystery still clings to the hearth, and it still is the centre of the world. It seems part of the Aryan inheritance; for while the nations were as yet unseparated, 'the hearth was in the midst of the dwelling; . . . as it were, an *umbilicus orbis,* or navel of the earth' . . . Hence it is frequently indicated by poets and philosophers as the navel or centre of the house.[27]

Here, then, were enough precedents to realize a device – the great stack which is, of course, the exterior expression of the hearth, and the Manners peacocks – that unified the epic and the functional, and made Avon Tyrrell the symbolic hub and navel of the family. Because this bold emblem is placed over the entrance it is just recognizably linked, in the usual Lethaby fashion, with the past; that is, with the similar practice in Jacobean times of placing a heraldic device above the main door.

Esoteric elements also complement the Ruskinian influence in the design of the façade of the Eagle Insurance building. The starting-point of Lethaby's inspiration was the ancient association of the crested

PLATE 129.   Liverpool Cathedral. West front.

eagle with the sun god. Of the great eastern door of the Temple of the Sun at Baalbek, he had written: 'on the lower surface lintel of the door is the celebrated figure of the crested eagle . . . The crest shows that it is not the Roman eagle; but . . . the oriental eagle consecrated to the sun.'[28] Two crested eagles figure in the earliest of Lethaby's drawings for this building (Plate 98); one on the parapet and the other standing on a sun disc above the door to the Eagle Company office, which is in a similar position to that illustrated in Wood's and Dawkins's *The Temples of Palmyra* (1753). Sun discs occur too at the top of the façade and on the double doors to the two entrances. The most likely source for these symbols is either a drawing of a Syrian tomb (Plate 131) or of a Buddhist gateway (Plate 132) both by Lethaby, but this last with its 'triple

166

lintels' is also the source for the complex form of the lintels of the two entrances (Plate 133). Though these esoteric elements are present in the design they are, however, much reduced in its execution; for the crested eagles have disappeared and the discs carry little of their original inspiration.

PLATE 130.   The Central Stone at Delphi.

PLATE 131. (*right*)   Syrian tomb, Galilee.

In All Saints' church, too, though Christian symbolism of course predominates, it mingles with more ancient and occult symbolism. Thus, at the east end the triple-light window above, like that at SS Colm and Margaret, symbolizes Christ at Nativity and Epiphany. When the dawn light enters the church, it realizes this sentence from the Revelation of St John: 'I am the root and offspring of David and the bright and Morning Star.'[29]

Then too from the centre of the crossing and hanging plumb in the middle of the church is a large chandelier having that significance which Lethaby described in *Architecture, Mysticism, and Myth*:

It is curious to notice how the hanging lamp affects the form of the egg with which it is often associated in the East . . . It may be that the shape is aesthetically the best for suspension, the form of every drop of water as it falls. It is sufficient for us that the egg was used as an architectural symbol of the origin of the world suspended from the sky-like dome, record of a genesis and emblem of the mystery of life, and a hope of resurrection.[30]

The forms which perhaps interested him most, since they occur in many of his buildings, were the square and the cube; it was not their association with classicism that attracted him, but their symbolism.

167

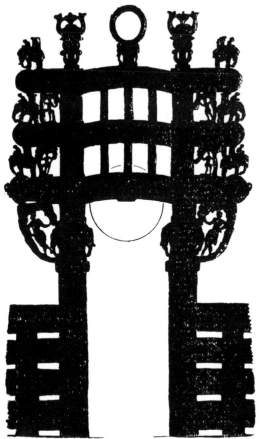

PLATE 132.   East Toran, Sanchi Tope.

PLATE 133.   Eagle Insurance Buildings. Detail of
door. The triple porch was derived from the
previous illustration and the door is embellished,
like the parapet above, with sun discs.

Here is his opening paragraph to 'Four Square', a chapter from *Architecture, Mysticism, and Myth*:

The perfect temple should stand at the centre of the world, a microcosm of the universal
fabric, its walls four square with the walls of heaven. And thus they stand the world over . . .
with the greatest uniformity and exactitude . . . Of all the forms, the cube and the hemisphere
are the most sacred![31]

Two examples of this 'world temple' are to be found in the bellcote (Plate 70) and the tea house at
Avon Tyrrell, but there are others in the square and cubes that occur in the designs of the Eagle and
All Saints'; in the latter, for example, the bell tower is made up of two superimposed cubes under a
pyramidal roof.

THE CENTRAL SCHOOL OF ARTS AND CRAFTS, SOUTHAMPTON WAY, LONDON 1907

The building as it stands today has been altered both internally and externally. Originally it was to house both the Central School and the London Day Continuation School for Teachers, which occupied the southern half along Southampton Way, so that there were two quite separate institutions with separate plans stuck together end to end behind a single unifying façade. Since then there have been many changes as a result of wartime bombing and extensive alteration after the Central took over the whole building, with the result that the present plan is an incoherent, rambling muddle.

It has been suggested that Lethaby was responsible for the design of the Central School. Although this is untrue he was, as Senior Art Inspector and Principal of the School, deeply involved from the start of planning in 1903. He formulated the requirements, drew together the various schedules that had been prepared by the staff who were to take charge of the various schools, as the departments were then called, and prepared sketch plans for the benefit of the Board.[32]

In March 1903 Halcrow Verstage, a Central student and an assistant in the second class in the Architects Department, was put in charge of the work[33] which was examined by Lethaby later in the year; as a result he proposed a number of changes designed to make a better use of the space and simpler arrangement of the exterior.[34] Two years later a letter from him expressed his doubts about the workings of the LCC and the progress of the design.

> The stupidity and ignorance is beyond human words and that makes me slow to hope – thus [for] the new Central School, an important Civic Building (say £72,000) on the most important street, they got in a new junior assistant (by chance a student here, and by greater chance an eager and capable youth). It is he who has planned and designed that building.[35]

While it is almost certain that this 'eager and capable youth' was Verstage it might have been Matthew Dawson, about whom Lethaby wrote in 1909,

> the plan is quite [Matthew] Dawson's own, all I suggested was the arrangements in groups of allied subjects . . . on separate floors. As to the outside and inside I only took a general sympathizing interest in, arguing that it should be like a nicely finished factory.[36]

The most likely explanation of the contradiction in these letters is that in the interval between the two, Lethaby had decided that a more experienced man was needed and accordingly had Dawson brought in, although he does not appear to have been in the employ of the LCC Architects Department.

Lethaby had written in 1903,

> As to the exterior, I am anxious, as the building will be associated with a school of design, that

it should be plain, reasonable, and well built, with as little of common place of so-called ornament as maybe. It should be substantial and of good materials, then, if it were just a set of well-built workshops, it would necessarily look well, and if beyond that certain spaces in panels were arranged for, in consultation with us at the school, we would without a doubt get them fairly filled with good sculpture (better than almost anything used on London buildings). The interior should also be severely plain, and if decorated at all, be done as time goes on by members of the school.[37]

This suggestion was accepted and both the interior and the exterior were provided with a variety of places designed to be carved. However, the scheme did not get very far for only a limited number of carvings, all on the inside, were executed. This sculptural decoration has survived, but the murals which once covered the walls have all been destroyed.

The involvement of two other architects, Percy Ginham, who taught at the School and H. Minton Taylor,[38] who is believed to have been a student, very much strengthened the School's direct connection with the design, so that it is reasonable to conclude that the building is as much the product of the Central's School of Architecture as it is of the LCC's Architects Department.

Lethaby's career as a creative architect is virtually confined to the closing years of the nineteenth century, for little work came his way after that, nor did he advertise, or visit fashionable places where moneyed clients might be encountered. 'How my sympathies leap up', Gimson wrote to him, 'when you talk about not being able to dine out for work or spend week-ends looking for it.'[39] The fact was that his work, like that of many other architects who practised what is now known as 'English Free Architecture', was becoming increasingly unfashionable, going down before the Wren Revival and the enthusiasm for Beaux-Arts classicism or, as he put it, 'Just as our English free building arrived, or at least "very, very nearly did", there came a timid reaction and the re-emergence of the catalogued "styles".'[40] As most of his peers retreated into the past – making historicism Britain's substitute for a modern architecture – so his work and ideas became increasingly unacceptable. Despite this growing isolation from the thought and activities of the majority of the profession, he never became bitter but continued to argue both in lectures and in the press for a new architecture appropriate to the twentieth century.

There were other and more personal reasons for not entering the arena; by the turn of the century he had become a well-known and widely respected teacher, doing a job which he thought was of the greatest importance, since he was helping to form the ideas of a new generation of art and design teachers. Moreover, it was work that was secure – he was by then middle-aged – and which he thoroughly enjoyed. He had lost, too, as he remarked, the wish 'to force his views on employers as a nostrum'.[41] But probably the most telling reason was that he felt himself inadequate to design a modern building as he was convinced it should be done. Inadequate both temperamentally – 'I would rather be dealing', he admitted, 'with rubble and thatch than with concrete and steel'[42] – and technically; it was absurd, he thought, that he should have been allowed to study cathedrals from Kirkwall to Rome and from Quimper to Constantinople; it would have been far better to have an equivalent knowledge of steel and concrete.[43]

If I were again learning to be a modern architect I'd exchange taste and design and all that stuff and learn engineering, with plenty of mathematics and hard building experience. Hardness, facts, experiments: that should be architecture, not taste.[44]

These feelings of inadequacy had nevertheless not prevented him from fathering the most daring structure of any English architect of his time – the design for Liverpool Cathedral described earlier in the chapter. Alas, that it remains an idea only! Had it been built, it would have been an inspiration to posterity.

CHAPTER FIVE

WORK FOR THE
LONDON COUNTY COUNCIL

THE DEVELOPMENT OF LETHABY'S PHILOS-
OPHY IS DISCUSSED ELSEWHERE; HERE IT IS ONLY NECESSARY TO SAY
THAT HIS IDEAS ON EDUCATION, AS ON MOST OTHER THINGS, WERE IN
complete opposition to the general trends of the age, and though his ideas paralleled those of better-known reformers he seems to have reached his own conclusions unaided. His public work must be counted as of some importance in getting general acceptance for these new and revolutionary teachings, but even today some of his own notions are still considered to be far too unconventional. For example, his belief that art schools, as centres of culture, should play a vital rôle in the local community seems today as far as ever from realization:

> Schools of Art in the past . . . were deeply injured by the tradition that no real work was to be produced in them, any more than in the workhouse: that the work done was not real work, which might be done for definite purposes or sold, induced a disease of unreality. The time has come when the Art Schools everywhere should be expected to produce for service. There are many ways in which production for the service of the community might be accomplished without raising the undoubted difficulties of sale . . .

> The Art Schools should be centres where advice might be obtained on questions of design: they should function more than they do in the activities of their towns, and they should endeavour to force forward civic culture in every possible way . . . [they] could under due safeguards produce for sale . . . [and] a small shop might be attached to the Art School where works might be sold, perhaps students themselves could be encouraged to hold exhibitions of finished and practical works . . . Perhaps gifted students might be assisted into 'setting up' as little masters. A setting-up-in-business fund would be far more valuable than most scholarships in leading students into a career. Schools of art should become centres of experiment.[1]

His earliest experience as a teacher must have come when, as Shaw's chief assistant, he was responsible for the practical training of the junior clerks, a task which Shaw later described as having been very successfully accomplished.[2] But it was probably not until he became a leading opponent of the RIBA's attempts to make a career in architecture open only to those who passed a theory examination that he became seriously committed. Nor could he, an architect and craftsman, have been unaware of the collapse of the old apprenticeship methods of training craftsmen and of the urgent need to find satisfactory alternatives. Gradually he was drawn towards teaching, encouraged by friends who had long recognized his unique gifts. The little technical training then available was of a sterile, theoretical kind, but new men like Sidney Webb, who had been elected to the London County Council in 1891, gave promise of great changes and reforms. Soon a Technical Education Board was set up and Lethaby was induced to become an art inspector for it. He was destined to be, within a very few years, responsible for the capital's art education.

As the nineteenth century progressed, several concerned observers had noted uneasily that Britain's trade rivals were beginning to equal or surpass her in certain respects. In particular, the growing success of competitors was seen in those industries where the form and decoration of the product were of first importance, and it was attributed to the fact that technical education on the Continent, especially in Germany, was far ahead of that in Britain.

Though the continental superiority in this field was indeed manifest, the attribution was in fact mistaken. The commercial success of rivals was much more closely connected with the far-sightedness of the industrialists who were ready to put money into the new products, and to the better organization of financial resources. In this country, however, public anxieties about technical skills were voiced in an increasing demand for state participation in art training. As early as 1837 the Normal School of Design was opened and in the year after the Great Exhibition of 1851, the Department of Practical Art, soon to be reorganized as the Department of Science and Art, was established. This was largely the brainchild of Henry Cole and remained in existence until the end of the century, when it was absorbed by the newly created Board of Education. (Because of the site of its offices the Department was often referred to as 'South Kensington'.) At the outset it aimed to improve national taste and the standards of manufacture by widespread art teaching, the training of art teachers, the production of designs and instruction in the manufacturing processes.

Unfortunately, despite such splendid ambitions, its aesthetic theory was as limiting as it was limited. For it was made up, first, of a smattering of debased neo-platonism – the belief that there existed ideal forms which, independent of materials and manufacture, could be represented by mere two-dimensional arrangement of lines or by three-dimensional models. Secondly, it embodied the notion of a canon of taste, of historically sanctioned and perennially perfect prototypes, from which virtually alone could new designs be generated. Its curriculum and administration were rigidly controlled by a system of rewards, based on examination results. The consequent educational mode amounted to an extension to visual material of the Victorian system of rote learning. The aims were 'precision, exactness, correct appreciation and imitation of form, careful and severe training and the inculcation of the right principles'.[3] As he acquired the right vocabulary and the means of execution the tyro could begin to design for the manufacturers – thus art could be applied to industry.

Well before the end of the century most of the Department's objectives either had proved unattainable or, through the determined opposition of the manufacturers, had been aborted. What little remained of its larger intentions – though a good deal depended on the initiative of the teacher – was in the teaching of geometry and drawing, and even this was mostly reduced to copying. Thus, in every art school in the country the student learned no more than would satisfy the very limited demands of industry.

To the new craftsmen and art workers of the last quarter of the century the Department's work seemed, at best, totally irrelevant and misguided. In other places, too, its work was very widely criticized. Typical indeed was this angry and probably not exaggerated attack by Augustus Spencer, the newly appointed Principal of the Royal College of Art. 'South Kensington' teaching was, he said, 'slow, vicious, feeble and antiquated. What takes place . . . is that the students are set to copy an apple or a sphere, or a cone, on which they spend a year, a second year is spent on copying a bad torso and thus the student reaches 30 and knows nothing.'[4]

With the passing of the Technical Education Act in 1889, local authorities were given the power to levy a penny rate to aid technical or manual instruction; but they showed no enthusiasm for it, despite increasing pressure from such bodies as The National Association for the Promotion of Technical Education. Among the most backward was London County Council, which refused to do anything until money became available that was not a charge on the rates. It was eventually through the opportunism of Arthur Acland MP, then chairman of the Association, that the finance finally became available and in a somewhat comical fashion. During a parliamentary debate on how the revenue of a beer and spirit duty (known as the Whiskey Money) should be spent, he jumped in and persuaded the Government to make this available to the County Councils. Education was, of course, something upon which such money could be spent.

Even then, the London County Council was not stirred to action until after the second Council was elected in 1892. Then at last, on the proposal of two councillors, Sidney Webb and Quintin Hogg, a special committee of enquiry into technical education was set up. Webb, who was elected to chair it, engaged Hubert Llewellyn Smith, a young man then acting as Acland's lieutenant, to survey the actual state of affairs and make recommendations for their improvement.

Smith already had experience of craft training at Ashbee's School of Handicraft and the White Chapel Craft School in the East End. His Report was ready within a year and is remarkable for the detailed picture it gives of the state and distribution of the capital's trades. London's technical education, he said, 'is not only far behind Germany and France in quantity and quality, but also far behind our chief provincial towns'.[5]

On the publication of this report, the LCC set up a powerful and largely independent body, the Technical Education Board. It consisted of twenty councillors and fifteen other members (all appointed annually by the Council), who represented the London Schools Board, the City and Guilds Institute, the City Parochial Trustees, the London Trades Council, the Headmasters' Association and the National Union of Teachers. It was to pursue, in the exciting, pioneering days ahead, a bold and determined policy.

To help with the preparation of the section on art education Smith had called in Edward Taylor, the headmaster of the Birmingham School of Art, one of the more successful state schools. The preamble, which probably reflects Taylor's views, attacked the 'South Kensington' doctrine that there was some fundamental difference between 'pure' and 'applied' art, and the notion that design could be taught only by rules. The authors of the Report found that the Department's London art schools had many faults in teaching and administration, largely since the teachers' wages depended on 'payment by results'. In effect this made a school's income entirely dependent on the number of examination passes obtained in the previous period. The financial grant was in theory given at first to the local management committee, who passed it and a proportion of the fees on to the teachers, keeping the remainder to pay expenses. But what usually happened was that these committees were completely inactive and simply handed the schools over to the teachers, who paid all the expenses and pocketed the grants and fees. 'If the schools are to be developed as the crown of public art teaching', wrote Smith, 'the Council has the right to demand a change', and he added that 'the most conspicuous weakness is the absence of adequate teaching of design and modelling, and for the most part of any attempt to develop particular applications of design to special manufacturing processes'.[6]

Smith's, and presumably Taylor's, proposals are merely reformist and imply no fundamental changes in theory and practice. If any existing schools would provide proper facilities for systematic study 'and teach design and its application ... to at least one manufacturing process' they should become Technical Art Schools, the new category of institution proposed by Smith. They were to be financed by special grants, one annually of £100, another on capitation, with an addition if craft classes were held, and a third for the purchase of equipment. Similar grants were proposed for Department of Science and Art classes not held in art schools, and for those in elementary schools. Smith pointed out that not even at the Royal College of Art was there adequate teacher training, and that, since this was of great importance, the Council should appoint a specialist to hold classes and give demonstrations for teachers. He also proposed an extensive scholarship scheme in addition to the very inadequate existing provision.

The Board immediately adopted the Report, which is scarcely surprising since many of its recommendations must have originated with Webb, who had become the chairman of the Technical Education Board. Webb chose as its secretary the formidable university administrator William Garnett, who had already built up Nottingham University College and Durham College of Science in Newcastle. With tremendous energy and despatch the two men set about the successful transforming of London's technical education.

Soon the reform of the first art schools (though not, as yet, their curricular transformation) was begun: local committees were reorganized to include a member or servant of the Board, both 'farming out' and 'payment by results' were abolished, the various recommended allowances were paid and attempts were made to improve the standard of teaching.

Many of the older Gothic Revival architects and most of the artist craftsmen – the people who constituted the Arts and Crafts movement – were deeply concerned to quicken the moribund crafts and encourage training for them. These men, like their exemplar Morris, had usually acquired their own skills through practical study and seeking out what survived of the native tradition; not, in other words, through a traditional apprenticeship, but through a more or less selfconscious artificial activity. (Their lack of systematic training was one of the reasons for the founding of the Art-Workers' Guild.) To them all, without exception, the phrase 'technical education' meant what passed for art training in the Department's schools which, since it was completely removed from any notion of the acquisition of a skilled craft, seemed to them to be monumentally irrelevant. They believed that Morris had been right when he said:

> I am convinced that it is from some form of apprenticeship, i.e. working in a workshop and gradually doing bits of it, and by that means only, that crafts can be taught. The theory may be learned afterwards, but cannot supplant the gradual acquirement of the habit of hand and eye which makes a craftsman.[7]

In essence the philosophy of the Arts and Crafts movement was at the opposite pole to the academic: design, it was argued, depended neither on a cultivated taste nor on drawing skill, but on an intimate knowledge of tools and materials. The movement was, in other words, anti-academic, concrete and non-intellectual; it is here described by Lethaby, who contrasts it with the practice of the state schools:

> Design was not the abstract exercise of a faculty plus a pair of compasses, nor even this faculty working on data of purpose, position and proportion. It was insight as to the capabilities of material for expression when submitted to certain forms of handiwork. It was the *imaginative* foresight which came of the designer's experience of his former results; when the subject, as Charles Lamb says, 'has so acted that it has seemed to direct *him* – not to be arranged by him . . . so tyrannically that he dare not treat it otherwise, lest he should falsify a revelation'.[8]

The Art-Workers' Guild decided to debate the Report, and invited Smith to address the Guild on 'Design and its Relation to the Proposed Technical Schools'. Probably to the surprise of his audience, who would automatically have identified him in advance as another ignoramus in the 'South Kensington' mould, he described the Department's work as reactionary, and stated his belief that, though design was at present badly taught, it did not in the least follow that it was unteachable.

His audience must have been delighted. True, most of them would have agreed with Morris and would have added that, to practical men, work done in school must by its very nature be but an exercise. Vital work, in contrast, could only be done under a master in a workshop, where real things for use were

179

made and had in consequence to be done right. Nevertheless, the age-old apprenticeship system was by then either dying or dead, killed off by the relentless pressure of commerce. Thus it was clear to realists like Smith that some form of schooling would have to form an essential feature of entry into the skilled trades, even if it did not replace the old ways altogether. There is little doubt that he took the occasion to point out that the Board was to pursue new policies. He probably asked what, in the face of this great opportunity, guildsmen were prepared to contribute in order to have a hand in shaping future education policy. Argument must have been intense, for it flowed over into a second meeting. The effect on Lethaby, who had been billed to speak *against* technical education, was to produce a change of heart. 'As a matter of fact', wrote Smith (with slight exaggeration) many years later, 'the result was to induce [him] to accept the post of Art Inspector for the London County Council' (i.e. The Technical Education Board).[9] This was the job that Taylor had been doing with Garnett since the Board had been set up, but which he had had to resign, since the work, in addition to running Birmingham School of Art, had soon proved too much.

From the advertisement for an inspector, which appeared six months after the Guild's discussions, it is clear that the incumbent was to have a good deal of authority in setting up and developing the Capital's art education.

> In addition to inspecting and reporting upon various Art Schools and Classes receiving or asking aid from the Board, the inspector should advise the Board in all matters relating to art teaching, should assist in the conduct of examinations for Art Scholarships and Exhibitions, and in procuring casts and other art objects for the use of the London Schools, and if required should undertake normal classes for teachers.[10]

Out of the 166 applicants, about three-quarters were either headmasters, mostly of art schools, or certificated art teachers and therefore products of the 'South Kensington' system. Not one of these was interviewed. The five shortlisted were all either successful designers for industry like Andrew Langman or S. Meteyard, or craftsmen like Frederick Robinson, a practising jeweller, George Frampton, a sculptor, who was supposed to be familiar with art training in France (then highly thought of), and Lethaby.[11] One could hardly find a clearer indication that the Board had chosen a policy for art education in direct opposition to that of the Department of Science and Art.

It cannot have been any secret, at least on the Left – that is, among Morris's friends and supporters and Sidney Webb's Fabians (at that time frequently the same people) – that this job was in the air, and many of them had pressed Lethaby to apply. When at last he did, he told Morris that he was not thinking of taking it as a last resort because of having no other work at the time. On the contrary, 'I feel', he said, 'I could do the work with real enthusiasm; for I believe I could succeed in interesting the pupils; I should at the same time do myself a lot of good in being dragged out of my present cul-de-bag.'[12] His application was supported by Norman Shaw, Sir Edward Burne-Jones, Philip Webb, Walter Crane, Heywood Sumner, William Richmond and William Morris, who wrote with enthusiasm of his many gifts.[13] On 19 November 1894 the Board announced that both Lethaby and Frampton had been appointed joint part-time art inspectors. The two were felt to be complementary and, since both wanted to continue to practise their respective arts, each was to work three evenings and two half-days a week for three hundred pounds a year.[14] Though the evidence is incomplete, enough remains to show that it was Lethaby who took the lion's share in the work of policy-making and reform. In any case, Frampton was to drop out within a year or two.

What were the convictions that Lethaby was to bring to the Technical Education Board and which in the ensuing years he was to turn into a teaching theory? In the first place the ideas that had originated in 'The Nature of Gothic' were to be explored, and secondly he had to test his conviction that design must be closely associated with the working of tools and materials. Though it was written the year before this appointment, it seems appropriate to reproduce part of the introduction of his influential book *Leadwork* (1893), for it exactly describes his thoughts as he took up his new appointment.

It cannot be too strongly asserted that the *forms* of past art cannot be *copied;* that certain things have been done is evidence to show that we cannot do them over again. Reproduction is impossible; to attempt it is but to make a poor diagram at the best.

Commercially produced imitations of ornamental works are infinitely beneath the merely utilitarian object which serves its purpose and nothing more. Behind all design there must be a personality expressing himself; but certain principles of treatment and methods of working may be understood in some degree by a study of past work without going all through it again.

New design must ever be founded on strict consideration of the exact purpose to be fulfilled by the proposed object, of how it will serve its purpose best, and show perfect suitability to the end in view, when made in this or that material by easy means. This, not the torturing of a material into forms which have not before been used, is the true ground of beauty, and this to a certain extent is enough without any ornamentation. Ornament is quite another matter, it has no justification in service, it can only justify itself by being beautiful.[15]

The recently created scholarships and exhibitions of the Technical Education Board had been awarded on the results of a 'South Kensington' type of examination, but the new inspectors immediately introduced an alternative, in which capacities were to be measured by very different criteria: evidence of imagination and the understanding of tools, processes and materials were substituted for tests of mechanical skill.[16] Complete change was impossible immediately. Not only were all the students and teachers trained on the old system, but it would have antagonized the latter, who sometimes saw the impending revolution as a threat to their livelihood.

Soon the inspectors were asking for new art examples quite different from the old. Lethaby's observations to the Board not only explain exactly why, but are of particular interest to us for their philosophical implications.

The casts also need careful revision, no care seems to be taken that they shall be good and stimulating, as long as they serve as drawing copies, it seems to be thought that they have served their purpose . . . The schools are now being flooded with 'elementary examples of ornament' which are so entirely bad – they [are] in fact manufactured expressly as 'ornamental' designs for school purposes. Nothing could be more destructive of the sense of beauty in the pupils. Examples should be fresh and vital . . . and of acknowledged works of art. Moreover they should be made interesting and instructive, all along the line, besides serving as drawing copies. At present the students know nothing of the examples, whether they come from Italy or England, whether exterior or interior work, whether far or near or remote position, whether in wood or marble, all is unknown; they are simply so much plaster 'ornament', whatever 'ornament' means under these conditions.[17]

We can see that the objects described came, in the spirit of the debased neo-platonism already mentioned, as near as possible to embodying an abstraction. They existed *only* as casts; entirely anonymous objects, divorced from materials, tools and purpose. Everything had been stripped away, leaving only the plaster bones of the 'principles of design'. The inspectors wanted, they declared, vital things

that should be good in themselves, of various schools and classes of design and workmanship, and their purpose and material clearly stated. Instead of being mere drawing copies, they should be definite classes of production.

Besides the reproductions of really good and stimulating works of art . . . we would largely use real examples . . . of wood carving, embroidery, pottery, book illustration, metal work, etc.

Such real examples would be of the greatest use to those who are studying special crafts and would suggest to the unattached student that the schools are established for other purposes than the teaching of drawing.

Then they made the very significant decision 'to buy occasionally . . . exceptionally interesting designs or examples executed in the schools. Modern design can only in great part be built up by studying current effort.'[18]

At about this time Lethaby submitted to the Board an undated report on The Schools of Art which contained many proposals for reform far more radical than anything Smith had recommended. It is a document of some importance, since not only does it make the most damning criticism of 'South Kensington', but it also appears to be the first statement of that practical forward-looking programme on which modern art education is based. Existing art schools, he wrote, aimed only at producing more certificated teachers, very few of whom were creative artists; the curriculum, too, was not only totally unreal, but destroyed the students' originality and spontaneity. Its highest aim was to obtain another examination pass and thus, by virtue of the 'payment by results' policy, earn more money for the school. (He must have been referring here to schools as yet unrecognized by the Board.) He proposed that the Board's grant should depend on the school's general conduct, the ability and enthusiasm of the staff, the standard of students' work and its appropriate practical application to the crafts. He continued:

> I would suggest that we need a clear distinction between the general Art School Teaching of South Kensington and the Technical Art Teaching of the Board. This will be especially necessary if payment by general results, such as I have suggested above, be made, for that will require a system of art-school inspection.
>
> In regard to this I feel strongly that the inspectors should be producing artists and have duties of a teaching kind, visiting and stimulating the schools periodically.
>
> I believe that this South Kensington Art School teaching and inspection should not attempt to cover any of the ground taken up by the 'Technical Art' instruction: such instruction is worse than useless unless it is given by actual craftsmen producers who live by their work. On the other hand the TEB while still assisting the Art Schools with grants and inspecting them as feeders of the Technical classes would be able to apply themselves more particularly to the Technical schools and classes. The special purpose of the Art Schools should be to provide wide and sound general instruction in art, specializing to some extent for those who are to follow certain callings but not attempting craft teaching by the certificated teacher method . . . I think there should be no increase of Art Schools in London on the present footing until we see what the Polytechnics and craft schools do. The point I want to make clear, is my view that an attempt under the present certificated teacher régime to transform them into craft schools would be vain. I feel that an effort should be made to make them do preliminary or at least more abstract work better, while experiment is being made with other types of instruction.
>
> Any attempt to radically alter the type of instruction must begin with the masters; . . . The attempt should be made to make the professional teacher competent in certain small groups of subjects and an artist in at least one branch. It cannot be too strongly enforced that an artist must be a producer and at the present time few of the masters are art producers. In the Technical Art classes the effort must be made by the TEB to get actual producers to teach in the schools, Architects, Sculptors and Craftsmen.

He went on to make detailed criticisms of the teaching, pointing out that much of it was inept and employed methods never used by craftsmen.

> [The teaching of] drawing needs compression and the removal, as far as possible, of artificial

code distinctions. Colours should be introduced at the earliest stage as it is found to amuse the young student. 'Freehand' from the flat should be largely eliminated in favour of relief casts of good ornament. In the higher stages much variety of methods should be encouraged. The 'shaded drawing' in chalk done by the stump which seems to be specially called for in the schools is entirely artificial and deadening, what is wanted is to train the students' observation, skill of hand and individual gift of expression.

Design: so far as it can be taught apart from special application needs most careful consideration and a clear understanding on the part of the teacher of the object to be aimed at. The endeavour should be to educate, not to teach supposed rules and possibly mistaken theories, but to bring out the individual sense of beauty. In many cases mere children in the classes show remarkable aptitude for making designs which really give delight; in too many cases this fresh beauty is not perceived by the teacher and he proceeds to crush it out by rule, correctness and historic styles. In design the greatest latitude should be allowed to immature power and poor drawing; suitability and freshness, in a word, beauty in the design is the one thing necessary. Neatly drawn exercises in combining historical forms usually get the most praise as designs and the thing of beauty stands much chance of being set aside as ignorant and ill-drawn work.

Flat copies, so far as they remain in the schools, should be in the form of interesting things finely drawn and with accompanying information. There is much loss of interest and power in the dry arrangements of abstract lines which largely serve as copies.[19]

To accommodate the Board's Central Art Department, the former Stationers' Hall in Bolt Court, off Fleet Street, was rented. Here the inspectors had an office, a workshop and a store for the collection of art objects. The lithographic classes held by the National Society of Lithographic Artists and Engravers were also transferred there from their original premises in Clerkenwell Road. When the inspectors proposed that these classes should form the kernel of a specialist school the plan was immediately adopted, and they were constituted a Technical Art School, jointly controlled by the lithographers and the Board, represented by Lethaby and Frampton. Subsequently enlarged to contain other printing processes, and named the Bolt Court Technical School, it was a unique and, at the time, a daring teaching experiment, being entirely independent of the Department of Science and Art. It has its place too in the history of technical education, for it was the first school in London to have specially equipped workshops, run by craftsmen for craftsmen, where teaching was related directly to the demands of printing and printers. It set the pattern for all future art schools, including the schools of art and crafts.

Three years previously E.J. Wall, editor of *Amateur Photographer,* had painted a gloomy but correct picture when he said:

The improvements in photography are coming from abroad and in photographical work the

Germans . . . are our actual workmen and managers. English firms are employing Germans, because they cannot get Englishmen who know anything . . . There is no school where they can be thoroughly taught in England.[20]

So successful, however, was the Bolt Court experiment that when the Director of the Photoprocessing Department, Charles Gamble, went to inspect printing education in Germany and Austria a few years later, he was able to report that only one European establishment – the Imperial Royal Educational Testing Establishment for Photo and Printing Processes in Vienna – was now more advanced, and that he could find nowhere in Germany evening classes of a comparable standard.[21]

In April 1896, Webb, prompted by Frampton and Lethaby, submitted a memorandum headed 'Central Art School' in which he wrote:

If . . . the Board gives up the hope that the existing schools of art can do all that is required for the application of art to industry it is imperative that an attempt should be made in another direction. I am driven to the conclusion that the Board should extend its very successful experiment at Bolt Court, and set up in some central situation an art school of its own. Such a school would serve many purposes. It would be a model for others, and thus greatly support the counsels of the Board's inspectors. It would be a centre at which the Board's art scholars and other picked pupils from the local schools could be brought under the influence of the best artists, who cannot be got to visit out-of-the-way suburbs. At present the good done by the Board's Art Scholarships is largely neutralized by the scholars having to go back to the routine art work of the local schools, from which it was intended to divert them. Moreover, such a school would enable the Board to provide *specialized art teaching in its application to particular industries* in close relation with the employers and workmen in those industries . . . as in the lithographic school at Bolt Court and in the St Bride Foundation Institute. This, which can only be done in some central institution, is the kind of art instruction which Messrs Frampton and Lethaby regard as most likely to succeed in really influencing industry. It is almost certainly the only thing which the workmen can be induced to attend.

Such a school might in time grow into a central municipal art school of the type of that at Birmingham, to which the local schools would serve as branches and 'feeders'.[22]

This memorandum was considered by the Board in conjunction with a report from the Inspectors on work submitted for scholarships, which, they wrote, showed

that we have not as yet to any large extent been able to lay hold of the ordinary artisan or even the craftsman engaged in the more ornamental crafts . . . before the crafts can be greatly influenced, more institutions of Bolt Court type must be established which will not be mere *drawing schools*, but schools where special arts and crafts are systematically studied.

It must be remembered that the large majority of those already attending the present schools of art are not engaged in industrial employments, they are 'art students', and often remain so to an advanced age. At present there is no way of leading those in the schools to take up specific crafts and arts . . . We are anxious that an experiment should be made with an art and craft school . . . for specialized art teaching in its application to particular industries.

The school should be complete and conveniently placed so that however many offshoots might ultimately spring up it would remain to some extent the central and typical school. The teaching should consist of experimental workshop practice with concurrent dwelling on theory; the teaching should in every case be by practical artists and craftsmen. We would suggest that it should comprise architecture and the building crafts, and sculpture and the decorative crafts. We believe it would be best to put the management of the school into the hands of a principal who should be responsible for the general discipline and all business, leaving the instruction to be given by independent artists and craftsmen. We need hardly say that we hope to be allowed to direct the studies. It is our view that architecture should be taught in the school as experimental building with as many workshops representing building crafts as room might permit; but at least masonry, bricklaying and plastering, with some carpentry and plumbing.[23]

Soon afterwards the Board heard of some premises that might be suitable: Morley Hall, situated in Regent Street opposite the Polytechnic. A subcommittee set up to consider the suitability of this property reported that it consisted of 'a house, 316 Regent Street, a private house in Little Portland Street, a two-storey building fronting in Little Portland Street and a series of saloons and corridors in the rear'. There were a number of large and small rooms, but the great advantage was that: 'The chief rooms are . . . in the rear . . . each room being lit by a lantern roof. This suite of saloons offers an opportunity for the establishment of art studios which is perhaps unequalled in the west end of London.'[24] The Board's minutes for the 18 May 1896 read:

We think it impossible to establish a central school under more favourable conditions . . . and it is very desirable that an experiment should be tried on a sufficiently large scale, in premises hired on a short tenancy, before the Board is committed to a scheme of a more costly and permanent character.

It went on to recommend renting Morley Hall for the new school to be opened the following October, and the preparation of a scheme for its administration and the conduct of the classes. The School's intention was not to supplant but to supplement apprenticeship, by enabling students to learn design and those branches of their craft which, owing to the subdivision of the production processes, they could not learn in the workshop. It was to provide for apprentices and workmen engaged in, or connected with, artistic handicrafts.

No attempt will be made to meet the requirements of the amateur, or to do the work of the teacher of figure and landscape drawing . . . nor is instruction given . . . in preparation for exams. The special business of the School will be the industrial application of decorative design [and] students . . . will concentrate on industries in which they are engaged.

The work of the school . . . will be for those employed in the building trades, architects and designers, workers in glass, bronze and lead, enamellers . . . branches of gold and silver trades.[25]

The proposals for the administration of the school and the conduct of the classes seem to have been mainly the work of the art advisers (Lethaby and Frampton), who proposed the appointment of a principal who, in addition to running the school, should 'teach some branch of art in its application to architecture or the crafts' – should be, in other words, a practising craftsman. As to the school, they recommended that it

should be open for class work on five evenings and at least three days in the week to begin with, and that it should be opened every day eventually if there is sufficient demand for instruction. We think, however, that the school should be open for the private practice of students every day from the commencement.

We think it extremely important that the principal should be well in touch with London artists, craftsmen and designers, so as to be in a position to bring the work of the school prominently before those most capable of profiting by it, and also to be able to advise the Board with reference to the appointment of professional teachers. It would be an advantage if the principal himself were an architect, or had been practically engaged in some of the arts and crafts connected with architecture . . . The teaching would be conducted in most cases, we think, by practical craftsmen acting under visitors or co-teachers who would treat of design; at the present time very few men can both teach design and practise a craft.[26]

In July the Board announced that the new school would be called the Central School of Arts and Crafts, and in the advertisement for a principal stated that its general conduct would be 'in the hands of the Board's Art advisers, G. Frampton and W.R. Lethaby'.[27] Three men, including W.B. Dalton, who subsequently became head of Camberwell School of Arts and Crafts, were interviewed but no appointment was made. A short while later the Board announced that Frampton and Lethaby would direct the School and appoint the staff.[28] They appointed Halsey Ricardo to teach architecture; drawing, colour, and decoration and design for cabinet-making and metal-working were to be taught by William Margetson, R. Catterson Smith and Archibald Christie; modelling and ornament, as applied to architecture and the allied crafts, by E. Ruscoe Mullins; enamelling by Alexander Fisher; lead casting and ornamental leadwork by Francis Troup and William Dodds; stained-glass work by Christopher Whall; stoneworking for architects by R.H. Hook; silversmithing by Augustus Seward; and building mechanics by R.B.

Molesworth. When these craftsmen were joined by Charles Beckett, who had been secretary of the Arts and Crafts Exhibition Society, but now became the School's curator, staff meetings must have seemed like meetings of the Society itself.

Here then was the making of a totally new departure in teaching – the fulfilment of one of Lethaby's dreams. The students were to learn their entire craft through workshop practice and the direct handling of materials and tools. The rigid theoretical abstractions of South Kensington's drawing syllabus were replaced by practical disciplines of making such things as a well-fitting dovetail or a *cire perdue* mould. The staff were not full-time teachers, but men who earned their livelihood with their hands and were employed for only a few hours a week, so that they could continue as craftsmen. One, William Dodds, was a certificated plumber and his employment must have been at that time an even more astonishing innovation. Nor did the School give diplomas or set any exams (and this meant that it was not eligible for any Government aid) – craftsmen continued to come as long as they thought the classes useful. It was to establish these precedents so successfully that they were to become part of the normal way in which art schools of the future were to be conducted. Under the influence of the Arts and Crafts movement, the curriculum of these schools was gradually transformed.

But this was all in the future. When the school opened its doors for registration on the 30 October, the assembled staff wondered whether anyone would enter, even with the encouragement of *Punch* which, summarizing one of Lethaby's comments – that 'Design . . . is simply arranging how work shall be well done' – published the following verses:

'Charge, Frampton, Charge! On, Lethaby, on!'
Are the first words of Punchius,
May you do just the thing which requires to be done,
With wisdom and wit and without noisy fuss.
The stubborn Britain is falling behind:
'Our fathers' custom' won't serve us today;
And to keep his front place Bull *must make up his mind*
For technical training to strive and pay!
British workmen don't lead where so long they have led;
The foreigner's filching our honour and hoard
Let us hope that our national wooden-head
May be cured by the Technical Board.[29]

The staff need not have worried. The School grew so fast that after six months there were over 250 students on the books and by the end of 1897 the Board was beginning seriously to think of finding a new site for a much larger building. Its tentative experiment had become an outstanding success.

Frampton resigned from the Inspectorate in 1889 and, though he remained a director of the School, he seems to have played very little part in its affairs. 'From the first,' wrote Noel Rooke (who had been an early student, then a teacher, and finally became vice-principal), 'the work, the creative ability, and the force were Lethaby's. I never saw Frampton there and only met one man who said he had.'[30] Edward Johnston's daughter Priscilla described the School:

> The building was a kind of improvisation of two houses joined together by a dilapidated conservatory, full of odd corners, creaking wooden staircases and small rooms packed as full as they could hold with eager students. Over it all presided Lethaby, who brought it into being and who must have filled it with an extraordinary sense of unity, for all, staff and students alike, were united in their love for him. His staff, it was said, never felt that they were working *under* him, but *with* him. Even the students felt themselves to be pioneers taking part in an exciting experiment.[31]

Lethaby's abilities as the *de facto* principal (he was not officially appointed until six years later) were outstanding. He was, wrote Rooke, the best chairman he had ever known. 'He had the wholly exceptional power of extracting the varied opinions from all sides of the table and of gathering them rapidly into a focus and a decision, without ever enforcing "Chairman's wishes" on a hesitant minority.'

Halcrow Verstage, an architectural student who was later to assist in the design of the new Central School building was equally impressed by Lethaby and his idiosyncrasies:

> The memory is still so fresh and strong of his voice, his phrases, his enthusiasms, and above all his charming modesty. Who can forget how he would punctuate the conclusion of a most acute and illuminating criticism with that disarming phrase, 'But there – I don't know.'
>
> Once I remember as I was busy on a design from a frieze based on the strawberry which Ricardo had set, I became conscious of Lethaby standing silently behind me. He looked over my shoulder for a time and then said, 'That's rather jolly; you must model it.' He hauled me along to the modelling room and got another student to show me how to prepare the clay. When the little frieze was finished, Lethaby carried it off to be baked. He was like that, encouraging students to develop all ways. 'Art, construction, architecture, they are all one,' he would say. 'You must go upstairs and see how stained-glass windows are made and books are bound and gilding done.'[32]

It is perhaps accidental that we know more about two particular classes than any others: those in architecture, discussed below, and those connected with the printing trades; these two seem in retrospect to have been the most influential. The first of the printing-trade classes was in bookbinding, a craft that had fallen very low by the end of the century, being driven down further by ignorance and the competition to produce ever cheaper bindings; this in turn led increasingly to the use of inferior materials and methods. It was a calamity compounded by the minute subdivision of labour, which rendered many an apprentice so incompetent that he did not even know how to stitch a book. Lethaby, determined that the tradition of making good books should not be lost, brought in Douglas Cockerell, who had been trained by J. Cobden Sanderson at the Doves Bindery, to start the first class in bookbinding in 1897. This class, in which the student carried through the binding of a book from start to finish, became so popular that the chief bookbinding enterprises regularly sent their young men to it for training.

From the first, even in his earliest competition drawings, it had been clear that Lethaby was interested in the design of lettering; and he lost no time in telling the Board that every kind used in art schools was, almost without exception, very bad. 'The way to "write" lettering', he stated, in a significant sentence, 'is to take some well recognized good example and practise "writing" that until a thorough knowledge of the forms is attained.'[33] Shortly afterwards he interviewed a hopeful young man who

> told him stumblingly, that he thought of 'going in for Art'. No doubt Lethaby groaned
> inwardly. 'What particular branch of Art, Mr Johnston?' he must have asked, and the young
> man replied that he understood he ought to 'learn to draw'. Lethaby leaned back in his chair and
> closed his eyes and he uttered what were to prove some of the most memorable words that his
> listener ever heard. 'Learning to draw,' he murmured, intoning it almost in a chant, 'Learning
> to draw! Thousands of young men and women *learning to draw*.'[34]

He was, of course, thinking of all those students up and down the country sitting in DSA classes and executing, one after another, totally useless and unproductive exercises in drawing. He urged Johnston to give up such vague ideas. Perhaps he could take up a craft? This led the young man to admit that he had 'played about with some parchments', and he asked if he could bring th⁀m round for the great man to see. Lethaby looked at the work he brought, ordered a manuscript for himself and said, with the most astonishing foresight, 'You will do very beautiful work if you stick to it.' When Lethaby started the new 'Illuminating class', as it was first called, he put Johnston in charge of it. (Plate 134.) There were seven students. The story of Johnston's subsequent work as a teacher, calligrapher and the designer of the London Underground type, among others, has already been admirably told in his daughter Priscilla's biography, *Edward Johnston*. Suffice it to say here that from his class came a whole school of calligraphers, and a renaissance in handwriting and type design. Eric Gill, the designer of many fine alphabets, was an early Central student. Gill wrote:

> I came along just at the moment when the work done by William Morris was bearing fruit in
> the minds of architects and the influence of Edward Johnston supported by that of W. Lethaby
> (who shall measure the greatness of this man – one of the few men of the nineteenth century
> whose minds were enlightened directly by the Holy Spirit) was making it clear that fine printing
> was only one of a thousand forms of fine lettering.[35]

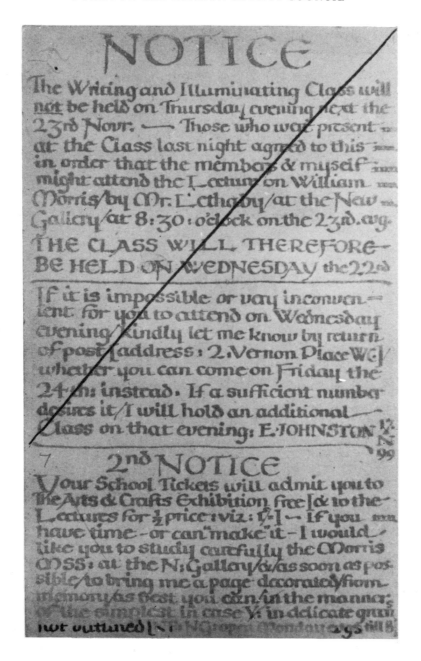

Two more classes in illustration and typography were started in 1905. The first was taught by Noel Rooke who was mainly responsible for the revival of the craft, at that time almost extinct, of wood engraving as an illustrative medium in its own right. In the nineteenth century books were largely illustrated with wood engravings, the product of the artist who provided the drawing, and the artisan who engraved it on the wooden block to reproduce a faithful copy of the original. But because the pen draws a black line and the graver a white one, there is a fundamental difference between the two media, which all too often went unrecognized by the artist and resulted in the making of unsuitable designs. These, in turn, were often made worse by feeble and mechanical engraving. In the last two decades of the nineteenth century, when photomechanical reproduction gradually replaced the engravers, the standard of these illustrations fell even further. Yet at the same time there was a revival of interest in fifteenth- and sixteenth-century cuts and their study persuaded a few people that, in the first place, the only true way to illustrate a book was with wood engravings, and second that such illustrations had to be designed and engraved by the same person. William Morris had already begun this with an illustration for his poem *The Earthly Paradise* in 1868 and he later cut several initials and borders for his Kelmscott Press; but the first real progress came about through the work of Ricketts and Shannon for the Vale Press and Lucien Pissarro at the Eragny Press. Even so wood engraving attracted little attention until Noel Rooke realized its potential and began in 1912 to teach it as part of his 'Book illustration and Poster design Class' in the Central's School of Book Production. He had to face widespread disbelief in the possibilities of such a revival, but received encouragement when most needed from Johnston and Lethaby.[36] The class soon flourished and most of the artist-engravers on wood of the next two decades received their early training in it.

The School was so crowded that the new typography class had to be held in a room above a shop in a nearby street. It was, wrote Lethaby,

> actually engaged in the trade and aims at supplying instruction in the highest type of book work
> . . . It is felt that in view of the most recent revival in printing the establishment of such a class
> which would co-operate with classes in book production, lettering and black and white
> illustration, etc., would form a complete school.[37]

The teacher was J.H. Mason, formerly the chief compositor of the Doves Press, which was conducted by J. Cobden Sanderson and Emery Walker. The Press was well known for the superb quality of its printing, in a type designed by Walker and, like Morris's Kelmscott Press Golden Type, based on one made by Nicholas Jensen. It may have been the production of its greatest work, the five volume Bible, then just completed, with its excellent setting and press work, that persuaded Lethaby to employ Mason. He carried into the School the austere ideals of the Press and chose to make Caslon Old Face the basic type to work in, because he believed its simple beauty made it the ideal teaching letter.

For some time Lethaby had been pressing, with little success, for specialist trade schools. He had originally suggested that St Bride's could be developed into a school of book production but, when the Board took no action, determined to set up such a school himself in the new Central School building which was being planned in 1903. The detailed schedule he submitted provided space for printing, engraving, writing and illuminating, lithography, colour printing, drawing and design and bookbinding, with a laboratory for research and materials testing. Douglas Cockerell's memorandum to the Board made the case for unifying the classes:

> Owing to the entire separation of the various book-producing crafts we find that the printer selects his paper and improves his type entirely from his own standpoint, with but little regard to the finished book. The paper used is often wholly unsuitable for binding by reason of its thickness or want of fibre, and plates and maps are often so printed that they cannot be satisfactorily bound up while in other ways quite unnecessary difficulties are made for the binder. On the other hand, the binder is apt to ignore the proportions of the printer's carefully arranged margins, and generally sacrifice the book to his conventional ideal . . . grouping the book-producing crafts together would produce uniformity of aim . . . If . . . these could be brought together under one general head so that by mutual interchange of ideas between masters and pupils of the different classes the relative needs of each craft might come to be generally understood.[38]

The typical product of the School will stand comparison with that of the best private press work of the time, for it was an expertly printed, closely set and well-made book, sometimes with woodcut or engraved illustrations. But for all that, its true significance lay in the standard of quality that it embodied; young printers and illustrators took what they had learned away with them and diffused it into commercial printing and publishing.

The School of Book Production was just one of the new departments Lethaby planned for the new building, which gave him the opportunity to weld together the various classes that had been started as and when there was a demand into schools where the whole of a craft could be taught. The new School should be, he wrote, 'an associated group of representative schools for particular industries', and he and his staff drew up detailed schedules (besides that for bookbinding) for silversmithing and metalworking, building design and decoration, cabinet work, textiles and architectural modelling.[39]

As a result of new Government legislation, the LCC became responsible for all the capital's education from elementary school to polytechnic and, in 1904, set up the Education Committee, with a number of subcommittees, such as the one for the Polytechnic and Evening Schools, which had taken over the work of the Technical Education Board. Soon it was considering who the new principal of the Central should be for it was obvious that, since the School was now housed in a new and expensively equipped building, it had to be fully used during daytime. For some committee members this meant a full-time principal: Lethaby, therefore, because he was prepared only to work part-time, was considered unsuitable. But Garnett, now the Education Committee's Adviser, successfully persuaded the subcommittee that it would be foolish to dismiss him. Pointing out that Lethaby intended to retire in two or three years in any case, Garnett wrote of the advantages of continuing a policy which had 'hitherto been eminently successful'; they could not afford, he said, to lose Lethaby's unique knowledge of the crafts and craftsmen, his skill and experience as a teacher, the loyalty of his present staff and the 'confidence with which he was regarded by art workers generally'.[40] The problem was resolved when Noel Rooke was appointed vice-principal, to take over responsibility for the daytime work.

The new dispensation was very different from that of the old Board, whose work had been done with such efficiency by Garnett and a tiny staff, and Lethaby soon began to experience the LCC's educational machine. He felt particularly the pinpricks of an individual he dubbed 'Mr Inkpots'. Nor, it seems, did his activities as chief inspector endear him to committee members. Shortly after the new building, with all its added cares, was opened, he wrote to Cockerell: 'I am thinking of resigning . . . I am worn out with night work and with all the reactions going on, they won't have anything from one except [red] tape . . . I am not a person high in favour – given to smelling around and looking at the things.'[41] A month later he did resign, but as a result of a protest by Cockerell and others to Lord Henry Bentinck, the Committee's chairman he was persuaded to stay on until 1911.[42]

What happened to the School and the changes that took place after Lethaby retired cannot concern us here. But under his direction it continued to grow and its influence to increase. The School's reputation abroad brought visitors from as far away as Japan. The young came to study – some from Germany, brought, no doubt, by the words of Hermann Muthesius, the architect attached to the German embassy to report on English architecture and design, who described it as 'probably the best organized contemporary art school in Europe'.[43]

At the beginning of the century Lethaby's authority in education was greatly extended by two successive appointments. In 1902, when he was officially made principal of the Central School, he was also appointed the Council's Art Adviser and charged 'to inspect any schools or classes referred to him and to consult and advise the Board's art inspector Christie . . . and advise on any questions of art instruction . . . to attend meetings of the Board . . . when required'.[44] Two years later, when the LCC took over all the capital's education, he was promoted to chief inspector, and thus given a say in art teaching in primary and secondary schools. With Christie he immediately issued a Report, *Art Instruction in Schools*, which suggested some radical changes:

> Art Schools should be developed as Arts and Crafts Schools . . . of course, picture painting
> and academic sculpture may be taken in certain of these higher schools and should count as

special arts to be taught along with others, but it is necessary to impress on the heads of art schools that there is no such calling as art-in-general, that general is only a preparatory stage to specific art.[45]

The Report criticized the art teaching for children, which was of a very low standard, lower if anything than in the DSA's art schools. It was made worse by ill-trained teachers and poor equipment, and had little to stimulate the child's imagination save the same dull models and plaster casts that Lethaby had attacked a decade before. The report recommended that, to make teaching more effective, there should be supplementary courses for teachers and, though making it clear that it was more valuable to draw from natural objects, advised setting up a circulating department to supply schools with art examples.

The fact that immediate change was not likely must have encouraged Lethaby and Christie to try to fill the gap by publishing *School Copies and Examples*, an inexpensive folder of large reproductions, which included the earliest English coat of arms, a sixteenth-century Italian alphabet, a design from a Spanish Armada tapestry, a St George and the Dragon, and reproductions from Bewick and the *Flora Londinensis*. It was accompanied by the following note:

> In this series it is intended to make available for school purposes fine works of Art in facsimile and also bring together Examples carefully chosen as being educational and suggestive. It has been so much the habit in Drawing copies to sacrifice the Beauty of the Example to some theory of method in instruction, as balance, clearness of outline and so on. It is our purpose, on the other hand, to put fine suggestive and useful material before the student so that he may at once have Drawing-copies of a real kind, Standard of Excellence and Examples of Historic Art, which would stir his imagination and suggest the very purpose of Art.

This book, with its lively illustrations, had a different purpose from most art manuals; its place is indicated by the laconic sentence with which Lethaby once summed up his thought on art education: 'Educate, suggest, encourage . . . Portfolios, Gill's letter cutting, Johnston's lettering, all good as ideals, all bad as imposed tyranny'.[46]

Meanwhile, Lethaby continued to visit the capital's other art schools and take steps to improve them. But since he was convinced that they were run on entirely wrong lines, he believed that the degree to which they could be changed was limited. The policy he recommended was planned to encourage the students in them to work directly from nature, and to practise designing, for example, a simple repeat pattern which depended not on a knowledge of a historical style or received form, but on a natural one. From some of the classes he brought students' work and, putting examples together, invited the masters of art schools to see them, with a view to elementary design being studied on some such principle in all schools.[47] (It is important to remember that at this time, and especially in 'South Kensington' circles, the notion of a 'design' meant almost exclusively a drawing on paper of a decoration.) A recommendation reiterated much that he had already said to Edward Johnston and no doubt to many other students. Pupils at all art schools,

should be urged to attach themselves to definite lines of study, and above all to enter into employment *as soon as possible*, letting their art school studies second their daily experience, and not be their main object. A large proportion of art school students seem to have the view that at the end of an art school course they will be able to earn their living as 'designers', they hardly ask themselves what they are going to 'design', and do not reckon on the difficulty of making a connection and getting work. Except in a small margin of instances – for such things as pattern design for wall papers and textiles – this view is entirely impracticable, all design being founded on an intimate knowledge of actual production in the *ordinary channels*.[48]

Lethaby believed that real design was the result of a proper understanding of tools, materials and function. Strongly supported by the outstanding success of the Central and later also the Camberwell School of Arts and Crafts, he was able to argue that art schools should be developed as arts and crafts schools. In such schools the 'fine arts' must have their place along with the practical arts, and each taught as a specific art: there was no such thing as general art. If headmasters did not agree with him, he was ready to sack them!

To analyse the influence of the Arts and Crafts movement on art education would mean a study in itself, and here it can only be hinted at. The Central School maintained its position, so that in 1946 *The Visual Arts: an enquiry* found that 'in the last fifteen or so years it has successfully trained designers for industry. It is better equipped than the Royal College; and its training more realistic. Many Royal College students have taken part-time courses at the Central School.'[49] It is undoubtedly true too that the Central had an enormous amount of influence. Dr Bernard Allen, who had been Garnett's assistant and later deputy education officer to Sir Robert Blair, the Executive Officer of the LCC Education Department, wrote:

The present generation has no notion of the state of things before the change. . . which was most dramatic . . . took place. Art teachers imagine that things were much the same as they are now; and have no idea what they owe to the pioneers of the latter part of the century. What was achieved by the Central School in the first few years of its existence was simply miraculous. It had profound effects all over Europe.[50]

Although two important art schools at Birmingham and Leicester run by great admirers of Lethaby were very successful, for the most part it would be true to say that, though the Arts and Crafts movement eventually transformed art education, the transformation was slow and sometimes painful. Few of the men involved had Lethaby's radical ideas, and the officers and many of the older teachers, trained on a different system, were no less entrenched in conservatism than were the Ministry of Education officials

Copy in pencil, with a clear outline, this diagram, slightly increasing the size.

ORNAMENT FROM A GREEK VASE

Candidates are required to copy the above drawing, increasing the size about one-third.
(*Candidates are not permitted to use rulers or drawing instruments.*)

PLATE 135. Two TEB examination papers from 1899 and 1902. The first is a typical DSA exercise using drawing instruments, the second, with its lively drawing of a real thing to be copied freehand, demonstrates the onset of the changes Lethaby and his allies were bringing about.

197

(Plate 135). Although most of Lethaby's ideas were eventually implemented, in some cases this did not happen till fifty years after they had first been aired. For example, not until 1946 was the Ministry's drawing examination replaced by one which was very much broader and included many extra subjects.

After Lethaby resigned from the Central School he was retained as the Council's art adviser until he retired in 1918, having spent a quarter of a century in the Council's services; twenty-five years in which its involvement in education grew from nothing to become the greatest in the world. When Lethaby applied for the Slade Professorship in 1910,[51] his claim that he had organized the Council's art education was well founded. In the minutes of the Technical Education Board and the Education Council there is a great deal more evidence of a similar nature, which has not been quoted here since, though it would enrich the tapestry it would not materially change it. When Lethaby retired, Blair wrote: 'I have always relied on you when dealing with problems with regard to which your wide knowledge and experience enabled you to speak with such authority.

I personally feel that your departure from the Council's service creates a gap which it will not be possible to fill.'[52]

CHAPTER SIX

ARCHITECTURAL EDUCATION

BETWEEN ROBERT ADAM AND RICHARD NOR-
MAN SHAW LAY A HUNDRED YEARS AND A WORLD OF DIFFERENCES. THE
ARCHITECT OF 1780 LIVED IN A SOCIETY WHICH HAD NOT MATERIALLY
changed for centuries; but the architect of 1880 was born of the flux of the Industrial Revolution. The eighteenth-century architect's main preoccupation was with Renaissance conceptions of space and the correct classical dress for his building. For its construction he depended on the traditional skills of the master craftsmen – masons, carpenters or bricklayers – who employed methods of construction that had changed little over the years. Suddenly everything changed. New towns came into being and old ones expanded enormously; the building contractor took over from the craftsman; novel building types emerged, there were new building techniques and up-to-date technology. Then the system of aesthetics – the Rule of Taste – that had been dominant since the Renaissance, collapsed. Novelty and diversity became the order of the day. The architect was thus faced with different responsibilities; he was now expected to negotiate with contractors and, in the absence of public legislation, to be responsible for the safety, quality and durability of his work. On top of all this he was often faced with the demand for a style appropriate to the age.

Though the architectural profession continued to expand, the old ways of training whereby a young man was articled to a principal continued to decay or became increasingly abused. Few can have been as lucky as the young Lethaby, who worked for seven years for a man both conscientious and deeply concerned about craftsmanship. Far more typical must have been the experience of Eric Gill who worked in W.D. Caroë's office:

> I saw the boss very rarely. He had no time to teach his pupils and least of all the sons of poor
> clergymen who paid reduced premiums. I don't say this in malice – in this kind of world, it must
> be so. After all it was my privilege to be allowed to work in his office and under the instruction of
> competent draughtsmen.[1]

In London, for the few, there was the teaching of the Architectural Association and the Royal Academy Schools of Architecture, which was conducted by Richard Phené Spiers, assisted by the Visitors, who were the architect Royal Academicians. In the modern sense it could hardly be called a school at all, since there were classes only on three evenings a week from six to eight, and practically the only subject taught was 'designing'. Spiers, who had been trained at the Paris Ecole des Beaux-Arts, tried to run the Schools on the same lines; but his attempts were doomed because there was no longer a 'correct' classic style to be taught. In due course he ceased to regret this loss, since it shifted the emphasis on to sound construction:

> There is no National School of Architecture here . . . no traditional teaching of 200 years as in France. So far as architectural design is concerned, I am inclined to think this a positive advantage and that in consequence English architecture is in a much more healthy state than either France or Germany.[2]

Spiers went on to say that he believed we owed the foundation of the modern school to the Gothic Revival and the intense study of ancient work that went with it. Thus English architects had not trusted to pattern books for the principles of design but had found them in the realities of mediaeval architecture. His account of the conduct of the classes described how the Visitor

> took the student's idea and suggested how it could be improved . . . It is on this principle that . . . instruction is given and . . . if the student is required to frame his plan on actual requirements and their best distribution, to base his elevation on the plan and to keep the whole design within the limits of sound construction it is better to leave alone the question of style . . . If for instance a student brings down a design bristling with Dutch impurities (and I am afraid Mr Norman Shaw has passed many a *mauvais quart d'heure* over some) it is no use trying to make it pure Italian . . . insist upon the construction being properly shown . . . So far as construction is concerned there is rarely a drawing sent in by an Academy student which would not make a much better *working drawing* than the finest example sent up in a competition in the Ecole des Beaux-Arts . . .[3]

Complementary to this is Lethaby's description, written from the point of view of a student:

> The method was to work out certain 'subjects' under the advice of RA Visitors . . . It was good fun, but it was anarchy. The constant master [Spiers] was, of course, overruled by the various opinions of the succession of Visitors, and thus the influence of the one man who could have taught us something of system and linked us to the larger European tradition of the time was rendered unavailing.
>
> Yet he was wonderfully modest . . . and talked with us with less than no sign of the superior, overbearing manner. That indeed was his weak spot(!), he did not care for riding over people. As to his helpfulness in advising generations of students where to go and where to find what they wanted his patience is hardly to be believed.[4]

As the various claims on architects multiplied and combined with the desires of many of them to better their social standing, so did the notion of professionalism emerge; the desire grew for a body of skilled practitioners who would be responsible for regulating the profession and by their skill and wisdom protect the public from any kind of building failure. Of course if anything of this kind were to come about, then architecture would have to become a closed profession, admission to which was regulated by some kind of authority. From this would inevitably follow several requirements: first, a national authority;

second, agreement on a definition of architecture; and third, some system of examination to determine whether the candidate for admission to the profession had acquired the necessary skills. Not surprisingly, no agreement was found to be possible, and when in 1891 an unsuccessful attempt was made to get parliamentary sanction for a Bill to close the profession, there was much public debate, which brought from the opposition a collection of essays edited by Shaw and T. G. Jackson entitled *Architecture a Profession or an Art* (1892). Although the main questions remained unresolved, it became clear that one of the bodies that claimed to regulate the profession – the Institute of Architects – had an examination for admission which was hardly adequate for the desired professional standard, and that, furthemore, it could be shown that membership of that body was no guarantee of competence.

It is important to distinguish between the great and growing demand for architectural *education* in the face of declining apprenticeship, and attempts to regulate the *profession* by examination. The only significant efforts for educational improvement in the last decade of the nineteenth century came not from the Institute but from the Architectural Association, the Art-Workers' Guild and the LCC Technical Education Board. The views of the Art-Workers' Guild were well represented in *Architecture a Profession or an Art*, since ten out of the thirteen contributors, including Lethaby, Macartney, Newton, Prior, Horsley and Blomfield, were guildsmen. Though all these men were to play a part in the national organization of architectural education, only the essays written by Lethaby and Jackson are significant, since they contain important new thought on education. Jackson wrote:

> Imagine some National School of Architecture, to which anyone connected with building could have access, whether he intended to be an architect, or a builder, or a craftsman. Let there be no conventional distinction of profession, no barriers of etiquette to divide the students. Furnish the school with competent teachers and appliances for study in every branch of the art. Let it be possible to learn all the mystery of good construction, but let construction never be taught except in connection with design, nor design except in connection with proper and natural use of material. Let the school be regularly visited by those who are recognized as masters of the art . . . Let students have every opportunity given them of seeing work actually done, and of themselves putting their hand to it . . . Let there be . . . school workshops where the process of every handicraft could be demonstrated, where masonry, carpentry, joinery could be taught, and a forge where iron could be wrought . . . Drawing of a practical kind would of course be taught, so that every student might be able to get out and explain his ideas to the workman or himself. Here those who mean to be ordinary builders might if they pleased, stop . . . The great thing would be that up to this point all should have been trained up alike without distinction, and that the Builder should have associated with those who aimed at higher flights, and should have shared in the same training under the best masters of the art.[5]

Once at the LCC, Lethaby had the ear of the ambitious and growing Technical Education Board, a public body prepared to take real action and with money to spend. No other architect had ever been in such a powerful position to do something, at last, for architectural education. The way had been prepared by Llewellyn Smith, who had reported:

> The provision for the training of architects in London is scandalously inadequate; such training, if improved, would raise the standard of the whole of the building crafts, and that a school of architecture and the building trades could become a centre of influence, giving tone and dignity to all the scattered classes for the various branches of the building trades throughout London; that such training as is being done is chiefly done by a voluntary society with no guarantee for its permanence, and is confined to its members, and that if a move is made to realize the idea of a great school of architecture, the Council would do well to help the project in every way in its power . . . The creation of a Municipal School of Architecture would be a splendid achievement for the London Council.[6]

Elsewhere in the Report he suggested attaching the Westminster Architectural Museum to the Architectural Association – the 'voluntary society' already mentioned – and developing the two as a single school. This plan received the general support of the Board who, a year later, stated that the Architectural Museum would be 'a splendid foundation for a school of architecture'.[7]

For Lethaby, however, this would not do at all. He was after something far more radical, even revolutionary. To understand his subsequent actions one must start from his criticism of contemporary architecture and his first blistering attack on the profession, the chapter entitled 'The Builder's Art and the Craftsman', which was his contribution to *Architecture a Profession or an Art*. His main argument comes again from 'The Nature of Gothic'. The profession, he wrote, could not be other than the enemy of good building since in practice one man's thought, framed in a dead language, was executed by another. And this was equally true of the

> so-called training of architects at the present time [which] consists not in their being taught their art, but in learning more or less by rote out of books some facts about it *when their art was an art*. The study of 'architecture' now is the study of lists of old buildings and their parts, classified and tabulated under every conceivable cross-indexing of features, styles, place, and date. 'Design' is now taught as being the 'scholarly' rearrangement of drawn representations of these 'features' in a new *drawing*. As a result of this utterly absurd and misleading method, young students . . . may now be examined and pronounced proficient architects – on paper.[8]

The examination he was referring to was probably that for admission to the RIBA, although it could equally well have been one set by the Department of Science and Art. Either would have demonstrated precisely the same split between the style or decoration of a building and its construction as there was between design and manufacture.

Soon after his appointment to the Board he produced a plan which gave practical expression to the ideas in 'The Builder's Art and the Craftsman'. It was based not on any existing architectural school but on the actual technical classes in the various branches of building construction. He seldom wasted time on disagreement but usually took from another's argument those points with which he agreed. Llewellyn Smith's Report was no exception, for out of it he picked what could just be interpreted as supporting his own view: 'I fully endorse Llewellyn Smith's view . . . that to leave the teaching of architecture to merely academic bodies is extremely undesirable. In the Polytechnics we have . . . what is required to [initiate] a scheme of instruction in practical architecture.'[9]

His proposal was to run at the Board's Central Art Department at Bolt Court, a programme which put into practice the view that there was in

good building, sympathetic choice and handling of materials and sensibility as to expression by means of colour, texture and form; all the factors necessary for building up a *positive architecture* such as is at present nowhere taught – an architecture entirely different to that of 'revival' and fashion which is responsible for much of the present chaos in the crafts . . . I recommend that an endeavour be made in the coming winter to establish a consistent course of training for architects; and to form a nucleus of a central *higher Polytechnic* . . . I make the following suggestions . . . courses in 'practical architecture' be commenced, embracing (a) technical training in masonry, carpentry, etc., (b) building construction . . . and design . . . in reference to the two former and to practical requirements, not in reference to archaeology as at present, and (c) that students be advised to become specialists in one [of the more ornamental crafts] . . . It is of the uttermost importance that the architect and workman should be in these technical classes together, . . . and that as an introduction, two or three lectures be given on 'Positive' or 'Constructive Architecture'. Such a scheme . . . has been in my mind for many years.[10]

It seems that the Board found this scheme rather too bold and unconventional for it was referred to Thomas Blashill, the LCC's chief architect, who did his best to kill it. It would, he said, cost a lot of money, lead to rivalry (presumably with the AA, of which he was a member) and possibly to impracticable ways. What was needed was that the architect should work 'in close contact not only with the workman, but with the contractors, lawyers, surveyors, parochial and county authorities . . . The most important agency for the training of the architect is the architect's office.'[11] Here, clearly, was a man who thought architecture no art but a profession! The Architectural Association itself was up in arms, and sent the Board a delegation which probably suggested that it would be far better to spend public money on supporting the AA rather than competing with it. Its own School, said W.D. Caroë, the president, was 'highly organized, full of life and vigour and whose teaching is based on half a century's experience'.[12] But although Lethaby's scheme was dropped, he could not be suppressed. His response was to give the lectures on 'Constructive Architecture' and call them 'Modern Building Design'.

In the first he reviewed the state of contemporary architecture – the built environment – and, in what was at the same time a theoretical statement of the nature of architecture, advanced reasons for its present failure. His first point was that architecture could not be divorced from building; the 'huge sloughs of squalor [which were] the imbecility and horror' of London were just as much examples of contemporary architecture as was the grandest architect-designed work.

It was the gravest mistake to foster the idea that there was a sort of building called 'architecture', superior in kind to ordinary building; the serious problem was how this 'ordinary building' might be well done, for without that as a basis no higher building or 'architecture' would be possible.

Although the skill of architects was unsurpassed, it had not resulted in a noble school of building. The principal mistakes had been the attempt to design in an historical style and to separate art from science. The first of these had produced the 'horrors' of ornamentation and the second had fostered the idea that *art* meant *books* about architecture of the past, and *science* meant *books* about building construction. Lethaby quoted Morris:

The art that is to come will not be an esoteric mystery shared by a little band of superior beings; it will be a gift of the people to the people, a thing which everyone can understand and everyone surround with love . . . A building is made up of millions of hammer strokes, chisel strokes and the movements of the hand. Because a man sits in an office and makes a design it does not follow that you get a fine building.

The lesson taught by the Arts and Crafts movement – so his argument ran – was that the only true style, a style with vital beauty, must be the result of experiments with material made by a man who was both its designer and maker.

It was important, he said, for a building to express its function, and 'the true mission of the architect was to lift these ideas themselves to nobler issues – to be Expressionist'. It is surprising to find him using what was then a new word probably for the first time in this context in English. More than a decade later, it was to have a similar meaning in Germany when applied to Peter Behren's AEG Turbine Factory, Berlin, that early monument to Expressionism. At the end of the lecture he gave this summary:

All buildings carry their characters written on their fronts. Students of architecture must learn to read these documents, questioning the right to exist of this or that so-called ornament or feature. This reading was a proper criticism. There were only two purposes for a building, service and delight, and that instructed pleasure could only be derived from a building when it fulfilled certain positive conditions. There was now no general interest in building, because design was irrational and workmanship not pleasant.

Those, not architects, who had taken the trouble to think about building, said very plainly that they had no pleasure in us. There were only two methods of design possible, the fresh experimental work of an artist, thinking in terms of materials, or the recombination on paper of the results of old artisan work. A small handiwork knowledge was so far better than none, but generally a fine work of art could only be produced by a workman. Beauty was not a luxury, but was inseparably bound up with quality. We who were selfishly interested in beauty could not content ourselves with less than the endeavour to bring back beauty to *all building*, and thereby beautify the earth and not desecrate it.[13]

His second lecture was devoted to architectural education and the way that he thought such teaching might be implemented. It must, he said, 'be based on constant and positive conditions of handiwork, utility, stability, and lastly on reverence for tradition and nature. Harmony with the rest of nature was the great rule of art.' In his opinion there were four 'positive conditions' for the creation of a truly modern architecture. The first was harmony with nature, which provided 'a vast reservoir of artistic ideas'; it gave material for local building types and in its 'actual facts of form, colour, and arrangement, the plan and pattern of things', was an inexhaustable source for decoration. Tradition furnished the second group of conditions.

The methods of studying the art must be reversed; instead of classifying their observations historically by time, place, and different styles [architects] must consider them as constructive expedients to meet definite requirements . . . Out of a critical use of past tradition, they must build up a tradition of their own.

Thirdly came 'need or utility' and fourthly 'materials and the manner of working them'.

Modern building design, he said, would be greatly improved if architects and buildings had 'practical workshop training seconded by office and workshop experience'. Architecture, which was 'a proportionate association of the crafts', should be taught in a crafts college, as part of a comprehensive scheme of craft education and in association with 'painting, sculpture, silverwork and so on'. Here builders, architects, artists and other workmen would meet on a common ground, where the best hope of stimulating a common effort to beautify public and private art would be established.

The four 'positive conditions' determined the curriculum. With the building trades workshop as the necessary basis and starting-point there would be a threefold course of instruction – manipulative, constructive and graphic. 'A young architect who had spent a year in a school of masonry, and a second year in plastering, plumbing and woodcarving classes would thereafter stand in quite a different relation to material and so-called design.' The student should also learn one of the artistic crafts such as 'modelling for plaster work, woodcarving and so on . . . To add something by one's own hand to a building under our care is a great pleasure, and production is a necessary discipline for the artist.' Parallel with workshop training would go the practical study of building construction, which would mean analysing methods, investigating possibilities and making evaluations based not on aesthetic judgements but on sound building practice and direct experiment: 'Construction might be carried much further by an extended analysis of the possibilities open to it . . .' Lethaby continued with a list of functional and practical questions which he thought it would be profitable to investigate, concluding: 'A thousand such problems should be attacked from the point of view of beautiful serviceableness.'

The student should practise not architectural drawing but drawing from nature in the widest sense: at the same time, a special architectural solid geometry, which explored such forms as arches, cycloids, etc., should be worked out. While going through such an intellectual training the student should be surrounded by 'examples, the loveliest that could be gathered, casts, large photographs, finely wrought drawings; but these should be for spiritual stimulus, a tree of life the fruit of which is beautiful, but not to be plucked'. As far as books were concerned, he recommended 'an accessible version of [Pugin's] main line of thought', Ruskin's *The Seven Lamps of Architecture* and *The Stones of Venice*, especially the chapter 'The Nature of Gothic'; Morris's essays 'Hopes and Fears for Art' and 'Gothic Architecture'; Viollet-le-Duc's article on Gothic Construction from his dictionary, which had just been translated with the title *Rational Architecture*; and finally Choisy's work on Roman and Byzantine building. In conclusion, he said that what was wanted

> was good building; architecture, not designs; accomplishment, not projects; experiences, not
> hearsay. Design could not be taught, it could only be suggested as primarily the outcome of
> requirements, material, traditions and pleasant workmanship under the inspiration of nature
> and tradition. These had been the conditions of every living school of architecture, and only by
> getting into relations with such ruling facts could we hope to build up an architecture at once
> scientific and beautiful – a Positive School of Architecture.[14]

These lectures, held at Bolt Court, which made such an uncompromising and critical attack on the architectural profession, were heard by between thirty and forty people and, as might be expected, were hardly well received by the older men, two of whom were heard to complain of the lecturer's 'terrible wrongheadedness'.[15] The editor of *The Builder*, H.H. Statham, in his rather guarded vote of thanks, was more cautious. These lectures, he said, had been 'very remarkable, eloquent and interesting . . . although, in certain points he was inclined to differ'.[16] Whatever the older generation may have thought, younger architects were not at all of the same mind: Blomfield, at that time still numbered among the radicals, said: 'So far as we . . . were concerned it was Lethaby who more than anyone coloured our ideas'.[17]

Meanwhile, the Architectural Association, seeing the possibility of another school at its gates, decided to forestall Lethaby's plans and introduce a new feature that had been, as W.D. Caroë said in his presidential address, 'almost a dream . . . for those connected with the management of the AA'.[18] This new feature consisted of workshop classes, which were known as The School of Design and Handicraft, and were intended to 'train students in the nature of materials . . . and their methods of construction'.[19] In the first three years of its short existence Lethaby, though not an AA member, was invited to inaugurate the session with an address, though what he said can hardly have been welcome to the older members. He attacked the whole panoply of academic teaching theory; systems of proportion, the value of sketching architecture, the ability to make an architectural perspective and so on – the very things, in fact, that he himself had once held dear.

At first the students in the School of Handicraft were admitted to building construction classes in the Great Tichfield Street Technical School, but the next year Lethaby provided, especially for them, workshop demonstrations at the newly opened Central School of Arts and Crafts. For reasons that have not been established, though they may be connected with the changes that were taking place· in fashion at the beginning of this century, when architectural style was heading back into the seventeenth and eighteenth centuries, the School was short-lived. By 1904 all its original teachers with the exception of Prior had resigned, and the class concerned itself exclusively with designing on paper.

When Lethaby found that his scheme for a Building School was not to go ahead he tried a new tack, while continuing to remind the Board of its responsibilities. He wrote, in a typical memorandum, 'The Board ought to do something to guide the studies of a large number of young builders and architects who are at present in the various . . . schools . . . There is no school where young builders, not calling themselves architects, can obtain good instruction.'[20] 'Young builders, not calling themselves architects' is a deliberate allusion to the beliefs of the Arts and Crafts movement, whose architect members generally disapproved of the notion of a *profession* and preferred to think of themselves as builders.

Six months later, the Craft College for which Lethaby had so long argued came into existence, but with a slightly different emphasis; for whereas in his Modern Building Design lectures he had proposed a school of building, with dependent classes in the artistic crafts, here the school – the Central School of Arts and Crafts – though under the aegis of the mother of the arts, was 'adapted to the needs of those engaged in the different departments of building work (Architects, Builders, Modellers and Carvers, Decorators, Metalworkers, etc.)'.[21] As already mentioned, the architectural design classes were run by Halsey Ricardo, an architect who greatly admired Philip Webb, from 'the point of view that they should respond directly to the facts of modern life'.[22] In describing his course, Ricardo said:

Architectural design is taught by setting subjects to the student to be worked out: as many determined conditions, as to cost, nature of site and materials, etc., being given as practicable. The conditions of the problem under hand are to govern its solution, and the design is made to arise from honest and proper acceptance and appreciation of these conditions.[23]

I am afraid you must not come to us to learn 'styles' . . . for we are a very practical and elementary class, I assure you we approach the subject entirely from the builder's point of view. That is to say we base our designs on necessity; we know what is wanted for a particular house, within certain limits of space and material, and we study how to arrange it in the most convenient and suitable way. We don't profess to study beauty of form and decoration as such; whatever beauty we may gain is such as springs naturally out of utility, and, perhaps, that is the truest way of teaching beauty after all.[24]

Even the architecture of the past was studied as Lethaby had proposed, from

examples of architecture, of Roman and Gothic times, mainly based on Choisy's analysis of Roman construction and Viollet-le-Duc's mediaeval buildings, . . . and the history of the conditions under which these examples were raised is dwelt upon. Stress is laid on the kinds of knowledge and thought exercised by those nations as being prime elements in the growth and beauty of their architecture.[25]

From the beginning, young architects were the second largest group of students, and the class eventually became so successful that Archibald Christie was brought in to help, to be followed in 1900 by Percy Ginham who, like Christie, had trained in Shaw's office under Lethaby. In the original school building the architectural studio was a large octagonal room with a leaky glass roof, so that when it rained students had to put up their umbrellas – an irony that will have added point to lectures on the importance of sound construction.

At first there were classes in modelling and ornament as applied to architecture and the allied crafts, lead-casting and ornamental leadwork, stone-working for architects and the mechanics of building. Others followed on building construction and structural mechanics, in which students experimented with 'models and apparatus to determine stresses and deflections, beams, roof principles, shoring and the stability of buttresses, retaining walls, arches and domes', and the chemistry of materials. There were also the artistic craft classes in stone and wood carving, decorative plaster, ironwork and metal-casting. The leadwork class deserves special mention, because, like Lethaby's book on this subject, it greatly assisted the revival of this craft for decoration, especially of houses.[26] It was taught by the architect F.W. Troup who had, at Lethaby's request, studied all the traditional methods of working lead, and William Dodds, a registered plumber, who became a highly accomplished lead-caster (Plates 136, 137, 138). Like the calligraphy class, it was the first of its kind and it was also the first time that a designer and a skilled artisan had taught side by side. Though now commonplace in schools of design, it was then almost unheard of.

PLATE 136. Lead flower vase.
This and the flower tub were designed and modelled by
Lethaby. Executed by Wenham and Waters.

PLATE 137. Lead flower tub.

Perhaps because the work was so down to earth it was almost ignored by the architectural press, and sadly little has been discovered about it. Students designed small or medium-sized town or country houses, railway stations, schools and the like, and such unfashionable things as methods of construction and cost were paramount considerations. At an exhibition of students' work *Building News* wrote that it was an

> honest effort applied to buildings of modest everyday use, instead of pretentious edifices . . .
> These are straightforward and exceedingly simple drawings, and would not perhaps commend
> themselves to those accustomed to the work sent in for National Competition prizes, but they
> are practical and the details are all shown to a good scale.[27]

PLATE 138.   Lead rainhead. Designed by F. Troup. Executed by W. Dodds. Reverse of postcard from
Troup to Lethaby, dated January 1903, reads: 'I hear the A[rts] & C[rafts] Exhibn. is swamped with up-to-
date highest art lead. *I* didn't begin it you know.'

A few years later, in 1909, when the tide of the Georgian revival was beginning to flow strongly, the
criticism became sharper and the journal thought that the designs exhibited showed signs of an 'endeavour
on the part of the teachers to impress students with the cult of simplicity, carried to the extreme of showing
bare construction without satisfactory and necessary ornament, and certainly without an underlying
knowledge of the bases of architectural style'.[28]
   Within the limits of its being part-time the Central's School of Architecture and the Building Trades
offered a building design course second to none and probably more comprehensive than in any other
institution with the possible exception of University College, Liverpool. Yet, in terms of the capital's
actual need for a higher polytechnic for the building trades, it was a drop in the bucket. It remained so

until 1904. Then the LCC at last founded the Brixton School of Building, and the kind of institution that Jackson had envisaged and Lethaby consistently advocated came into being. Lethaby had criticized Jackson's essay for not clearly stating the need for a scientific training, but at Brixton that was attempted too. The School's purpose was

> training junior members of the trade in principles and the relationship of these to other allied trades, training potential foremen and clerks of works, the training of architects in the principles of construction and in all matters, in which in the exercise of their profession they come directly into contact with several branches of the building trade, experimental research of an educational type in connection with builders' materials and composite structures.[29]

By the time the Brixton School was completed the LCC had given the capital, in a decade, a richer training in building and architecture than ever before; but away from London, in the provinces, hardly anything existed. It was becoming increasingly obvious to progessive architects that education would have to be organized on a national scale with an authoritative controlling body.

An examination of what was desirable in the education of the architect depended at the very least on a definition of architecture, a critique of its builders and the possibilities and limitations of contemporary society – in short, on a theory of architecture. For without some guiding principles how could what was taught be evaluated? In Lethaby's first lecture on modern building design he had largely confined himself to a critical attack on contemporary architecture in general, but in 'The Builder's Art and The Craftsman', and in 'Education in Building', an important lecture given at the RIBA in 1901, his theory of architecture was more fully developed, as will be seen in a later chapter. In conclusion he spoke again of the need for a Building polytechnic, and added this timely reminder of the Institute's shirked responsibilities:

> The question of education in building to be solved must reach all classes of men engaged in building, and it must set itself to improve all the mass of building done in England. If we are to claim public help, I feel that we should get rid of visionary ideals and sectarian narrowness, and stand to gain with the common gain. It would have been well if we could have been ready with a scheme in which all might join a dozen years ago, when Technical Education was first being 'practically dealt with; but I fear unless we are less vague in our aims nothing will be done for a further dozen years, and that I feel would be a calamity.[30]

The Guild architects were no longer content to let the matter rest there and, whilst one knows very little of what was discussed in the architects' group, it seems clear that, although some of them were extremely wary of the Institute because of its attitude to registration, they did agree that the RIBA was the only body capable of organization on a national scale. Accordingly in June 1903 these men (Blomfield, Champneys, Horsley, Lethaby, May, Newton, Ricardo and Prior) approached Aston Webb, the president of the Institute, with some proposals, and he agreed to call an informal conference between them and the officers of the Institute. Subsequently, a committee was set up – it included Blomfield, Champneys, Lethaby, Macartney and Ricardo – to prepare a discussion document for the RIBA's Council. If it was not drafted by Lethaby himself, it shows his influence. The first of its two main points was that articled pupilage failed because it gave no grounding in construction and left too much to individual initiative and chance, and that lack of preliminary training prevented the pupil from taking advantage of his office experience. The second was that polytechnic classes failed because the student was not in touch with the conditions under which real work was actually designed and produced. Its last paragraph follows Jackson quite closely:

> It is suggested that the object . . . [should be] the training of all who propose to deal with Building . . . and should be mainly directed to the practical side of architecture and what should be called the ground work common to both architecture and the building trades . . . Admission should be open to anyone . . . with the necessary education. (Students should take the Preliminary course before working in an office and subsequently follow the advanced course.) Architects taking pupils should insist on their pupils having gone through the preliminary course.[31]

Soon an RIBA Board of Education was established which, since only a minority of its members were members of the Institute, was at least nominally independent and able to co-opt architects who were not of the Institute. Immediately the Board set to work to draft a teaching syllabus – and made a good start by voting down a proposal from Lethaby! The reference in the minutes reads:

> Mr Lethaby considers laboratory training is the most important part of the whole scheme. He says (it is hardly realized how many well-appointed shops in masonry, plumbing, etc., there are in the Polytechnics) . . . there should be kept in view the necessity of raising up experts who will undertake research in building science. We want to train expert constructors, engineers of building, men of initiative and daring . . . Mr Lethaby suggests that the principal institutions concerned, London University, the RIBA, the LCC be invited to confer as to the establishment of a Central School of Building Science (the phrase is Mr Lethaby's) to deal with experiments in advanced building science.[32]

Vigorous discussion continued, and in November 1905 the dozen leading Guild architects, which included Lethaby and others who had worked on the original scheme, publicly accepted that any scheme of education could be effective only if carried through by the Institute. They agreed to join (or in some cases rejoin) it, on the understanding, first, that it would zealously support the scheme and, secondly, that their strong opposition to any legislative restrictions in the practice of architecture would be understood and respected.[33]

When the syllabus was eventually published in 1906, it was clearly a compromise between the views of those who might be called the constructionalists and the academics, as can be shown by comparing it with Lethaby's own teaching syllabus that had just been published by the *Architectural Review*.[34] The middle course taken by the Board is clearly demonstrated by the way the following two propositions from the preamble are arranged cheek by jowl: '[Training should be] governed by the principle that construction is the basis of architecture and by its correlative principle that architecture is the interpretation of construction into forms of aesthetic value.'[35]

The Board started work in the same year as the syllabus was published, but before long Lethaby, who was a member, was pointing out there was a discrepancy between the syllabus and the RIBA's examination questions, which seemed to arise from insufficient contact between the Examiners and the Board of Education.[36] A joint conference resolved this conflict, to the triumph of the reactionaries; the syllabus was rewritten, construction took a back seat and the acquisition of drawing skills became once again the supreme aim. 'Expertise was', in the words of Goodhart-Rendel, 'restored.' Lethaby must have been many times on the point of resigning, but decided in the end that he could do more good inside than out.

At Board meetings, where his minority view can have carried little weight, he contrasted the superior technical training on the Continent and in America with training in this country, criticizing the common tendency of English schools to ignore practical and scientific training in favour of 'the academic, which itself is made to consist of "designing" on paper'.[37] Heads of schools, presumably prompted by the examiners, encouraged students in grandiose feats of draughtsmanship for the Prix de Rome and the Institute's own prizes and medals, in a variety of revived English and French Renaissance styles. Encouragement must also have come from men like Blomfield, also a member of the Board, who, though he had for a time supported Lethabean ideas, now threw his considerable weight behind the revival of 'styles' and a futile attempt to establish the Beaux-Arts system of teaching here. Lethaby naturally attacked the move.

In 1917, at an RIBA Conference and just before he resigned from the Board, he delivered his parting shot:

> Modern architects have to deal with very complex and technical matters, the building on congested sites of great hotels, railway stations, factories, business premises, and the like, and for this it is clear to me that there must be highly organized scientific training . . . What are the main divisions into which different faculties might run? There seem to me to be about five; the expert constructor and planner, the finisher and furnisher, the expert in old buildings, the man of business and the country builder and general practitioner . . . the first and the last should be the main concern of this Institute.

I have been asked why I would 'concentrate on structural perfection' and why I do not advance to 'some theory by which to express ideas . . . the science of aesthetics, psychology, and human nature'. Now, because I don't think there can be any agreement on aesthetics and human nature so that they can be taught at this Institute, it does not follow that these things do not interest me profoundly. Indeed, it is just because I want a true artistic or human nature content given to our buildings that I would sweep away the teachings of grandiose bunkum as architectural style . . . I want the most exquisite poetic beauty, but I do not see how this Institute is to teach how to produce it. Therefore I say train us to practical power, make us great builders and adventurous experimenters, then each of us can supply his own poetry to taste.[38]

Lethaby came to believe that no architectural revival could take place without a common programme, and it was this that led him to originate The Modern Architecture Constructive Group; an informal group, it has left few records but must have been based originally on the Art-Workers' Guild. The scheme was perhaps first aired in 1922 in this letter to Pite:

> This year I do want to get one dozen men (good quality as may be!) together in a room just to *agree* that they believe in building, experiment, tidyness and adaptation &c (no vows forswearing 'Gothic' or 'Renaissance' or anything) but just as far as maybe we will agree. You'd come wouldn't you and not raise posers?! Put posers in Pocket! (Motto). I want you to say to being what you are – remember the young are as cattle without a drover – and no Bishop but Paul Waterhouse.[39]

The first meeting of the Group was probably held in March 1923, for Lethaby's manifesto, which will be found on pages 295–6, was issued two weeks later. Only one account of any of the meetings survives, given by Sidney Loweth, then a young assistant in the Architectural Department of the LCC:

> I am amazed to find that in a group of about 20 architects – there were 6 to 8 Professors of Architecture – several of whom I knew – Pite and Richardson.
>
> The meetings were 'about' once a month and I was thrilled to be so honoured and never missed one . . . I was charmed by Lethaby . . . One evening I got there early and had a chat with Professor Richardson . . . he told me that we were both honoured to know Lethaby – and that he was ten years ahead of any other architect in the country.[40]

Lethaby's opinions were unlikely to be supported by many successful architects because, while he was concerned with service and science, they considered architecture to be primarily a vehicle for aesthetic self-expression – as many architectural students are still taught to do. When, in 1917, Lethaby wrote to Blomfield and asked him to support some earlier statement similar to that of the manifesto, he received a particularly illuminating reply:

> I have twice read through your very interesting memorandum . . . with much of it I am in sympathy . . . but I cannot turn my back on the past . . . (and) I will not limit science merely to

laws of fact ascertained by experiment. There are the unascertainable facts of human emotion and temperament which are the basis of all art, including architecture, and these are to be reckoned with too by the architect and that is why he is not an engineer . . . I have been writing my ideas of the history of architecture for thirty years or so and am I now to sign a palinode? I have just completed the second part of my history of French architecture . . . and am I now to sign a clause that the whole thing is bunkum? What it comes to is this, that substantially I am with you, as far as you go, but I want to go further and combine with your practical drift, the recognition of that emotional basis without which architecture has no particular interest for me. To put it crudely in another way, fine architecture is as much the expression of personality as fine painting or sculpture or any other art. You see my individualism is in the bone.[41]

Lethaby addressed his propaganda for modern architecture and design to the general public and to young architects and students, for he expected little support from his contemporaries. Two of them – Blomfield and Goodhart-Rendel – provide equally disparaging though different views of Lethaby's philosophy. Blomfield thought that Lethaby had 'never woken from the trance into which Ruskin's eloquence had thrown him'.[42] But Goodhart-Rendel's criticism was, though more intelligent, equally damning:

Functionalism may be regarded as a close architectural analogue of Puritanism, with its insistence upon moral values, its distaste for aesthetic values, its righteous slow-wittedness, and its abhorrence of gaiety. Like Puritanism it offered the consolations of assured virtue to those whom a naughty world might otherwise abash . . . It was first preached in England by Professor W.R. Lethaby many years ago, but enjoyed no vogue until it was restated more recently by M. Le Corbusier, and by him put into practice . . . Although the theory of Functionalism was Lethaby's and therefore English, it nevertheless seemed for many years as though the country of its origin was the only part of Europe in which it never was to be put into practice.[43]

Lethaby's theory of architecture is discussed elsewhere, but may here be summarized by saying that he believed that the first essential in the creation of a modern style was wide agreement on a definition of the nature of architecture and the second putting into practice an enduring programme of work inspired by it. Today, it was no longer possible that this definition could be other than scientific since one based on aesthetics was too subjective and vague to gain the widespread acceptance that Lethaby believed essential. The idea of such a rational definition was, however, unacceptable to romantics like Goodhart-Rendel who, despite familiarity with Lethaby's arguments in favour of 'structural perfection' (page 253 et seq.) preferred, as in the above passage, to simplify them to the point of misrepresentation.

CHAPTER SEVEN

THE ROYAL COLLEGE OF ART

AT THE PINNACLE OF BRITAIN'S STATE-
SUPPORTED ART EDUCATION STOOD THE NATIONAL ART TRAINING
SCHOOL WHICH HAD BEEN RENAMED THE ROYAL COLLEGE OF ART IN 1897.
This impressive sounding institution in South Kensington was meanly housed. It lacked a lecture theatre, a refreshment room and other amenities, and what rooms it had were grossly overcrowded, badly ventilated and ill-lit; the fabric was in such a poor state of repair that work had to be moved from the upper floor when it rained. Conditions must have been intolerable.

> The advanced rooms are placed over the Barracks of the Engineers, whence come the noise of crying children, and the smell of cooking food. On the same side is the road around the Museum and on this road the traffic is considerable . . . Coals are delivered under the windows during which operation the idiomatic English of the men delivering them, among themselves and to their horses, it not instructive to anyone, especially the young ladies of the school. Immediately opposite the windows is a large steam engine and [its] machinery . . . also a blacksmith's forge with anvil and chimney . . . so arranged that the dense smoke drives into the windows . . . These inconveniences are outside, but on the courtyard face the odours from the restaurant . . . make it impossible to open the windows.[1]

So shabby was the entrance to the College that even the name on the building could not persuade foreign visitors that it was the entrance to England's sovereign art school. As a symbol of the national concern for living art, it could not be bettered.

Initially the School had been founded to train designers for industry, but well before the end of the century it turned more and more to the education of teachers. The syllabus was necessarily laid down by the Department of Science and Art, which meant that students' time was spent almost exclusively in the production of the highly finished drawings that were required to gain the Art Class Teacher's Certificate or the Art Master's Certificate, which for future teachers were of vital importance, since their income would depend on having as many qualifications as possible. Towards the close of the century, increasingly critical reports showed that the College was badly run down and that the teaching, lacking both direction and any real system, was at a low ebb. Even comments such as the following were not untypical:

> The time devoted to elaborate drawings for certificates was often beyond the stage when the student ceased to derive any educational benefit from them. The monotony and uniformity of the work, and the anxiety of the student to gain another 5 shillings per week [a grant made by the Board for each additional certificate] brought about a dead level of indifference to Art. Any subject which did not appear among the requirements for the certificate was studiously

avoided. The history and tradition of Art had no interest for the student. Nor was he sympathetically inclined toward applied Art, but rather the reverse; it was looked upon as foreign to his profession, something quite outside the range of subjects with which he would eventually have to deal. No system could be invented better calculated to produce untrained, narrow minded men. The certificates had become such fetters that a broader outlook upon the field of Art was almost an impossibility. Students who intended to become teachers could scarcely have been more unfortunately situated . . . Art was never approached from an educational point of view; it never entered into part of the curriculum.[2]

When in 1898 the Department of Science and Art appointed Walter Crane as headmaster, it was an admission of failure and of the bankruptcy of its policies. As one of William Morris's most ardent disciples, he stood firmly in the opposite camp. Not surprisingly, he advocated the rival system of art education fostered by the Arts and Crafts movement in the increasingly successful crafts schools. 'The curriculum seemed', wrote Crane, 'terribly mechanical and lifeless'; and as far as the existing constitution allowed he tried to expand it.[3] But in trying to run the college he found himself up against a suffocating bureaucracy whose red tape ultimately proved too much for him; so, diplomatically pleading pressure of work, he resigned. He left behind a scheme to reorganize the College, which had been prepared with Alan Cole and was designed to turn the RCA into a high school for decorative design and handicraft.[4] The syllabus started with classes in drawing and in architecture, as 'mother of the arts', which were followed by others in all the crafts connected with the decoration of buildings. Even painting was to be studied 'strictly from its mural and decorative side'. There were to be practical workshop facilities for all the crafts and a large empty space or temporary building in which the students could collaborate annually in the design and execution of a complete scheme of decoration. But the Department responded with a firm NO, not surprisingly since it would have meant overturning the existing syllabus and admitting its own failure even more openly.

When, at the turn of the century, the Board of Education superseded the Department of Science and Art and took over the responsibility for its work, it immediately set up a Council of Art to reorganize the College. The members of this Council, apart from the Board's officials, were Crane, T.G. Jackson, Onslow Ford and W.B. Richmond, all drawn from the Art-Workers' Guild. On their recommendation the College was divided into four schools – architecture, decorative painting, sculpture and modelling, and ornament and design. Beresford Pite, G. Moira, E. Lanteri and Lethaby were respectively appointed to take charge of them under the new headmaster, Augustus Spencer. Standards were raised, the number of students was greatly reduced and an entirely new curriculum, far broader and more systematic than the old, was introduced. In this new curriculum students did a short architectural course before specializing, but those who wished to become teachers had to spend some time in each of the Schools.

Lethaby's reports for the London Technical Education Board had shown that the low quality of art education came just as much from the methods used as from the theories of the Department of Science and Art; it was largely to counteract such methods that the arts and crafts schools (the Central School and Camberwell) outside the control of 'South Kensington' had been opened. The abolition of the DSA meant that all the old problems could be brought to light and examined and that different methods of training could at last be established. Consequently, when Lethaby was offered the new post of Professor of Ornament and Design in 1900, he jumped at it, though he had few illusions about the difficulties he might face. 'At the moment', he said, 'it is the worst school in England . . . I feel a call, like Livingstone to the heart of darkest Africa. They'll probably try to eat me.'[5]

Lethaby's curriculum had to be different from that pursued at the arts and crafts schools, where the students were already craftsmen or apprentices in specific trades. Since the Royal College students were potential teachers, he believed they should receive a wide visual education, be encouraged to produce independent design work and become masters of at least the rudiments of a craft. What he tried to do was to find means that would reverse his previous judgement on art teachers, by making these student teachers 'competent in a certain small group of subjects and an artist in at least one branch. It cannot be too strongly enforced that an artist must be a producer and that at the present time few of the masters are art producers.'[6]

To the modern mind his syllabus, which rested on 'a study of practical needs in production . . . the study of fine examples and drawing from nature'[7] must seem remarkably unambitious but set against previous syllabuses it was revolutionary. For the former painstaking copying of drawings and plaster casts he substituted the direct drawing of living plants, a method which upset some of the older students, such as the young woman who had complained to the headmaster that the new professor wanted her to draw watercress, which was such a comedown from the high art she was used to.[8] Again, museum objects were studied in quite a different way, no longer as examples of historic style but in the same manner as the architectural students at the Central School studied architectural history; that is, as characteristic products of a certain set of unrepeatable circumstances, which nevertheless had things to teach in terms of techniques, pattern distribution and so on. In Lethaby's words: 'Out of the critical use of past tradition, [students] must build up a tradition of their own'.[9] His third innovation, the introduction of craft teaching, was badly hampered by the parsimony of the Board, and it was to be many years before anything like real craft training became possible.

Since the Board of Education would allow only those craft classes that needed little or no expensive equipment, a decade after the reorganization there was still but a handful of them – in stained glass, simple metalwork, calligraphy, embroidery, carving and gesso work, and pottery where the students did little more than tile painting. Explaining to the Board the function of the classes, Lethaby wrote that they laid down the practical basis of many forms of design, and in teaching technique and necessary limitations by actual demonstration and experiment. By this direct access to the material conditions the meaning and purpose of design as arrangement for real work is brought home to the students, it corrects the erroneous idea that design is an abstract thing, and convinces them that suitability and pleasant fitness are the main considerations.[10]

He personally taught what would now be called an elementary course in basic design, in which students learned the method of formation and distribution of repeating patterns, did a variety of exercises which he called 'games', such as the making of constructions out of 'a bundle of little rods', and played with simple units of form in a variety of colours.[11]

The objectives of his syllabus were set out in a paper on design education which begins with a definition of 'design' as

some intention in regard to work, as special arrangement, or an adaption to meet given ends. Perhaps the best definition . . . would be – the arrangement of how work should be well done . . . Drawing is a useful aid in recording ideas, but much the best work has been done directly without it, the design and workmanship being inseparable . . . The closer design and workmanship can be associated the better in every case: for only by being an expert in the work required can one properly arrange how it shall be done.[12]

In discussing the vexing question of originality, he wrote:

The work is the reality; designing is but the means; and the first need for the designer for any craft is to know thoroughly the methods and traditions of that craft. We associate originality with design, but original ideas of any value are likely to come only to the designer who knows, and to him they will come more or less spontaneously in solving special problems or reaching desirable ends. Violent and affected distortions to attain the appearance of originality . . . are the mistakes of the ignorant.[13]

In his teaching he discouraged 'originality' as it is now commonly understood – that is, a novel and wilful distortion of surface appearance, aimed at producing an object that is superficially different. He objected as much to the excesses of what is now called 'the arts and crafts style' as he did to *art noveau*. Once he warned Edward Johnston, 'If you draw a straight line with a heart at the top and a bunch of worms at the bottom and call it a tree, I've done with you.'[14] But it was only the extremes that he disliked; for he acknowledged Alfred Gilbert to be the best modern sculptor, though, to modern eyes, Gilbert seems strongly influenced by the *art nouveau* style. For Lethaby the designer was

the explorer, the experimenter, the inventor. His special faculty is to wonder how things would be 'like this' or 'like that'; and he is not content to take them as they are . . .

What we have to aim at is not the rigid application of any rule, nor even the training of model prize-earning students, but rather the forming of competent and resourceful men. Always remember that design does not necessarily imply decoration – service comes first.[15]

Ten years after the reorganization, the Board of Education set up an enquiry into the working of the College, in which staff, students, manufacturers and others, including the successful commercial designer Lewis F. Day, gave evidence. As was to be expected, the College sought to present as convincing a picture as possible of the activities of the decade and produced statistics to show how much more successful the students, including designers, had been in finding employment than under the previous administration. Most of the evidence concerned the School of Ornament and Design, since it was in connection with the work of this School that all the important questions about 'applied art' were debated, and it had come in for some strong attacks. Some of these attacks came from the manufacturers, who complained that 'the public which they serve will have the "styles" and the RCA students have a wholly negligible knowledge of the history of design';[16] meaning that the students were unable faithfully to reproduce the decorative styles of the past – a defect which, since Lethaby preached that eclecticism in any form was death, was hardly surprising. But the most articulate attack came from Lewis Day, the author of a number of design manuals. He believed that 'design intelligence' could be inculcated as an attribute in its own right and, once acquired, could be employed at will on any material or technique. Thus, by the making of drawn representations of decoration, art could be applied to industry. It was a view then commonly held, and characteristic of the philosophy of the old 'South Kensington' circle. According to this theory, tools and materials tended to be seen as limiting factors in designing. In opposition to this view the Arts and Crafts movement held that in these very restraints lay wonderful opportunities to give expression to unique qualities and methods of working.

After several visits to the College, Day wrote to Robert Morant at the Board of Education more or less accusing the design teachers of snobbish disdain for industrial design:

Design and Ornament, so far as they are taught at all, are taught in relation to Architectural decoration, so that in reality Ornament is very little considered and its practical application to Industry is entirely neglected.

It could not be otherwise with Professor Lethaby and his staff . . . The very fact that Ornament and Design are connected with Trade and that the Royal Academy ignores them makes it, I know, difficult to do anything for the subject. And the Arts and Crafts Movement, instead of helping it, has drawn what artistic sympathy there may be for it away from Industry and towards the more or less amateurish pursuit of little Handicrafts – which to my mind matter much less. But I hold very strongly that the Board of Education ought to consider the question of design teaching in relation to the larger interests of the country.[17]

In his report to the Board Day wrote:

I doubt if any of those in charge of design teaching realizes the conditions under which a great part of practical design is done . . . So little [are the industrial arts] understood that it seems to be taken for granted that before a man can design for the trade he must practise it with his own hands. That is not, and never has been so. What is necessary is that he should understand it. And an intelligent designer has only to visit the workshop of the factory for a while to see the thing done, and to have the opportunity of cross-questioning the doer of it, and he will be able to adapt his design to the inevitable conditions. Insight, readiness and suppleness of mind are indispensable to the designer, and these practical faculties, no less than the artistic, it should be the aim of design teaching to bring out. So far from this being realized, I find it suggested that, in order to design for textiles, a man must work at a loom . . . Of the many trades for which I have designed I have scarcely practised any.[18]

Day, in short, conceived design as an abstraction, and the process of what he called 'practical designing' primarily as drawing or painting decorative schemes on paper, the results afterwards being adapted to the technique and material of manufacture, which were thought to be of secondary importance. Evidence for the truth of this interpretation of his position is found in his books and in the fact of his resignation from the Arts and Crafts Exhibition Society when the committee refused to exhibit drawings of ornamental designs (what Lethaby always referred to as 'paper promises'). When, therefore, Day wrote, 'It is not technical education, but education in practical design which seems to me to be the thing to aim at in the College'[19] he was not, as the modern reader would suppose, referring to mastery of tools and materials, but to the acquisition of skills in drawing and pattern-making.

All this evidence was sifted and issued in 1911 as a Government Report on the Royal College of Art. The Report is by no means as clear-headed as it might be, nor does it come to grips with the most important questions. The first of these was whether the College existed primarily to train teachers or designers; the second was whether Day or Lethaby was right. In those days the two 'design philosophies' were thought to be very different and, in terms of the artifacts that were the products of these rival theories, they were. Today, it can be seen that they actually shared certain common ground, though the Arts and Crafts movement has been the source of modern design education.

The Government Report was generally addlepated and certain passages, which probably reflect the thinking of the Board of Education as well, only go to emphasize this:

The methods of handicrafts have long been replaced by those of the factory . . . form and pattern are subject to definite mechanical limitations which have to be learned, so that the designer who controls them must study the conditions of the textile power loom rather than the embroidery frame, of the metal spinning lathe rather than of the hammer and forge, and of the mould and the transfer print rather than the potter's wheel and the paint brush.

These parallels were of course nonsense. The equivalent of the power loom is not the embroidery frame but the hand loom. Again, many craft metal workers used a lathe, and many of the pot-making processes were simply the mechanization of hand work; even pottery transfers were hand-engraved and printed.

There were, however, expert witnesses quoted within the Report who put the record straight. One was the head of the design studio of several prosperous distributing houses, who had had exceptional success in training designers. He spoke good sense in saying that

> design for handicraft, just as much as design for manufacture, has to accommodate itself . . . to the limitations and conditions imposed by the appliances used. A hand loom or a potter's wheel is, after all, although it allows the hand to contribute more, no less a machine than is a power loom.

The most serious criticism made by the Report was that

> much of the inventive design remains unpractical, and may be described as design in the abstract, rather than design for some actual and clearly understood technical process. This weakness is admitted . . . by the College who would remedy it by an extension of the Craft Classes.

On this matter the Report was in favour of the College's request and, as Crane had done a decade before, recommended

> a Craft School of an *entirely practical nature*. The Craft shops should be real, the student working with the instructors and their assistants. If the College were an assemblage of studios and workshops, like a guild, the idea of a 'school' would disappear, the true feeling of apprenticeship taking its place.

It also recommended that 'the training of designers for the manufacturing industries should be specialized and should be undertaken by provincial colleges [who were] to devote attention to dominant local need'.[20]

The ambiguous quality of part of the Report was reflected in the indecision within the Board, where confusion reigned. Sir Robert Morant wrote of the difficulty in setting up

> a Committee to consider the way in which the RCA carries out its functions . . . So long as the Board have no authoritative position (as is now the case) it is sadly difficult to be sure that criticism is justified.
>
> At the same time it would be hardly decent, would it, to refer to a committee the fundamental question of what the Government ought to have in view as the purpose of the RCA.[21]

The proposal for the training of designers was accepted, and became the professed national policy. It was intended to mean that certain provincial art schools should, with the support of local manufacturers and artisans, become what we might term monotechnics, where all the scientific and practical aspects of a particular industry would be taught. But it remained largely a policy in name only. The Government was not prepared to allocate sufficient funds to make it effective; and as for local manufacturers, they remained indifferent.

The proposal for craft workshops was not accepted. Even had it been, it was most unlikely that the Government would have found the money. The Board's lack of direction became, in fact, a policy of *laissez-faire*. 'I do not believe', wrote Selby Bigge, the Permanent Under-Secretary for Education, in 1918,

> that it is essential for a designer of textiles to be a practical weaver or a designer of wallpaper to be a practical printer, in any case the RCA cannot undertake to make him one. . .
>
> I do not think we need contemplate any great extension of Craft Classes as has been proposed by Crane and the Principal in the direction of weaving, lithography, wallpaper printing and so forth . . . students [should] learn in local art schools . . . the RCA is to widen and improve them as designers. For them the RCA should be a finishing school.[22]

It is worth examining some of the opinions expressed on this matter. There were what, in retrospect, can be seen as the reactionary arguments of Day and his comrades who, conceiving design almost exclusively as flat decorative pattern, thought that the College should be developed on an improved 'South Kensington' model. Then there was the Report's recommendation that the College should become a handicraft training centre, and this in turn may be contrasted with the Board's notion of a kind of post-graduate finishing school. Finally, there was Lethaby, whose first concern was with service and function; the evidence shows that nobody else saw craft training as the proper beginning for successful industrial design. Writing to the Board, Lethaby said:

> In regard to the relation of Machine industry and design . . . for experiment and demonstration a few simple and comparatively inexpensive appliances are all that is necessary to carry on experimental work. Designing is not done in the great power workshops and the first experiments are always akin to hand industry. The most pressing need at present is for practical experimental classes.[23]

In March 1914 Lethaby wrote a long letter to the Board in which he spoke of his wish that training at the College should be made to bear 'as immediately as possible on the manufactures and the art and crafts of this country'. He went on to explain the difficulties facing the young designer in the face of the general indifference and backwardness of British manufacturers who tried 'to maintain the existing customs, and . . . are naturally shy of new ways and new experts'. The rest of the letter warned how some Continental, and particularly German, industrialists were harnessing the Arts and Crafts movement in the service of industrial education and product design. Foreign manufacturers, he wrote,

> in pushing an attack make every kind of experiment and absorb every kind of knowledge. . . .
>
> The Germans have made it their business to understand English experiments in Art training

with a view to applying them directly to Commerce. While I was at the LCC Central School of Arts and Crafts I found that the people most interested in its work were Germans, Americans, and Japanese. Numbers of schools of the Arts and Crafts type are now established in Germany, one of the last being an enormous school opened in Hamburg last year.[24]

Despite the threat of increasingly successful competition from abroad, the British Government, like industry, appear to have been as indifferent to the quality of our products as they were to their design, and neither Government nor manufacturers were able to understand the true relationship between craft training and design for industry. It was impossible at that time really to test Lethaby's thesis, for the College had no workshops, and manufacturers had small place for the independently minded designer.

Design training at the College may have been inappropriate or backward, but the real reason for the small number of designers being trained lay in the actual world where women and men earned their livings. Although the rewards for the few successful designers were higher than for teachers, they were far more uncertain and the profession itself was far less reputable. There was greater prestige and security in being a teacher. On top of this, the teacher believed he had some social purpose, but the designer was frequently made to feel socially irrelevant.

In the years following Lethaby's retirement, the College became one of the leading schools for the study of painting and sculpture, but that reputation was gained at the expense of design training. To some extent this was inevitable. Even as late as 1946 there was little demand

from industry for creative artist–designers: and many students who found employment gave it up after a few years because its conditions were unsatisfactory. But the Royal College was also to blame . . . its training in design lacked realism, unsuitable premises and inadequate equipment hindered development at every turn; many students were not even able to experiment with the necessary materials and technical processes . . .

The administration of the College has . . . been a longstanding reproach to the Ministry of Education.

The [Hambleden Committee], like so many of its predecessors, recommended [in 1936] that the College should regard its primary function to be that of training designers for industry. To achieve this end the industrial design school should be expanded to cover all the principal industries needing designers; fully equipped workshops should be provided.[25]

Not very long after *Visual Arts: an enquiry* (1946) was published, the College was again reorganized; and on the same lines as Lethaby had, years before, organized the Central School, the Design School was divided into separate sections, each with its own workshops. An appropriate comment was made in a letter to *The Times*: 'The new constitution of the Royal College of Art appears likely to bring into force several of

Lethaby's ideas of 1901 . . . the authorities are to be congratulated on this very short time lag of only forty-seven years behind their best teacher.'[26]

And, in an unconscious echo of Lethaby's words, the new Principal Robin Darwin wrote:

Of the academic changes, much the most important was my decision to pursue a policy of rigid specialization in all fields of design, to discard responsibility towards the teaching profession and to provide courses of a thoroughly practical nature in all primary industrial fields.[27]

Lethaby was not popular with the Board of Education whose records contain disparaging references to him. It is not difficult to see why. His opinions clashed with those of some of its officers, a proportion of whom must have been inherited from the Department of Science and Art. He could not abide red tape, and was becoming increasingly impatient with the ministerial indifference to civic affairs, upon which his by now quite widely read tracts commented unfavourably. To cap it all, he had had much to do with the founding of the Design and Industries Association, an organization whose forceful and outspoken opinions had caused some highly unfavourable comment within the Board. It may indeed have been the Association's unsuccessful attempts to get ministerial intervention in the cause of better design that prompted his comments to his friend Sydney Cockerell in Cambridge:

There is something profoundly wrong . . . in our type of organization by which the able man is swamped under detail, which narrows him to a withered stick and he has not time for aims and ideas and really no power. More and more the stink of slums which our towns are, oppresses me. Don't the universities see anything and couldn't they set [up] an infant class in civilization. You know, order, tidyness, brightness in everything, can't you tell Cambridge of the swinish horror of the railway station. Oxford in the approach and High Street has gone lower than we ever supposed might be – so imbecile, blatant, shoddy.[28]

So, in 1918, at the earliest possible moment, the Board forced his retirement on him. His students gave him a bicycle as a parting gift. They clearly thought more highly of him than did his employers.

CHAPTER EIGHT

WESTMINSTER ABBEY
AND THE
CARE OF OLD BUILDINGS

THE GOTHIC REVIVAL COVERED ENGLAND

WITH A VARIETY OF ECCLESIASTICAL AND SECULAR BUILDINGS INSPIRED BY A ROMANTIC NOSTALGIA FOR THE MIDDLE AGES AND BUILT WITH AN increasingly accurate understanding of mediaeval style and methods of construction. This movement was responsible for giving Victorian towns their characteristic appearance, but also for the wanton destruction of a great many genuine Gothic buildings. To zealous and well-meaning churchmen and architects it seemed good that ancient monuments should be restored to some ideal state of perfection by stripping away the slow accretions of time and correcting the bungling workmanship of mediaeval masons. It was then hardly understood that these buildings are not simply items in a catalogue of historical styles, but, as Lethaby put it,

> witnesses which cannot lie; they are indeed, not so much records of the past as samples of actual history. Westminster Abbey is a great piece of the middle of the thirteenth century still projecting above the lower strata of English life and effort.[1]

In an explanation of what 'restoration' could then mean, he wrote,

> an old building could be tricked out to appear like a new thing provided by contract from the best London shops – a Saxon or Norman church might be made to look as if it had been gone over by machinery, and people loved to have it so.
>
> It is impossible to give any notion of the violence and stupidities which were done in the name of 'restoration'. The crude idea seems to have been born of the root absurdity that art was shape and not substance; our ancient buildings were appearances of what was called 'style'. When the architect had learned what his text-books taught of the styles he then could provide thirteenth- or fourteenth-century 'features' at pleasure, and even correct the authentic old ones. Professional reports would run: 'The Tudor roof is incongruous with the Early English chancel arch, and it should be replaced by a thirteenth-century roof of steep pitch.' At Canterbury a wonderful twelfth-century tower was destroyed to put in its place a nineteenth-century 'fifteenth-century' erection. At St Albans eleventh-century and fifteenth-century work were both destroyed to satisfy the whims of a lawyer-lord. It never struck anyone that antiquity is being old.[2]

The feeling against restoration had been gathering for some time. Since the 1840s Ruskin had continued to attack the vandals, but he had found little widespread public support until it was proposed that Tewkesbury Abbey should be handed over to Gilbert Scott, the man who had thoroughly organized the Cathedral restoring business.[3] Morris immediately published an angry protest. His letter in *The*

Athenaeum also contains the first serious proposal for an association to protect old buildings. The idea caught fire. Less than a month later, the Society for the Protection af Ancient Buildings (known to its devotees as 'Antiscrape') was founded, and Morris had set out its principles, which called upon all those who had to deal with ancient buildings to put

> Protection in the place of Restoration, to stave off by daily care, to prop a perilous wall, mend a leaky roof by such means as are obviously meant for support or covering, and show no pretence of other art, and otherwise to resist all tampering with either the fabric or ornament of the building as it stands . . . in fine to treat our ancient buildings as monuments of a bygone art, created by bygone manners, that modern art cannot meddle with without destroying.[4]

THE SOCIETY FOR THE PROTECTION OF ANCIENT BUILDINGS (SPAB)

It was a holiday with Gimson that brought Lethaby into the Society. The two men, who were staying near Fountains Abbey, went together to see the old pack-horse bridge at Pateley which Gimson, a committee member, was to inspect on the Society's behalf.[5] Lethaby, his interest aroused, soon joined the Society, and in a short time was co-opted on to the committee. In the following forty years he was to put in many hours of uphill and frequently heartbreaking work for the Cause.

By the turn of the century, Lethaby had become the most influential propagandist for SPAB policies, and it is significant that at the seventh session of the International Congress of Architects in 1906 he was invited to give, as its representative, one of the key papers on *The Preservation of Ancient Architecture*. The invitation suggests that the RIBA had by then accepted conservation, rather than restoration, as the proper way of caring for old buildings.

> The historical and poetical aspects of old buildings are, it is self-evident, very largely dependent upon their authenticity as handed down from age to age. Such monuments, it must be realized, are not mere records, they are survivals, and a land in which they had been carefully conserved would carry on its past in actual being. We want not mere models and abstract shapes of buildings, but the very handiwork of the men of old, and the stones they laid. On the historical side, nothing else is a valid document to be reasoned on, and, on the side of feeling and beauty, nothing else can really touch our imaginations.
>
> You have noticed some masterpieces in our Museums – the Venus of Milo at the Louvre, fragmentary sculptures from the Parthenon at the British Museum, the faded frescoes at the Brera – and felt that by the care taken of them they seemed all the more precious for showing a

history of antiquity, loss, and disintegration. How precious must the armless Venus be which is set in such a place of honour in the greatest Museum in the world! Why are tiny pieces of red and black pottery brought from Greece and stuck together with such infinite pains, and placed so carefully in costly cases? They must surely have great historical value and beauty. So an old building, however much is lost, whatever be its state, should be cared for, in this spirit of proud guardianship; and then no necessary strengthening and upholding will harm it.[6]

To give an account of Lethaby's activities in this field would be to catalogue a large part of the work of the Society which saved so many fine buildings from destruction. Such a cataloguing is impossible here, but merely to mention it is to acknowledge the debt to Lethaby. Lethaby's contribution can be shown by two examples of his work for the Society, one a failure the other a success. The first, which attracted great public attention in the nineties, was the attempt to stop the architect J.L. Pearson from re-building part of the west front of Peterborough Cathedral. The following comment by Hermann Muthesius is doubly interesting, since it was made by an outsider with a wide knowledge of the English scene who wished, by it, to move German opinion towards the acceptance of 'Antiscrape's' philosophy. 'It will repay us', he wrote, 'to look closer into this matter', continuing:

> The architects of England are divided into two camps. The larger side with Mr Pearson who has a considerable following amongst the men of the RIBA. On the other side are ranged all those architects who have identified themselves with the new art movement who advocate freer and more general artistic ideas as to Architecture and together with the painters, sculptors and craftsmen of the new Art-Tendency form one large community. This community is unanimous as regards protesting and it is pleasant to see the disciples of a new and progressive movement holding out their hands to the appointed guardians of antiquity. Bitter words have fallen from both sides.[7]

He concluded that although the campaign had not been successful in preventing the destruction, it had succeeded in bringing it to the attention of the public, which would make such destruction more difficult in future.

Lethaby, who had with Philip Webb worked out a way of repairing the gable *in situ,* had attempted to get the support of eminent men. Some refusals were not always as courteous as Shaw's:

> No My Dear Lethaby
> I don't think I can sign that petition or memorial. In the first place I do not know enough about it. Not having seen Peterborough to look at for some thirty years. And so of course knowing nothing about the cracks, settlements etc. and then with this slight knowledge I really could not go against my Colleague – it would not look well!! and I should not like to do it. I thought the last letter, somewhere about Friday or Saturday last, from the Dean or one of those

parties, I mean the one in which he dwelt on the danger and the risk that the workmen would run of being crushed to death. I think it looks as if they were very weak, when they fall back on such twaddle as that – and then I am sorry for Pearson – I really am – he has been a good careful conscientious worker all his life – and is doing his best according to his lights – and his lights not small, and then in his extreme old age, he runs his head against this post. And so when he dies his name will stink in the nostrils of all the younger school and the Antiquarians – instead of scenting like a rose – as we learned from Dr Watts that it should.[8]

The fact that Lethaby and Webb had worked out the problem of repairing the gable was typical of the policy of the Society, which was always ready to offer highly skilled free advice and practical constructional solutions to any of the numerous and complicated problems of conservation.

The second example of Lethaby's work was the successful repair of part of Rochester Cathedral, where he was Surveyor to the Fabric from 1920 to 1927. It is explained in an official letter to the Society's secretary:

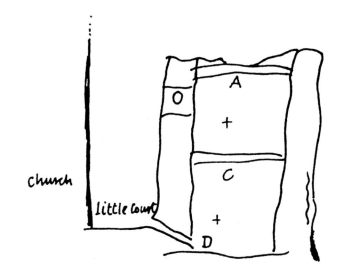

III Inverness Terrace

Dear Mr Powys   11 November 1922

Gundulf's tower is something like this. It is a low thick walled structure without any existing 'features'. It has been roofed for a long time and the space has been used for coal, scullery for Verger's sink etc. It is built with coarse rubble surfaces & concrete cores, the top is ragged and the inside casing is gone leaving the core to the wet and frost + +. It is proposed to put a roof [at] A, to make it sound and dry, but without altering *the ragged top*, unless when we come to it, it was thought best to mask the ragged top line and *within* that to build up a little rough new parapet B, which should be obvious repair. The scullery coal &c, they can't do without and the proposal is to put in an intermediate floor to line up the interior with brick, leaving arch spaces of the core here & here ** and to make it sound dry, tidy and useful in two floors. No openings are to be cut in the wall, except perhaps a coal shoot at ground level, in a hidden position, which may be thought better than carts drawing through an old archway as they do now. It is intended to light the interior by a top skylight and taking out the filling of an opening O & putting oak frame or something other than new stone. I should say that the inner side of the top is ruined low so that the concrete roof would run out over and the water would be taken off on the hidden side – more like this. At the same time the tops of the walls will be made sound by grouting and some lifting and re-setting and the wall will have open joints filled. My hope is that when done it will look cared for and be made sound but have no other sign of alteration. I wish you could go down and give us your advice or that you would ask Weir to go officially from you, I have said to him privately that we should be glad to see him.

Yours sincerely,

W.R. Lethaby

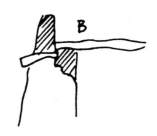

Possible coal shoot at D is *not* in little court as would seem from sketch but in another sheltered position.[9]

WESTMINSTER ABBEY

Before Lethaby came to work on Westminster Abbey, it had suffered at various stages of the nineteenth century at the hands of its previous Surveyors. By the beginning of the century, the whole of the exterior stonework had been replaced and some parts had been so altered as to bear very little resemblance to the originals. The most glaring example was the front of the north transept, which was the principal façade of the church as rebuilt by Henry III. By 1904 the exterior was, despite all this work, in a deplorable state, and J.T. Micklethwaite, the Surveyor of the Fabric, wrote: 'I have to call attention to the ruinous state of much of the outside stonework of the building. And in later years I have had to add that decay is now going on so much more quickly than the repair, that unless a remedy be found the state of things will soon become very serious.'[10] Fortunately the interior, despite years of neglect, soot and dirt, was still sound.

Micklethwaite died in 1906, the same year that Lethaby published a statement on the *Preservation of Ancient Architecture* and also his pioneering study, *Westminster Abbey and the Kings' Craftsmen*. These were certainly enough to convince his friends that he was the best man for the now vacant position, and they pressed him to apply for it. But he would not. He explained to Cockerell:

I am in doubt and confusion about W.A. because it would mean giving up this place [the Royal College of Art] and officing once more, if I were to get such an appt. Here I am settled and happy and feeling I am helping things in explaining them to young minds. There I should be in the coils of respectability and compelled even as caretaker into compromises and concessions and wrigglings . . .

Prior is as much to be trusted as I am, don't you think? I am in doubt. Did an 'Anti-things' ought to take such posts? I don't mean anti-scrape for that might be put in evidence, but anti-things as they be.[11]

Weir finally forced the issue. He visited Lethaby and refused to leave until he would allow his name to be put forward.[12] At about the same time Augustus Spencer, Lethaby's principal at the RCA, sent the Dean a copy of Lethaby's book *Westminster Abbey and the Kings' Craftsmen*;[13] this was a book which had already set out in very clear terms the policy he thought ought to be followed, and the force of this declaration necessitated some negotiations before he could be nominated. Its main points were:

that not one more monument or memorial window should be erected . . . The Church within and without should be kept continually in the most perfect repair . . . It should be kept clean . . . and a protective skin of limewash should be applied to the whole of the exterior stonework . . . instead of restoring decayed work, the original should be left untouched and a faithful record and copy made of it as it is.[14]

To the Dean's letter, which is lost, Lethaby replied with a detailed explanation and justification of his proposals, part of which ran as follows:

By an accident I have lately stated what I believe to be guiding principles. On thinking these over in relation to directly practical points which must arise, & are arising every day I find that they do represent my real thought and standpoint. Of course there are other considerations, & of course the Surveyor to the Fabric has in much to obey instructions which must depend upon these other considerations. Of course also, any particular suggestions must be subject to modifications in consequence of experiment & experience.

Where the old stone-work still exists the problem, as it presents itself to me, is to save every inch of it by almost any means. In our reverence for the Abbey on the historical side, the plain stones are hardly less valuable than the carvings. The saving of the very stones that the old masons laid will ever justify means that seem undesirable in themselves. I venture to take a case – that of the Cloister, which is obviously in a very serious state. Decay has here gone so far that it must speedily be arrested, or the work must be strengthened by supplementary support, or it must be renewed almost entirely.

Regarding the endeavour to arrest decay, I feel that experiments with lime-wash (I do not say White-wash for it may be of any colour) made at the Abbey & elsewhere, have proved satisfactory at least up to a point. It was thought from the beginning that the first applications would adhere in part, & in parts come away, & that the coatings of lime should be renewed from time to time. Lime-wash I believe, not only has the advantage that it nourishes the stone, but gives it a skin which protects it from the continuous effect of currents of air, & this no chemical application could do. It was the custom alike in classical times & in the Middle Ages to paint statues partly in view of the preservation. At present there are some parts of the Abbey buildings where there still remains some old wash of a dark ochre colour for instance, at the West end of the Vestibule to the Chapter House, & as far as can be judged from below I believe there is a similar wash on the inside of the walls of the South-east apsidal chapel.

It may become necessary or desirable to strengthen the existing ancient vaulting of the Cloister. In that case much might be done by getting at the upper side of the vaults &, carefully cleaning them out to grout the joints and apply a continuous backing of cement and concrete. Such a treatment would I am sure, make them absolutely secure, but even if it were not so, I do not think the Guardians of the Abbey would be compelled to rebuild them. Instead of that I believe it would be possible to devise additional supporting arches, neat & workman like, but obviously supplementary & thus not in the least interfering with the authenticity of the ancient work.

In the above paragraph he put forward a simple and comparatively inexpensive plan for making secure the Cloister vaults, which previous experts had all agreed could be saved only by a large scheme and the expenditure of a great deal of money. After these proposals he added:

> Considering the question of new work, I cannot think that others would care to see any of my designs in the Church any more than I would those of someone else. I feel that as little new work as possible should be undertaken at the present, and that the whole force of effort should be turned toward maintenance and record.[15]

What was being proposed was a conservation policy radically different from anything that had been done in the Abbey before. The Dean accepted it. He also accepted another of Lethaby's suggestions – that a 'capable young architect and practical builder' should be appointed as Assistant Surveyor; a man

> who should agree to give so many whole days in every week . . . to the work, constantly inspecting, measuring, drawing, and photographing, the entire building and its details in every particular, as well as looking after works in progress. In this way exact knowledge might be acquired, not to be gained in any other way.[16]

On 11 December 1906 the Dean and Chapter made the appointment, and a day later the new Surveyor made his first official visit to the Abbey: he was to continue to visit it twice a week for the next twenty-two years. He had spoken of his guiding principles some years before in 'Westminster Abbey and its Restoration', a paper prepared for 'Antiscrape'. If, said Lethaby,

> instead of theory, learning and caprice, this energy in pulling down and setting up – if instead of all this, there had been steadily carried on during the last century a system of patching, staying and repairs – a sort of building dentistry, how different it would have been with Westminster. Even so, if we could arrest the process of so-called improvement which is slowly creeping over the whole building in a sort of deadly paralysis, and substituting mere daily carefulness, much might be handed on for other ages.[17]

Lethaby's personality and his devotion to the Abbey stimulated new research, which had the enthusiastic support of Dean Armitage Robinson. He had, recalled Lawrence Tanner (former librarian of the Abbey), taught them all to see the building with new eyes, and had brought to its study both humility – a rare thing in Surveyors – and poetry. Tanner recalled Stanley Baldwin's delight at Lethaby's comment that Henry III had planted pear trees between his palace and the new abbey 'so that he might see it over a bank of blossom'. He added that he could no more imagine Gilbert Scott saying that than making Lethaby's observation, 'the interior ever surprised me by its loveliness'.[18] Tanner wrote:

> It was a delight to go round with him and see the care with which he studied every stone and detail, and to share his enthusiasm for some delicate piece of colouring or carving and to discuss

with him some of the problems and secrets which are part of the inexhaustible fascination of the Abbey.[19]

Lethaby loved caring for the old building, a trying task which must have called for all his tact and diplomacy, not only to get his ideas accepted but also to resist the constant demands for restoration and alteration. Nor was he always successful. R.B. Rackham, the Dean's secretary, recorded, of work on the north transept of the aisle in 1907, that

> the finials of the four easternmost buttresses had to be renewed. Mr Lethaby was at first going to put up quite plain work. But Mr Dean insisted on their being carved, so Mr Lethaby made a design. But as he had them limewashed, it was exceedingly hard to identify the two new finials which had been put up.[20]

People found it hard to accept that mediaeval buildings had once been whitened and gaily painted rather than, as in Victorian times, hidden in dirt and 'romantic' gloom. So, despite its increasingly obvious success in preserving stone, his policy of limewashing met with continued resistance.

Before 1922, the date of the first surviving Surveyor's report, the only record of Lethaby's 'daily carefulness' is Rackham's notes. However, from the terse phraseology of the 1923 Annual Report, it is obvious that Lethaby's plan to save the cloister had been accepted and that it was succeeding beyond all expectations:

> It will have been noticed that the repair of the Cloisters has just been completed for the whole length of the South walk. It is now proposed to work along the West walk from South to North. So far this has been a most satisfactory job and one which has amply repaid the care and patience of the men employed on it. All loose and fractured stones have been secured and the apex of the vault has been ventilated into the roof space above in the hope of reducing the effect of condensation. There is one small piece of gilding remaining on one of the bosses and some interesting remains of colour on the ribs in the S.E. corner.
>
> When these repairs have continued round to the earlier work of the North and East walks we propose to clean the old Purbeck marble shafts. It will then only remain to improve the organization for regular washing, sweeping and dusting of Cloisters.
>
> When it is remembered that only 18 years ago the wholesale rebuilding of the Cloisters was in serious contemplation and nearly came to be started, the recent work in the South walk becomes especially interesting as an example of what can be done in the way of preserving the original ancient work.[21]

The Report also records that stone decay had been successfully arrested with the application of limewash.

Mention must be made of Lethaby's reverence for workmanship of any age; he never attempted to alter previous restorations, believing that work done was relevant in its time and should not be tampered with. It was his opinion that 'all embodied labour should be held in reverence . . . and that is why a real Anti-scraper does not meddle with anything which once exists'.[22]

In June 1893, in a paper written for 'Antiscrape', Morris, who could admire little produced in England after the Middle Ages, had made a forceful attack on proposals for yet more 'restoration' at the Abbey and in speaking of the monuments, which were mostly post sixteenth century, he said:

> the burden of their ugliness must be endured, at any rate until the folly of restoration has died out. For the greater part of them have been built into the fabric, and their removal would leave gaps, not so unsightly indeed as these stupid masses of marble, but tempting to the restorer, who would not be content with merely patching them decently, but would make them excuses for further introduction of modern work. In short, disastrous and disgraceful as these pieces of undertaker's upholstery are, . . . they protect us from . . . a thorough restoration.'[23]

He sent a draft of this letter to Lethaby; while Lethaby agreed with Morris on most things, he appears to have disagreed on this occasion. His reply is lost, but it brought from Morris this riposte: 'I don't agree with you that I have said the worst of the monuments; I think on the contrary that I have let them down very easily.'[24]

There are many examples of Lethaby's all-embracing reverence for 'embodied labour' at the Abbey; one such example, from his 1922 Surveyor's Report – the saving of a mid-Victorian artifact – is revealing because such a gesture had been almost inconceivable before Lethaby's Surveyorship:

> After the grass has been sown in March in the little Cloister garth this will again be a fresh and bright corner of the Abbey buildings, and an example of how much can be done by a little addition, cleaning and orderly arrangement as opposed to reconstruction. I should like to preserve the fountain out of loyalty to those who put it there: it is one of the few Victorian attempts at making the place more delightful. Poor as it may be thought, it represents its time and it must be 60 or 80 years old.[25]

In about 1922 the cleaning of the soot-blackened interior began in earnest, which in time was gradually transformed to its present-day appearance. E.W. Tristram undertook the cleaning of some of the tombs and painting, and though modern restorers have criticized his methods they were at the time thought to be the best. New treasures were uncovered, notably a large part of a noble Annunciation group and the figures of St Peter and Edward the Confessor in the Inslip Chapel. When Tristram had made careful copies of the Abbey furnishings Lethaby was able to put into practice another part of the conservation policy he had explained nearly two decades before:

> Whatever we do, much will necessarily decay – painting, carvings, pavements, are quickly fading and wearing away from sight and memory; and a part of any general scheme of

preservation must include the recording of all these things, beginning with those that are likely to be most fugitive, the last traces of painting especially . . . To *restore* these things is to substitute a copy for what remains of an original, but to *copy* it is to preserve a faithful record of it, while leaving the original untouched, which will carry on its interest until it fades to a mere shadow. What will the next generation most thank us for?[26]

In 1926 Dean Foxley Norris offered to pay for the construction of a sacristy, which Lethaby believed could be achieved by making some changes within the Abbey buildings, without new construction or alterations to the fabric. But the Chapter decided to bring in another architect, Walter Tapper, to make the design and in October 1927 a site was chosen on the east side of the north transept. Lethaby's reaction was immediate and typical:

Dear Mr Dean

I was appointed Surveyor of the Fabric in November 1906 twenty-one years ago. As I have been growing older all the time it seems to me that I should retire not later than next November 1928, unless it is thought desirable that I should resign earlier. I need not speak of the privilege it has been to me to have some charge of the wonderful old place during these years and I trust very little harm has been done to it in that time.[27]

The following February the design for the Sacristy was published; as it was clear that his advice was no longer acceptable, Lethaby relinquished the post immediately, although his resignation was not announced until the following July. Meanwhile, a violent public debate had broken out about the proposed building; Lethaby, despite repeated appeals, declined to join in. His refusal was prompted partly by divided loyalties, but mainly by his conviction that a public quarrel was unlikely to settle anything. He chose to throw his weight into the SPAB attempts which, along with others, were eventually successful in getting the scheme abandoned.

Lethaby left the fabric of the Abbey church in an immeasurably better condition than he found it, and its present state is a tribute to his skill and to the tact with which he carried out the task. Indeed, it is a most convincing and first rate demonstration of the application of the principles of 'Antiscrape'. On his departure, Lethaby said, 'The systematic cleaning of the structure and monuments . . . has given me more pleasure during my little term than almost anything else – the one greater pleasure is new work I have *not* done in the ancient church.'[28] To all who follow, his work must remain a perpetual inspiration.

CHAPTER NINE

THEORIST AND WRITER

ARCHITECTURE WAS FOR LETHABY THE QUINTESSENTIAL ART, THE ULTIMATE EXPRESSION AND SUM OF CIVILIZED MAN'S SOCIAL ORGANIZATION; IT WAS 'HUMAN SKILL AND FEELing shown in the great necessary activity of building'.[1] Passionately devoted to this most catholic art, he created, in four decades of writing, a body of work consisting of a dozen books and three hundred articles as impressive as it was influential. It ranged from learned and highly original historical research to fervent preaching for better industrial design and a more ordered and beautiful town life. His writings on social and educational subjects are as relevant to the architectural theme as are those on aesthetics, economics and modern architecture which, though equally relevant, were often unacceptable to many of his contemporaries.

Preceding chapters have made frequent reference to Lethaby's books, lectures and articles; his theories and beliefs are now well know. We can now supplement and draw together the various strands of his thought and expression.

Lethaby was a clear headed and unsentimental writer whose mature style was, even in his most passionate passages, apparently simple and direct: its cool limpedness caused many to miss the frequent irony, strongest when he was most serious. His writings may be divided roughly into three periods. In the first, up to the early nineties, the only major piece is in defence of the Renaissance style. In the second, which lasts until the First World War, the influence of the thought of Ruskin and Morris becomes increasingly apparent. As the third period begins, a change of emphasis is seen. At first Lethaby had written on such matters as style and craftsmanship, concentrating on questions of interest only to other architects or historians; but he was becoming increasingly concerned with tackling problems in a wider context of public morality. Architecture, he saw, could not be separated from society. The final dividing line occurs in about 1914. The war was a profound shock; amid the turmoil of thought, he became more than ever convinced that principles of social organization and civic responsibility were inseparable from the nation's architecture. In this third and last period, a spare style and sharper argument characterize his writing, which often reached a wider audience through periodicals such as *The Hibbert Journal* and *The London Mercury*.

Although Lethaby published only one lecture in the 1880s, it is especially noteworthy, for in it he recommended a somewhat eccentric form of the English Renaissance as the correct architectural style for the time. But between 1891 and 1895 he had published enough material to show evidence of a complete turnaround in his beliefs. Not until Lethaby reached his late thirties did the radical Arts and Crafts Socialism so much associated with him begin to manifest itself. This was undoubtedly in response to his increasing comprehension of the gulf between the designer and artisan in contemporary society.

Published in 1892 as 'The Builder's Art and the Craftsman' and previously referred to, the paper was one of the essays in Shaw and Jackson's book. The first statement of Lethaby's comprehensive doctrine, it is a slashing attack on contemporary architectural practice which consisted of rearranging elements of past styles gleaned from textbooks. Modern architecture, said Lethaby, was 'a superficial veneer, the supercilious trick and grimace of art . . . overlaid on the dreary work of drudges': drudges because, with these methods, the craftsman was reduced to a machine. Such mechanical work with its denial of free expression meant the death of building crafts and traditions.

> No man [except by suggestion] in these things can design for other than himself. Design progresses and changes through the suggestions gained from direct observation of special aptitudes and limitations in material and the instant ability to seize on a fortunate accident and to know when the work is properly finished. The separation of the two necessarily makes design doctrinaire – a hot-pressed-paper-craft and workmanship servile; degrading even in the ordinary necessities of building, destructive to ornamentation; a mere insult and pretence of art.[2]

Real architecture was, in contrast, 'the easy and expressive handling of materials in masterly experimental building . . . the construction of buildings done with such fine feeling for fitness, such ordinary traditional skill, selection, and insight, that the work was transformed into delight, and necessarily a delight to others'. Its design could be made only by a man with a direct understanding and practical knowledge of the properties and possibilities of materials, 'a real artist in building', and one who was 'a housewright'. Since the increase in mechanization, and social necessities which Ruskin had not taken into account, meant that much building construction had now, regrettably, to be 'by line and rule', it must at least be, like the Kenton furniture, of the utmost simplicity, with decoration restricted to what the architect–craftsman could execute himself or, in the last resort, 'trust to a free artist'. For smaller-scale works, the option of undivided operation was still open, as Lethaby intimated in a reply to Beresford Pite, who had asked him what policy should be adopted when an architect was asked to design a small work such as a reredos in a church. Lethaby suggested that the work should go to some practical worker who would carry it out entirely. For a medium-sized job like a tomb, he continued, the architect would offer the work to a sculptor with whom he could work on equal terms.[3]

Addressing himself to young architects, he asked in 'The Builder's Art': 'Will you sustain the "status of architects", the theory of the "good and noble profession"; or will you devote your whole strength to becoming an artist in building – a chief workman?'

> If your choice is entirely for your art, you will certainly be poor, because much work cannot be properly done by one person . . . But you will have the craftsman's joy in his craft. You will have a place in life for whole-hearted ambition, that greatest of all crying wants – a noble

ambition, to do good work before you die: to be a leader, perhaps, in the art of making those things by which man lives.[4]

The burden of this essay was that the construction and decoration of buildings could be successfully carried out only by architect–craftsmen, their associates and assistants, all working together. It was out of this thinking and the idea of a craftsmen's commune that the first proposal by Blow, Gimson and Lethaby to set up a cooperative workshop evolved.

The lectures on Modern Building Design which Lethaby gave at Bolt Court in 1895 were the first public statement of the revolutionary views that established him both as a powerful propagandist for a new architecture and as an important theoretician in the vanguard of London's architectural fraternity. They were published in shortened form in *The Builder,* which in its leading article (presumably by the editor, Statham) both welcomed and criticized them. In *Modern Architecture* (1897), Statham returned to the subject again when he picked out what he thought had been Lethaby's most important observation, as in many ways it was. Lethaby, he said, had 'proposed a method of exclusion for getting rid of all conventional features of architectural design and had proposed to reduce architecture to the simplest elements of construction with which it began'.[5]

Most writing in this second period of Lethaby's output concerns the history of architecture and the crafts. Buildings could never be for Lethaby, as they were so frequently for other historians, mere examples of style, elements in a tree of architectural genealogy. For him they were material testimony, still surviving and forming a part of modern life. Moreover, although Lethaby drew inferences from the past, he never used his writing or his knowledge to make moral judgements upon his own society. His work made an important contribution to the then still fairly new and burgeoning attempts at writing history dispassionately through the successful analysis of evidence. His methods may be inferred from his statement that

> every school of art is the product of the antecedent schools plus the national equation of the moment, and these two factors may be as almost distinct and existing side by side, or they may run together into a new compound form. So true is this that the history of art may be compared to chemical analysis; and one of the offices of its historian is to distinguish and weigh the components of any given example. If his tests were rigorous enough he should be able to trace every element.[6]

If the subject of Lethaby's first book, *Architecture, Mysticism, and Myth,* is not history in its strictest sense, *The Church of Sancta Sophia,* his second, certainly is. It was written in collaboration with Harold Swainson and published in 1894. Swainson had done most of the literary research and the translation, while Lethaby, who had conceived the book, had analysed the design, construction and the decoration of the church. Unlike his first book, it is a work of exact scholarship which allows the evidence to speak for itself: for no personal opinion is obtruded, save in the exciting way in which the great church is shown to have emerged from the material conditions of its time. By then he had reached the second stage in his development, and believed that the design of modern buildings depended on 'Positive' or 'Constructive' principles: they should have a comprehensible symbolism; be erected only by the cooperative activities of builder–craftsmen and free artists; and since there could be no separation between building and architecture, the architecture of any period comprised everything constructed in that period, from the meanest shed to the grandest princely or picture palace. These principles clearly inform this work; indeed one of the reasons for going to Constantinople in 1893 must have been to test their validity by such an historical study at a time when present social conditions were in the distant future. So much is implied in the book's subtitle – 'A Study in Byzantine Building' – and in the preface:

> A conviction of the necessity for finding the root of architecture once again in sound common-sense building and pleasurable craftsmanship remains as the final result of our study of S. Sophia . . . in estimating so highly the Byzantine method of building in its greatest example, we see that its forms and results directly depend on the present circumstances, and then ordinary materials.

By the end of Chapter IX, the reader has a complete picture of the church and the author turns from the evaluation of historical testimony to what is perhaps the most absorbing chapter in the book, 'Building Forms and the Builders', which describes the construction, the evolution of the style and, finally, the craftsmen who so successfully solved the problems. The architects, he said, were master builders, who had graduated as workmen and 'came and worked at every part of the building'; the workman was 'no passive instrument, obedient without regard to initiative or responsibility to the foreman, but was treated as an intelligent power and found in front of him liberty, and a field open to his imagination'. The workmen were all members of craft guilds and were hired directly, which Lethaby considered to be of fundamental importance: many new forms appeared. One of the most striking and vital was the new capital design, which the masons, throwing off Roman forms, had invented. They had, in fact, out of a critical use of past tradition invented a tradition of their own:

> After more than a thousand years of working marble through one complete development, Greek builders, by considering afresh the prime necessities of material, and a rational system of craftsmanship, opened the great quarry of ideas in constructive art which is exhaustless. In a hundred years architecture became truly *organic,* features that had become mere (vestiges) dropped away, and a new style was complete; one, not perhaps so completely winning as some forms of Gothic; but the supremely logical building art that has been.

> If anywhere this vitalizing had not been completed, it would have been in the more decorative forms; but here we find no mere exercise in applying architectural orders, every-

thing is as real and fresh as in the structure. Having the Corinthian and Ionic capitals before their eyes and without forgetting or rejecting them, the Byzantine builders invented and developed an entirely fresh group of capitals fitted in the most perfect way for arched brick construction.[7]

Where *Architecture, Mysticism, and Myth* had sought to present a philosophical justification of the use of symbols, *Sancta Sophia,* by identifying Byzantine building with the principles of rational construction and a dynamic understanding of materials, enriched contemporary interest in the Byzantine, and – ironically, in the light of the views expressed in the book – gave an added stimulus to neo-Byzantine architecture. J. F. Bentley, the designer of Westminster Cathedral, remarked that a visit to San Vitale at Ravenna and Lethaby's book had taught him all he wanted to know about Byzantine architecture. The final words of the preface show that Lethaby thought such revivals just another blind alley. 'It is evident that the style cannot be copied by our attempting to imitate Byzantine builders; only by being ourselves and free can our work be reasonable and if reasonable, like theirs universal. *L'art c'est d'être absolûment soi-même.'*

Writing of *Sancta Sophia* some sixty years later, the great Byzantine scholar D. Talbot Rice said:

In no work, French, German or English, does this superb building receive so sympathetic or so penetrating treatment. Quotations from early writers who described it when it was young are freely drawn on; the elements, Eastern, Western and local, which went to inspire it are carefully analysed and examined: the numerous works of art which adorn it are carefully described. But it is the subtle understanding of the building itself that is so particularly striking, and in a series of simple but profound sentences Lethaby succeeds in describing it and penetrating its spirit in a way which has subsequently never been equalled. Several books that have appeared in recent years, where abstruse analyses of basic aesthetics are embarked upon, fail strikingly in constrast with Lethaby's work, in spite (or because?) of their elaborate vocabularies and high sounding phraseology.[8]

Common-sense construction and pleasurable craftsmanship was also the theme of his contribution to *Plain Handicrafts* edited by A.H. Mackmurdo, misleadingly titled 'Cabinet making' which was later reissued by Dryad Handicrafts as *Simple Furniture.* Drawing on Lethaby's experience at Kenton & Co. it was the nearest thing to a manifesto ever issued by the partnership and, broadly speaking, in later years its theme remained the policy of Gimson and the Barnsley brothers.

Leadwork, though probably completed by 1889, was not published till 1893. It is not a straightforward history of the material, but rather an analysis of the art of leadworking, mainly for architectural enrichment, in the past. The book carries one of Lethaby's earliest appeals for rational, utilitarian design, and ends, characteristically, with the plea that someone may again take up this fine old craft of lead working as an artist and original worker, refusing to follow 'designs' compiled by another from imperfectly understood examples but expressing only himself – this has been my chief hope in preparing this little book.[9]

The *Magazine of Arts* reviewer had little belief in the artistic possibilities of lead, and thought artists unlikely to practise the craft. But Lawrence Weaver (author of the authoritative work *English Leadwork*) maintained that the influence of Lethaby's book on the revival of the architectural craft of leadworking had been dramatic: the book, he said, 'did more than anything to revive interest in the art of leadwork'.[10]

Mediaeval Art (1904) was one of the earliest attempts to write a concise history of European art from the Peace of the Church to the dawn of the Renaissance. It was probably his most influential work, a book which successfully advanced the then unorthodox view that the major influence on English art was French. Although some of it is now out of date, it is still a significant work of dispassionate but stimulating scholarship; an inexhaustible delight is his imaginative understanding of the everchanging uniqueness of things carried forward by what he liked to call the *force majeure* of history; the onward rush of man's endeavour: 'I . . . have tried to suggest that unity in diversity of the stream of art which flowed down the centuries, every age showing a different manifestation of one energy as the old tradition was ever shaped by the need and experiment of the moment.'[11]

Two years later he published *Westminster Abbey and the Kings' Craftsmen*, the fruit of years of study and an association that had probably begun with a study of the north transept front, made on a visit to London when he was a young man. He intended in this work

to give an account of the artists – masons, carpenters, sculptors, painters and other craftsmen – who built and decorated it . . . I want to show that, just as in the thirteenth century we assign certain works of art to Arnolfo, Niccolo or Giotto, so here we can identify the works of John of Gloucester, mason, John of St Albans, sculptor, and William of Westminster, painter. And as in Florence, so in Westminster, a personal human interest must add to our reverence for an otherwise abstract art.

I have wished also to get at the facts as to building organization – the 'economic basis' of Gothic art.[12]

Some of Lethaby's later Abbey writings, though not strictly of this period, are relevant. To complement the coronation of George V he wrote *Westminster Abbey and the Antiquities of the Coronation* (1911), which described the evolution, from pre-Norman times, of the religious ceremony with its various rites, customs and furnishings. His third study of the church, *Westminster Abbey Re-examined* (1924), was the result of his many years as Surveyor. Lawrence Tanner, the former keeper of the Abbey Muniments and a considerable scholar in his own right, considered that Lethaby's books broke entirely new ground and were the foundation upon which almost all subsequent research on Mediaeval craftsmen has been based. Here almost for the first time the veil of anonymity which it was assumed concealed those who designed and worked on Westminster and on other great mediaeval cathedrals was lifted. Lethaby showed that it was possible from surviving account rolls at Westminster and elsewhere not only to give their names, but in many cases to identify the same craftsmen at work, in different places.[13]

Other experts on mediaeval art have been equally impressed. John Harvey, author of *Gothic England* and other works, wrote recently that

Lethaby's books on Mediaeval architecture, especially the two on Westminster Abbey and Mediaeval Art, were the 'sacred scriptures' to me when I started to take an interest in the subject from the beginning of my training in 1928 and after more than 40 years of 'progress', including the publication of such classics as Knoop and Jones' *The Mediaeval Mason*, Salzman's *Building in England* and Hannloser's edition of Villard, it still seems to me that Lethaby had by far the deepest insight into mediaeval architecture (perhaps all architecture) of anyone who has ever written. This largely because he was himself an architect who was endowed with intellect, but mainly because he felt a real love of art and did not just take it as a subject for study or personal attitudinizing.[14]

At the end of the last century the great importance of Byzantine culture was virtually unrecognized. If thought of at all, it was in the same terms in which it had been seen by Gibbon; that is to say, as one long decline from the glories of Imperial Rome. The two men who most helped to reverse this notion were the great Austrian scholar Stryzogski and Lethaby; who were among the first to draw attention not only to the power and beauty of Byzantine art and architecture, but also to their fundamental influence on the culture of the West. In England much work to this end was carried out by the Byzantine Research Fund, which Lethaby helped to found.

In 'The Theory of Greek Architecture', a lecture given in 1908 to the RIBA, Lethaby delivered a characteristic attack on the then widely held view that classical systems of proportion were a determining factor in modern design. To contemporary neo-classical architects it was a matter of fundamental importance. To Lethaby it was nonsense; but he said so quite politely:

Proportion to the modern mind can, I think, mean in the main only organic fitness plus habit. To the ancients from their manner of thought it meant more; it was undoubtedly believed that the perfect work was conditioned by a scheme of related measurements. This idea of proportion meant first what was assumed to be a proper relation of parts to one another and to the whole – that is a ratio. It also seems to have meant the use of similar ratios in different parts, giving a series of dimensional echoes. Now, of course we all believe in 'organic fitness' and the 'proper relation of parts' but the insoluble queries are – What are they? How are we to find them? To the Greek mind proportion meant the discovery of a law of typical perfection like the laws of geometry, number and music: to apply it to building was the way to attain to an Absolute Architecture.

That simplicity, orderliness, discipline are best we can all acknowledge, but the modern man seeks right and fitness by direct experiments. From a long series of experiments he may at last deduce some general laws. He does not first assume some simple mathematical relation of the parts for his chemical compounds and experiment only along those lines.

In the modern bicycle, locomotive, or fiddle, for instance, a general relation of parts (*its* due proportions) has been reached. This ratio is the accident of the bicycle, but to the classical mind the bicycle would be the accident of some supposed perfect ratio.[15]

Two years later came a lecture on the 'Architecture of Adventure' in which Lethaby showed, with evidence drawn from many periods, but mostly from Wren's work, how in the past architecture and engineering were one. Wren was at that time considered, with Vanbrugh and Hawksmoor, to be one of the inventors of English Baroque architecture, a style then much copied. Lethaby, however, wanted to show him not as a stylist, but as a great engineer who was far more concerned with a daring solution to the structural problems of the dome of St Paul's Cathedral than with the conventions of fashion. This lecture showed the emergence of a sharper and simpler view of the problems of modern design in the face of the increasing success of style revivals. In the gentlest manner, he challenged, with his insistence on experimental science, the views of most of the members of the RIBA. 'The method of design to a modern mind can only be understood in the scientific, or in the engineer's sense, as a definite analysis of possibilities – not as a vague poetic dealing with poetic matters.' He posed the problem in this way:

Architecture or building, so far as at any given moment it deals with known traditional needs, should be customary; so far as it has to meet changing conditions and ideals it must be experimental. For the customary part practical craft education would be best; but how to meet changing needs, especially when one of the changes is the breakdown of custom itself, is a new and urgent question. However desirable it might be to continue in old ways or revert to past types, it is, I feel, on reviewing the attempts which have been made, impossible. We have passed into a scientific age, and the old practical arts, produced instinctively, belong to an entirely different era.

Then came the following statement, foreshadowing the Modern Architecture Constructive Group, which stressed the importance of a common programme of work. Historical research had led him to conclude

that any basis on which there can be some general agreement over a long space of time will produce architecture of a sort. The one thing that is essential is this agreement, so that a process of development may be set up by continuous experiment. A school of art is only generated by intensity, the heat of common pressure. The only possible basis of agreement at the present time is the scientific method.

There were current, he said, two commonly held views of the nature of architecture: the first that it was some kind of revealed truth, an absolute that could be discovered by some special sense in the artist; the second that the essence of architecture lay in systems of proportion and that by a use of definite ratios an absolute architecture might be embodied. To these he opposed his own view

> [that] architecture is primarily building according to the natural laws of structure and stability, according to need and order, and always with care and finish; that it must ever vary with ever-changing conditions, and that this ordinary building may have associated with it painted stories and sculptured stories, or inlays and fretted works and gildings, while the essential architecture is still structure, and the method of architectural growth is by continuous experiment in the possibilites of structure.

A conscious quest for a 'modern' or 'engineering' style was, however, self-defeating:

> I must safeguard myself from being thought to urge any quest of originality. Quite the reverse. I am satisfied that all search for it blocks the way, with our preconceptions and limitations, to any possibility of realizing a true originality, which properly is of the root, not of the appearance. True originality is to be found by those who, standing on the limits of the sphere of the known, reach out naturally to some apprehension and understanding of what is beyond; it is the next step in an orderly development.[16]

In 1912 came *Architecture: An Introduction to the History and Theory of the Art of Building*, in the Home University Library of Modern Knowledge, which was published in England and the USA. Each volume was to be 'a new work inspired by knowledge of the latest research and critical thought' and one in which 'the best voices of contemporary scholarship' would be heard. 'Each [is] to constitute a vivid introduction to its subject, throwing into relief its fundamental principles and ideas, to be an incentive to further study rather than a dry textbook.'[17] This work, wrote Lethaby, was planned to 'bring out principles and ideas' rather than describe examples of the past and from them suggest 'a general theory of architecture'. Great art, he concluded, 'is not a question of shapes and appearances . . . it is fine response to noble requirement; a living architecture is always being hurled forward from change to change'. The last chapter, 'Modern Position', is a résumé of much that he has said before, but more incisively put. On beauty, for example, he says:

> It cannot be other than the sum of many obvious desirable qualities, such as durability, spaciousness, order, masterly construction, and a score of other factors needful to a fine school of building. There is no beauty beyond these except in the expression of mind and of

temperament of the soul. Probably the less said about these the better. The temper of the national soul is likely to operate best in silence. Little could be gained by disquisitions on purpose, fitness, unity, vigour, simplicity, dignity, generosity and intelligibility.[18]

Whereas in earlier years Lethaby had been concerned to press for fresh first-hand decoration, he began to realize that its use was becoming increasingly unlikely with the return of classicism and the advances of industrial society. In this work he pressed his radical view that 'a work of art is first of all a well-made thing'. The dreary waste of past styles – the costume disguises which English architects hung on their steel-frame buildings – excited the contempt of many, besides Lethaby, who wanted a new art for a new time. One was the Vorticist painter Percy Wyndham Lewis who, in 1919, remarked about Lethaby's book:

Have you ever met an architect? I do not mean a well-paid *pasticheur,* who restores a house or runs one up, in Tudor, Italian, or any other style. But a creative architect, or a man with some new power in his craft, and concerned with the aesthetic as well as the practical needs of the mass sensibility of his time? I have not. And what is more, should you wish to approach this neglected subject and learn more about it, you will find nothing but a dismal series of very stupid books for your information and reference. The best treatise I have come across is . . . Lethaby's handbook . . . it appears to me to be as sound a book as possible: and if everybody were of Mr Lethaby's opinions we should soon find that the aspect of this lifeless scene had changed for the better.[19]

Unlike most other contemporary English architects Lethaby faced the reality of using modern materials, and in 1918 wrote

although all these modern activities frighten me, and I would rather be dealing with rubble and thatch than with concrete and steel, that I have seen much which causes one to look again, in great bridges spanning a valley like a rainbow; in roofs meshed across with thin threads of steel; in tall factory chimneys, great cranes and ships; or even in gasometers . . . , these things have vital interest for modern people because they are modern and part of our life . . . There is nothing necessarily evil in modern materials or requirements; it is the spirit that tells.

He saw concrete as a plastic material to be modelled by formwork and, like the Expressionist architects of the twenties (but for different reasons) had little interest in rectilinear structures: 'We have to bring out what it can best do on its own merits and put away any attempt at imitating forms developed in stone and brick building.' Concrete, Lethaby continued,

gives to us once more the possibility of erecting solid roofs. Such a system of homogeneous building, with roofs of cylindrical, conical, domical or other forms – the low dome, cone and pyramid seem especially suitable forms – taking the place of the poor wood and slate coverings we have been accustomed to, opens up large possibilities of more dignified and interesting types of planning as well as more monumental super-structures.

Curved lines in plan and slanting and curved surfaces would seem to be specially appropriate to this mud-like material which must be modelled as it were into form. Interior angles of Roman rooms were usually rounded. Corners might be rounded both within and outside; cornices, if any, might be simple coves or rounds . . . The aim should be to develop structures in which the walls and roofs are all of a piece; and there is surely something exciting in such a mode of building.

Concerning exterior ornament there should be no attempt at concealing the structure or burying it in undertakers' doleful trappings. Some modern buildings are naked and unashamed, while others are smothered with figments of so called 'architecture' . . . the unadorned ones show energy and experimental thinking, and so we cannot help being held by their interest. The adorned ones are nearly without exception sullen and stupid. [But] I do not ask for bare and bald buildings – an architecture of the simple life and all that; not at all. I want to open a way to intelligence, expression, life and even exuberance.

Speaking specifically of the decoration of the exterior he proposed various alternatives such as marble trims to the doors; a heraldic device or two; sculptural panels or medallions or a fine inscription. This he said 'would probably be enough, we don't want our buildings worried all over, we want richness and colour and food for thought; but we also need bareness and relief and peace'. One can see all these ideas of Lethaby's in the design for Liverpool Cathedral.

A related problem for Lethaby with his Socialist views was the continuing decline in the building industry of workmanship and the concurrent rise in unskilled labour with all its implications for society:

In a large and sociological sense the use of these materials may be found undesirable, ultimately, as calling for low types of labour; but we are not going to find this out for a long while yet, and in the meantime, we must do the best that may be with the different materials as they come into use.[20]

In the following years Lethaby published many more articles with the same theme – the creation of an architecture appropriate to the twentieth century. His arguments became more direct and he simplified his definition of architecture as 'a developing structural art mainly concerned with the building and bettering of cities and the provision of all the structures required in civilization'.[21] His philosophy could hardly have been more different from that of the majority of his peers, occupied as they were with futile attempts to introduce the ideas of the Beaux-Arts and the revival of various forms of classicism. It was their belief that by the conscious act of an artist, beauty and poetry could be breathed into a building; what Lethaby called 'architects' architecture' is here defined by that arch-eclectic, the later Blomfield: 'Architecture is the art *par excellence* of abstract form, which makes its impact on the emotions by sheer rhythmical form and composition of forms.'[22] From a study of the past Lethaby drew precisely the opposite conclusion. In 1923 he wrote: 'It is because I want poetry, humanity, and even sacredness in building that I see we must be experimental, courageous, serious, real. Archaeology has taught me "Modernism" – that is reality and no pretence.'[23]

In this final position Lethaby argued that architecture should be a national service and the architect a public servant, concerned primarily with the construction of humane and efficient towns, public buildings and housing. But behind these beliefs can be sensed something else: the idea of the architect not just as a member of an exclusive profession, but as something far greater, the archetype of man himself – man, the designer and creator, who in making his world makes himself. While believing that the onward rush of history constantly created new forms, he was very sceptical of deliberate attempts at the creation of a modern style. Man could act only as part of changing society. But (and this was his reason for the setting up of the Modern Architectural Constructive Group in 1922), with a common programme a new architecture would come about. It was a doctrine that seems to be contradictory. On the one hand he seems to be saying that all attempts to create what he once called 'ye olde modernist style' were founded in error and on the other that such a style could be brought about by a considered act of working on a common programme. There is, however, no contradiction. What he attacked was the notion that a style could be founded on an idea of modernism for its own sake, the result of an agreement on cosmetics, on an untestable hypothesis rather than real things. Commenting on Le Corbusier's phrase, 'A house is a machine to live in', he wrote,

It is striking and really suggestive when judiciously interpreted, but some attempted applications seem only to be a new kind of whim works in a Corbusier 'style'. First of all, should the phrase be read 'A house *is a machine* to live in', or 'A house is a machine to *live in*'? The 'living in' should be the operative part of the saying. It would be a pity if, in addition to sham Gothic and sham Classic, we were to have sham Modern as well. And after all, it is only a phrase. If we agreed that a plum pudding were a machine to eat, it would not be made so by designing it like a wheel or screw, but by making it to function properly for its own purpose.[24]

Lethaby's philosophy had essentially been formed by the early 1890s, but during the next decade it became richer as his view of the nature of architecture and the responsibilities of the architect became more far-reaching. Then it underwent further modification in encompassing the problems associated with hand and machine design. Because he wrote from a moral, and indeed socialist, rather than an aesthetic standpoint it adds up to a coherent body of thought, for he came to see clearly that art, society, the human environment and morality were inseparable elements making up the unified whole that was human life. The most influential thinkers who transformed his early evangelist Christianity were first Ruskin, then

Sedding, followed by those atheistical socialists Morris and Webb. Supplementing them were his own direct experiences as a builder and teacher.

The burgeoning cities that followed the Industrial Revolution were regarded with horrified fascination. The nature and purpose of cities in former times had been almost universally forgotten, especially by those *laissez-faire* politicians and others in positions of power who looked on the city as little more than the producer of money rents. But towards the end of the century more and more people – writers, artists and social reformers – though they shared the politicians' amazement, refused to accept their miserable philosophy of slothful do-nothing, and, in a dozen different ways, set out on a path that was to lead to civic recovery. One outcome was the Garden Cities movement; others were the birth of town planning and such organizations as the Civic Arts Association. The activities of the Art-Workers' Guild, too, reflected this concern. In 'The Masters of the Art-Workers' Guild' C.R. Ashbee, a very active member of the Guild, commented on the part Lethaby played:

> In the earlier writing comes that appeal to the conscience of London, the noble replanning he first suggested at the heart of the great city, at the centre of the arc of the Thames from the British Museum to Waterloo Bridge (Plate 139), an appeal and replanning so pitifully, so blindly neglected by the LCC and the RIBA. We note in it already that approach to a common mind we so need. In his later, post-war work, the appeal is emphasized. But he grows less technical, more metaphysical. The Guild Aesthetic takes form in words. But we note the inevitable cleavage of the War: 'We have lived under an anarchy of opinions', he says, speaking of the spirit of Rome, 'and have hardly yet risen to the idea that to produce finely we must first get some approach to the common mind which shall be set in that direction – a national and civic psychology which shall be interested in inducing a high tide in civilization, in art, learning, and life. If we would build up a noble civilization, we have to find and follow after a spirit, a spirit which shall express us, as Roman architecture expressed the Romans. When we have the concentrated mind it will find the proper form of things.' 'A town', he says, 'is a work of art according to its quality as a dwelling place for men.'
>
> His rather dry, and at times even style is constantly made vivid by suchlike flowers of wisdom . . . I have said he was a 'great Londoner'. It was because of this he could write so, for he saw the misery and humiliation of the mighty city that had come from the neglect of her aesthetics.[25]

Lethaby's conception of what towns had once been and might again be, must have had something to do with the almost religious awe with which he remembered his native Barnstaple as it had been in his youth. His notions had been feelingly expressed at an early stage in 'Beautiful Cities', a lecture delivered in 1896 at the Arts and Crafts Exhibition, which described the beauty of a number of cities

PLATE 139. A proposal for a Sacred Way, *c*. 1891, Lethaby described this town planning scheme for a new road from the British Museum to old Waterloo Bridge as a Sacred Way dedicated to the City and the men who built it. Such an avenue, which should be 'wisely extravagent, wide, full of trees, and preserved from carriage traffic, would almost alone give an organic system to London'.

of former times. But it was London that occupied his imagination, the city that he loved – and hated.

The earliest fruit of this constant source of interest and research was *London Before the Conquest* (1902), the first study of the city to treat its early topography as a whole and, in his words, an attempt at 'the decipherment of the great palimpsest'.

Recent discoveries, particularly facts revealed by wartime bombing, have changed and greatly added to his picture of King Alfred's city, but his careful examination of the evidence enabled him to correct a number of theories then current about the city's early days. He had a great sense of history, of the continuity of man's experience, and believed that it was important that modern society should recognize that it too was a part of England's story, the continuation of a great and rich tradition. In the introduction to a much later work, *Londinium, Architecture and the Crafts* (1923), he wrote:

'It is curious that Roman buildings and crafts in Britain have hardly been studied as part of the story of our national art. The subject has been neglected by architects and left aside for antiquaries . . . In attempting to give some account of Roman building and the minor arts in London, I wish to bring out and deepen our sense of antiquity and dignity of the City, so as to suggest an historical background against which we may see our modern ways and works in proper perspective and proportion.[26]

Lethaby's editorship of *The Artistic Crafts Series of Technical Handbooks*, published by John Hogg from about 1904, must be accounted the source of his most widespread influence on craft practice. The authors he chose for these manuals – 'trustworthy text-books of workshop practice' – were all first-class craftsmen and women, most of whom taught either at the Central School of Arts and Crafts or at the Royal College of Art. They included Douglas Cockerell, Mrs Archibald Christie, Chris Whall, Henry Wilson and Edward Johnston. Some volumes in this series, like Johnston's *Writing, Illuminating and Lettering*, have, despite the vagaries of fashion, remained in print, and others, in the wake of the present revival of interest in the crafts, have recently been reprinted. Tucked away in Lethaby's preface to Johnston's book is a most important statement, which illustrates the high quality of the series and was the fruit of his profound knowledge of the 'form-forming' nature of the tool. He argued that Roman capital letters were not, as Johnston suggested, developed under the chisel, but were simply the 'cutting in' of a written model:

They must have been formed by incessant practice with a flat, stiff brush, or some such tool. The disposition of the thicks and thins, and the exact shape of the curves, must have been settled by an instrument used rapidly; I suppose, indeed, that most of the great monumental inscriptions were designed *in situ* by a master writer, and only cut in by the mason, the cutting being merely a fixing, as it were, of the writing, and that cut inscriptions must always have been intended to be completed by painting.[27]

More recent archaeological discoveries have shown that his observation was correct.[28]

261

To Lethaby's middle period belong most of his educational writings. Many of these have already been mentioned in context. It is worthwhile considering his theories on education.

Lethaby disliked and distrusted the English educational system. From his own schooldays he had found what passed for education unacceptably dry. Later, after years of work for the LCC, he came to believe that everything taught in school was of little or no value as a training for life. He was, however, keenly aware of the problem which survives today, and in an accentuated form: to put it in old-fashioned terms, the conflict between the ideals of a 'liberal' and a 'technical' education:

> The aim of even Matthew Arnold was 'culture', the being able 'to move freely in the realm of ideas'. This is doubtless good enough in its way – one way – but we cannot all take the veil and retire from the often rough productive work of the world. Such education is very nice and proper, and it may be that this type, improved and amended, may be preserved as leading up to one kind of human training – the department of archaeological scholarship and historical culture.
>
> When we turn . . . to the world of labour, adventure, and invention, a very different type of education is needed from that in which the 'humanities' are identified with dreaming and divorced from doing. The control by academical scholars of the vast field of modern education must be loosened, for they start with an avowed doubt of all vocational education except that for their own narrow vocation of letters conceived in an historical spirit. General education has to be re-thought out as the preparation for various vocations, each of which is as cultural in its own way (more or less, and in some cases much more) as the vocation of scholarship. Education should be an apprenticeship to life and service, and workers will have to educate their would-be instructors to the knowledge that there are diversities of culture by the very nature of things.[29]

He considered the educational principles of his day, such as they were, to be imbued with the ideas and assumptions of the ruling class:

> The proposition . . . is that English education, as traditionally developed and guided from the old Universities, is not directed to production and to action. It is an education in appreciation and in a knowledge of what has been written. It is by its very nature retrospective, and at its best it is introspective – the proper introduction to a life of contemplation. It may be developed to so fine a point of 'pure scholarship' and elegant criticism as to become sterilizing and destructive. This type of education has become an English 'ceremonial institution'. It was the great class badge and the foundation for the old Civil Service and a Parliamentary career. At its worst (and that was very bad) it was an education in 'side', 'bluff', and voice production; its inward unrealized function was to provide a myth of superiority to those who could pay. Since mail went out of fashion it became the defensive armour of a class.[30]

In his capacity as art inspector he saw this notion of education filter down into the colleges of art and the schools. It had, he said, two outstanding faults: first, appreciation rather than production was its aim; secondly, it had become passive and sterile – in fact, a large part of teaching activities was directed towards crushing spontaneity and imagination. So narrow a concept was unthinkable for Lethaby. For him education must, rather, be concerned with 'the world of labour, adventure and invention where most men live their lives and give their contribution to society'.[31] Control of it had to be wrested from the academics.

His criticism, and his vision, in principle applied to the whole field of education in England; but it was, naturally, focused on art education. His specific comments[32] have already been discussed in Chapter 5.

He was entirely opposed to formulae and to the unreflective following of models. For example, in his work at the Royal College of Art, while doing his best to lead students away from both 'Arts and Crafts' styles and *art nouveau* and towards the beauty and dynamic nature of Roman letter forms, particularly Trajan, he nevertheless emphasized that models were inspirational, not prescriptive.[33]

In 1896, giving the annual opening address at the A A School of Design and Handicraft, he said that he 'would sweep away from the drawing-board all theory of art – design, proportion, picturesqueness, and pretty drawing – styles – and would identify architecture with reasonable building'. Design, he said, was properly only the making up of one's mind as to how a given work should be done under certain circumstances.[34]

On the other hand, in his view the power of a model to inspire and stimulate was quite inestimable, and he thought that children in every type of school should be in contact with beautiful objects.

He introduced an important and, for then, novel idea – to purchase work executed under the influence of a good teacher and exhibit it for the edification and guidance of other teachers:

> All students should be expected to do some elementary designing, if only to get rid of the idea that design is a mystery dependent on the 'styles'. I would specially here refer to the great success of the elementary designing stage as taught at Battersea by Mr Thomas. The principle is to take the quite elementary pupils and set them to draw from flowers, birds, etc., in *their own way*, and observing points of interest for themselves. These studies are brightly coloured, as much as possible being done with a single stroke of the brush. A problem is then set the student to apply these studies to certain conditions, such as a border of given width, the filling of a space on some simple repeating principle, etc., and these designs are also worked out with the brush in bright colours. A large proportion of the designs so obtained (and other exercises, such as filling a given space with a braided pattern in an endless line) are not only interesting as students' work, but are really in many cases beautiful, having a freshness like that which we

admire in old work. Pattern design is also being studied in an interesting way under Mr Whall, at the Central School. I am arranging with Mr Thomas to buy (at a merely nominal sum) some dozen or two of the exercises done at Battersea, and I propose to add to them some examples done in Mr Whall's class and by Mr Cooke's students at Bethnal Green, and to put them together and invite the masters of art-schools to see them, with a view of elementary design being studied on some such principle in all schools.[35]

Another idea in advance of his time was that students should form a group 'to talk over their own affairs and to make known any difficulty or any wish'. Nor was this a mere bright notion of novelty, but rather a consequence of his respect for the learner. 'The schools', he said, 'exist for the students, it is for them to improve them.'[36] Perhaps the verbal and rhythmical echo of 'The Sabbath was made for man, not man for the Sabbath' is not accidental.

Lethaby pondered deeply and constantly on the meaning of education. Because he believed so profoundly in its organic and dynamic nature, he resisted pressures to codify. He was well aware of the paradox that, in this resistance, he was bound to appear least precise just where in reality he saw most clearly for part of the question, what is education?: what is teachable? To this his reply was: 'Art is the active side of things, science is the contemplative. The most of art is science in operation, and a large part of science is reflection upon art. Properly, only science can be taught.'[37]

For Lethaby education was primarily a process of opening out, of growth, and he believed that everything possible should be done to encourage the learner's inventiveness, spontaneity and imagination. He was an early supporter of the theories and practice of the Austrian educationalist, Franz Čizek, who revolutionized European thinking about children's art and who was followed by such fine teachers in this country as Marion Richardson.

Lethaby was not proof against the attractions of that vision of culture, based upon 'the best that has been known and thought in the world' for which Matthew Arnold had pleaded so eloquently. But he was even more keenly aware of William Morris's reciprocal plea, made in his book *Hopes and Fears for Art* (1882): 'If art which is now sick is to live and not die, it must in the future be of the people, for the people, by the people; it must understand all and be understood by all.' Lethaby's reply to the Arnoldian position was:

> Literary organizers of education have a great dislike of empirical methods, but art itself is empirical, and our literary friends must not deceive themselves by their own phrases . . . I believe that we shall not get very far till we recognize that a literary education is only one of a dozen avenues leading to true but dissimilar culture.[38]

Arnold had written that culture sought to do away with classes, stating, 'This is the *social idea*; and the men of culture are the true apostles of equality.'[39] Morris, writing and teaching almost a generation later, had presented what might be regarded as the converse of this position: for him, the social idea was socialism. It is not known exactly when Lethaby became a Socialist, but as early as 1883 he went down to Hoxton to listen to Philip Webb speaking at a meeting of the Labour Emancipation League.[40] He was soon propounding the ethics of socialism to Shaw's clerks, and bringing some of them into the fold. Gimson recalled how in February 1888 he had had 'the delight of listening to Morris on art at the A W G [Art-Workers' Guild]. Lethaby and Schultz and Butler were in their element, applauding his socialism to the echo.'[41]

This lecture was probably 'Of the origins of Ornamental Art'[42] which, despite its inoffensive title, contained an outright attack on capitalism, offered a socialist alternative and concluded by telling the Guildsmen that at some point they would have to choose sides. No wonder Morris was unpopular with many, obtruding in this sharp way the claims of the workers and disturbing the citadel of art. Lethaby accepted Morris's socialism wholeheartedly, writing, 'I think that I shall never find any other exponent of religion – translated in terms of today – so altogether believable as Morris.'[43]

Lethaby had long since left behind the austere sectarian teachings of his childhood, and he remained agnostic to the end of his days. But he was religious by nature, and he seized upon Morris's teaching with almost devotional fervour, perhaps unconsciously transmitting it to something closer to his own needs. He saw the Morris doctrine not as 'the grabbing of material things by the lower classes of which we hear', but, rather, 'a giving up and giving back'.

It was a theory and practice of human brotherhood. The major theory included minor theories such as 'the nationalization of the land, capital, and means of production'; at least it implies the readiness to try what these would do to modify the types of capitalism which is near to cannibalism. The end of the aim, however, was Fellowship – 'Fellowship is Life and lack of fellowship is Death'. Seeing how we are constrained by the system under which we live it was plain that a changed system would set up changed relations. On one hand a more reasonable system might be expected to bring reactions of righteousness in the people: on the other hand the desire for righteousness would precede the system which would embody it. In some statements the mechanics of organization may seem to be set before the spirit but that was only a necessity of putting the case in a world where the opposition claims the highest motives, and all are honourable men. Further, to Morris and Webb 'nationalization' was not a counter in a game of politics but a communization indeed which left no room for exclusion or evasion.

Socialism was an 'interim ethic', not a final religion, but it was a needful idea; once embody that however and further height would appear. One time I heard Morris speak of the immediate need for a citizen religion and of how in the future a higher religious problem might be 'Why are we so happy?', not, 'Why are we so miserable?' The Socialism of Morris and Webb was a necessary part of a religion of righteousness.[44]

This is idealized Morris, the Morris of *News from Nowhere*. Morris had studied Marx, had accepted his doctrine of the inevitability of social revolution and expressed his belief in increasingly political terms. But his championship of human rights and his hope of an egalitarian society were inextricably interwoven with his view of art, and in this dual concern Lethaby was a true disciple.

Inevitably, therefore, Lethaby's educational theory and practice showed a blending of the functional concept of art with the social idea according to Morris rather than Arnold. When, as the leading authority on architectural education, he was invited in 1901 to lecture on this subject to the RIBA, he caused some anxiety by the very title he chose, *Education in Building*. In this lecture he said that in the past not only had the architect and engineer been the same person, but his authority had come through a mastery of building crafts; moreover, although in that situation the master builder was the directing foreman, there were 'little masters' working under him: 'It is impossible to bring back this state of things – it may be that it is not even a desirable state of things – but it is necessary to recognize that this evolution of masterly building is what we mean by the expression Ancient Architecture.[45]

The quality of workmanship rested, in the long run, on the economic base. The great art of the past had been produced in societies, whether tyrannies or democracies, in which the workers had pride and reward in their work; but now workers were so taken up with the struggle for a living wage that they had no heart for anything else. Lethaby pointed the moral: 'Where labour is honoured, there art will be found, for honourable labour *is* art.' Turning to the present, he continued: 'These unions, in a much narrowed form, represent the old guilds and . . . any real improvement in practical building will be accompanied by these unions assuming more and more the functions of the old guilds.' He ended by outlining the curriculum of his proposed institution and by reminding the Institute of its responsibilities:

> The question of education in building to be solved must reach all classes of men engaged in building, and it must set itself to improve all the mass of building done in England. If we are to claim public help, I feel that we should get rid of visionary ideals and sectarian narrowness, and stand to gain with the common gain.[46]

Lethaby saw the trade unions as agents of the utmost importance in the achieving of a just and beautiful society, and he hoped that they would be one of the most powerful educational media of the future. He returned to this theme constantly, as when lecturing in 1897 to the Royal Society of Arts:

> The building system of any time and country has always represented the state and activities of the guilds or unions . . . If ever a living style can again be made economically possible it is by the unions . . . assuming guild functions, seeing to the education of their learners, setting a

standard of quality in production – in a word assuming the entire responsibility for the whole conduct of their craft – and nothing effectual can be done without them.

The members of unions . . . must themselves consider the matter of education. This work done for them from without would be of comparatively little good.[47]

This review of Lethaby's educational position may suitably end with an extract from a paper read to an education conference in 1919, which is at once a summary and a comprehensive statement of his beliefs:

Education and production need to be brought together in new types of apprenticeship. It is absurd to aim at merely abstract and grammatical preparation until the age of twenty or thirty. Even for those who prefer to read books, the scholarship university should be a research workshop. The vocational ideal in education is not only a theory which would apply to a commercial and industrial people, but it would rationalize and make human the 'humanities' themselves. If we would seriously set about building up a productive epoch, we must begin by training and tempering the national mind, suggesting a strong desire for a noble type of life, which shall not only use the words of civilization, but produce all the works thereof as well. We must consciously aim at bringing in a great epoch, a period of culmination which will become historical. With such an idea and intensive training, we might in a single generation become quite a friendly, humanized, and civilized people.[48]

The third period of Lethaby's written work was primarily concerned with his belief in the inseparability of architecture and society.

'The lamps are going out all over Europe; we shall not see them lit again in our lifetime': Viscount Grey's words on the eve of the First World War must have lain heavily on Lethaby's heart. He had shared Ruskin's and Morris's dream of a just, beauty-loving and humane society and had worked strenuously towards its realization. He was not insular: his early travels had enabled him to appreciate the work of other European nations; his own work had inspired that of German architects, and he had been in close contact with the Werkbund and learnt much from it. The war stunned Lethaby. A glance at his bibliography shows that no substantial book appeared between *Architecture* (1912) and *Londinium* (1922). This gap is filled with a number of articles for journals, the majority (for example, *The Nereid Monument Re-examined*, *The Earlier Temple of Artemis of Ephesus*) on Greek archaeology. Wartime is, of course, an unpropitious time for book-publishing. But perhaps it may also be surmised that 'in time of the breaking of nations' it was stabilizing to busy oneself with tasks so objective, mentally demanding, and limited in scope.

The articles and pamphlets on Hellenic, educational and other subjects continued to be published after the war had ended. But from *Londinium* onwards, more books appeared. Those on Westminster Abbey have already been noted. To this period also belong his biographical writings, particularly his study of the life of Philip Webb. After Webb retired, Cockerell persuaded him to allow Lethaby to write an account of his work. No start was made until after Webb's death when, at an Art-Workers' Guild memorial meeting in 1915, Lethaby's contribution contained this observation, which was to become the main theme of the future biography *Philip Webb and His Work*: 'Browning brought Romanticism and Realism together: he tried to look at modern people and modern problems with clear eyes and an adventurous spirit. If you think something like that is true of Browning it may explain a little of what I think of Webb.' It was another decade before the work neared completion and, as no publisher could be found, *The Builder* issued most of it in instalments. The work was published as a book in 1935, after Lethaby's death; more recently it has been reissued with some additional material that the author had left in an incomplete draft. A delightful account of a great Victorian architect, it successfully drew together, in an apparently artless but actually deliberate way, the strands of Webb's life and times, giving expression to the questions of the value of tradition, of modernity and historicism, that faced all thoughtful architects.

In this last period (during most of which he was kept more than ordinarily busy with his work as educator and surveyor), Lethaby occupied himself with lectures and writing of a kind which to a conceited man might have seemed too modest to merit attention. He read a paper before the Conference of the Parents' National Educational Union; he wrote one of the Dryad Handicraft leaflets; he contributed to Salford Boy Scouts' 'Book of the Quest', and so on. He had been concerned from an early stage with the revival of the artistic crafts, but later he came to see also how important it was to encourage and preserve such simple everyday crafts as sewing, ploughing or baking as activities vital for a healthy society. He hoped also to prevent people from becoming simply consumers of machine-made objects, deprived of the powers of self-expression. It was for this reason that he agreed to write a series of articles for *Home and Country,* the journal of the National Federation Women's Institutes, which was later issued as *Home and Country Arts* (1923). One chapter begins:

One of the thoughts I am anxious to get expressed and understood is this – *It is the common things that matter most.* Of the several reasons which might be given for this, I will pick out two. Our lives are mainly concerned with the common things and the world is really carried on by them. Secondly, the few great exceptional things grow out of the widespread little ones. Thirdly, somehow it is the common things which are *poetic.*[49]

A comment from the *Spectator* was typical of the praise it received: 'This . . . little book contained more sound sense on such subjects as education and art in common things than can be found in most of the larger books written by specialists.'[50]

Perhaps he came to feel that the path of his quasi-religious socialism was to lead ultimately not to grandiose schemes, but to humble service in whatever region the human spirit was stirred to do something constructive and creative. Perhaps, after the shock of the war, he felt, as others have felt, that for the present the only hope available was in individuals and small groups working disinterestedly and patiently. Lethaby's *Form in Civilization,* which was published in celebration of his sixty-fifth birthday and contained, in a collection of previously published essays, the essence of his teaching. They were, he said, 'a crude attempt to set down what I seem to have found out about life'. The result was 'something like this':

1. Life is best thought of as service.

2. Service is, first of all and of greatest necessity, common productive work.

3. The best way to think of labour is as art. This was Ruskin's and Morris's great invention. By welcoming it and thinking of it as art the slavery of labour may be turned into joy.

4. Art is best thought of as fine and sound ordinary work. So understood it is the widest, best, and most necessary form of culture.

5. Culture should be thought of not only as book-learning and manners, but as a tempered human spirit. A shepherd, ship-skipper, or carpenter enjoys a different culture from that of the book-scholar, but it is none the less a true culture.

CHAPTER TEN

LETHABY – A RETROSPECT

PLATE 140.   The Town Hall, Guildford, Surrey. Watercolour.

LETHABY'S LIFE AND CAREER WERE BY ANY

STANDARDS – AND PARTICULARLY ACCORDING TO EDWARDIAN AND VIC-
TORIAN CONVENTIONS – RELATIVELY SUCCESSFUL AND HAPPY. A MAN OF
humble origins but of some ability, he survived conventional schooling, found congenial employment at
an early age, moved with ease among the cultivated middle classes, and earned public recognition through
his work. After a career as a productive and influential architect and designer, he became a leading figure
in art education and gave long service in the care of old buildings.

From records and personal testimonies we can put together a clear picture of Lethaby's life, from the
child raised in a kindly but puritanical household to the student who became Lauder's brilliant apprentice.
First jobs and travelling scholarships ran together, and soon Lethaby was shaking the conservatives a little
with his unconventional designs and exhibiting a decided will of his own. He went diffidently into Shaw's
office but once there his high spirits and jokes were unforgettable. As educator and Surveyor, he had many
brushes with officialdom and, although seldom openly aggressive, did not suffer gladly his experiences of
'Folly, doctor-like, controlling skill'; but as colleague and teacher he was admired and often loved.

Lethaby was evidently a delightful companion. At an exhibition of Lethaby's work, Alfred Powell
spoke of

> the jolliness of him; he never seems to have really grown up; he remained like a boy until the day
> of his death. He was full of exhilarating fun, and he would go into fits of laughter if anything
> struck him as amusing. I remember that once we went on the South Downs together, we had
> horses – goodness knows where we got them from – and to see him galloping along on a great red
> camel of a horse was wonderful. He was given a bicycle by his students after he had finished up
> at the school, and he revelled in that bicycle. And I have seen him on the river enjoying rowing
> in a boat as much as anybody. I once went to Yorkshire with him on a holiday. You see these
> paintings of his on the walls (Plates 140, 141); I tried to do something of the sort. He caught hold
> of my drawing and said, 'Alfred, you don't know how to do it; you want to get lather into it', and
> he picked up a bunch of grass, and, rubbing it over the drawing, produced a wonderful texture.
> That sort of thing kept things going tremendously for him. He was about the jolliest companion
> anybody could dream of, always full of life. It seemed as though his five wits were multiplied by
> eight or ten, he had so much sensation, and his senses were all so continuously alive. It was that
> which made him so sympathetic to everybody; there was no kind of person he could not
> sympathize with.[1]

Seen in action at the Art-Workers' Guild (or, possibly, the RIBA):

PLATE 141.   Landscape with trees. Watercolour.

[Lethaby's] genuine modesty and hatred of display must have made it very difficult for him to play a public part. It was his burning conviction, his passionate desire, to see wrongs put right that steeled him to do so, but often the involuntary rustling of the papers that he held in his hand betrayed the nervous strain that it cost him to address an audience. So, much of his influence was exercised underground, and it was no rare thing, when some useful piece of work was doing, to find Lethaby sitting unseen, content to pull the strings while others reaped the kudos . . . So many people sought his advice that he could not but know it was worth seeking, and his modesty never degenerated into mock-modesty. It was a delightful experience to go to Lethaby for advice, or indeed to listen to his conversation at any time. The generous warmth of his relations with his friends, the depth and width of his knowledge, the concentration of his mind on serious subjects, the ready play of his wit – now caustic, now fantastic – on lighter matters, the characteristic hesitation, followed by the equally characteristic pounce as he found the right phrase to make his meaning clear, gave a very special charm to his talk, and made it in the highest degree stimulating. But, above all, it was his sincerity and his utter want of self-seeking that endeared him to his friends and were the source of his power.[2]

At the Central School he could be seen in a different role, that of teacher and inspirer of others' creative gifts. 'He went round the classes', said Dora Billington, the potter, 'like a white-moustached rabbit, with a quick, dark eye.'[3] He seemed frequently to be able to strike fire off his listeners, as many have testified. Catterson Smith, for example, said, 'He always electrifies me.'[4]

Edward Johnston said that meeting Lethaby had been 'the greatest miracle of my life'.[5] George Clausen must have spoken for many when he remarked that whenever he asked a group of students from whom they had learnt the most, Lethaby was the name most frequently mentioned. 'It was not', said Clausen, 'that Lethaby showed you how to do anything. He just showed you how to think about the thing.'[6] Even when he disapproved of what a student did, he usually confined his criticism to 'If you must do this sort of thing, couldn't you do it at home?'

A. S. Hartrick, whose meetings with Lethaby – usually when the two went to Reading University to examine the work of the art classes – were always red-letter days, recorded that 'His eager "Yes, yes, yes!!" when you found something that excited him will remain with me always.' Lethaby had, he continued, 'one peculiarity: he was quite indifferent to what is known as "handling" in paint; I believe he actively disliked it. In looking at a candidate's work he frankly ignored it and left the appraisement to me alone.'[7] It is strange that Lethaby, so ready to praise and encourage expression in craft work, apparently felt unable to do so in painting or 'free' art. The reason may lie in his deep distrust of either 'originality' – that is, making wilful difference for its own sake – or of aesthetic experience.

Members' accounts of SPAB committee meetings paint a scene of cheerful conviviality. The committee met every Thursday evening. Promptly at seven o'clock Morris would adjourn the meeting and lead the way across the Strand to Gatti's Restaurant where supper was served by Ticino, the Italian waiter, who 'smiled on them like a host'. The party usually included Webb, Cockerell, Detmar Blow, Emery Walker and sometimes Cobden Sanderson and Theodore Rooke. These were often hilarious evenings, when the company would sit on for hours discussing an endless variety of aesthetic and ethical questions, though no doubt much of the talk ran on architecture. Pictures and photographs were brought along by returning holidaymakers, who described the buildings they had visited. Often, too, Morris would produce from his canvas satchel a new design or a mediaeval manuscript; even, on occasion, the latest book from the Kelmscott Press. It had all been, recalled Lethaby, 'a great time to me'.[8] Although there is much evidence of his eagerness and *joie de vivre,* it was in this same period that Lethaby wrote:

> From about 1890 to 1900 I frequently saw Spiers, who from this time was an older friend. I was welcome in his house and had many long and to me delightful conversations on our common friend Architecture. At that time I suppose he was the only man in England who took the whole world for his province . . . For his friendliness at that time I owe him very much, it was one of the things which made living in London just possible for a lonely person.[9]

In March 1893, not long after the completion of Avon Tyrrell, Lethaby and Swainson set off for Turkey to inspect Byzantine churches in and around Constantinople, Sancta Sophia in particular. But once there they were unable to get into the church, probably because of the damage visitors had been inflicting on the mosaics rather than because the building was now a mosque; for evidence suggests that until that time it had not been very difficult to get permission to inspect the interior.[10] Fortunately for the two men a recently widowed American named Margaret Crosby was staying in the same hotel, with her two daughters, Edith and Grace. They were probably returning from a visit to Margaret Crosby's son Ernest, at that time a judge in the international court at Alexandria. According to Crosby family records,[11] the restriction to visit the church fell most heavily on English *men*; the ladies therefore lent the two young men women's clothes, and with the men thus disguised they all went in together. To this we can add some fairly certain suppositions: first that the Crosbys got their permission through Ernest's influence with the Khedive,[12] and second that the Crosbys were still wearing mourning veils. Disguise was perhaps not too difficult, since the Crosbys were tall women; even so, it must have been a very thick veil to have concealed the Lethaby moustache. Perhaps, in the pursuit of truth, he made the great sacrifice of shaving it off! It is known that they were able to make only one visit, and it is a tribute to the men's powers of observation that they took in so much.

Leaving Constantinople after two weeks, Lethaby seems to have recorded his last impressions from the ship:

> See the blue sea washing ten miles of wall. Look at the thousand low domes, lead-grey or gilt, backed by tall cypresses and interrupted now and then by a tall statue-bearing column. Let our last look of all be at Sancta Sophia, which surmounts the scar and point. Its dome-star sprinkled to the interior – expanded above 'pastures' of marble on rainbow arches. The altar of jewelled gold standing under a canopy of silver. From the vaults hang down a multitude of lights so that at night the forty windows of the lighted dome seem like an illuminated coronet suspended in the sky.[13]

Edith Rutgers Crosby was born in 1850, the daughter of a Boston clergyman. An active social reformer, Howard Crosby had been a professor of Greek before his ordination. His daughter was a well-educated and intelligent woman who wrote verse and, with a friend, had published in 1892 a selection of quotations from the Bible entitled 'Blessed are They that Mourn' – probably in memory of her father. She had first met Lethaby in 1893 in Constantinople during the memorable visit to Sancta Sophia, and had kept in touch subsequently. From the surviving letters between Edith and her sister it seems that the marriage might have happened before, had her mother not been opposed to her alliance with a penniless architect. At last, however, Mrs Crosby was persuaded to change her mind, and in July 1901 the three women travelled with Lethaby to Switzerland where, in the American Episcopalian Church in Geneva, he and Edith were married on 1 August. Lethaby was forty-four, his wife fifty-one.[14]

Back in London, the Lethabys took rooms at 15 Duke Street, Manchester Square, while Edith went house hunting and entertained her husband's friends. Many, like Cockerell, their first visitor, immediately took to some of her American innovations. 'My patriotism had a triumph', she told Grace,

in the success of some American candies I had for dessert. I had gone to Fuller's and got popcorn and peanut candy and maple sugar and marshmallows – I wish you could have seen him and Richard devouring them. I have also sent a box of them to Barnstaple – they [Lethaby's parents] have been so kind in constantly sending us things – last week it was a great box of the most delicious plums – and the week before a tin of Devonshire cream, etc.[15]

By October they had found and bought 111 Inverness Terrace, near Kensington Gardens, which was to be their home for the rest of their lives. This early Victorian house was furnished with pieces from the disbanded Kenton & Co.; others were designed by Lethaby, who also gave Edith, as she told her sister,

the sweetest little old piano of 1791, the exact date of Haydn's first visit to England, so he may have played on it, for it must have been very 'grand' in its day – it has a handsome mahogany case, and funny long tail, like the pianos one sees Mozart playing at in the pictures, and fine gilt ornaments and satinwood front.[16]

Wallpapers and a tapestry came from Morris and Co., and a great many pictures, including drawings by Ruskin and Madox Brown. Lethaby maintained his usual energetic routine and for the first year had a separate office, which he subsequently transferred to his home.

He leaves at 9 – and doesn't get back till after 4 – then after tea he has to go to Gray's Inn to get his letters, etc., comes back at 6.30 and is off again till 9.45.[17]

Edith's letters tell of the day-to-day life of the household, of her difficulties in finding a church she liked and of her husband's indifference to organized religion. On Sundays she often had to attend church alone while he lay abed. Time, she prayed, would overcome his agnosticism, bringing faith which 'will fill his whole nature as his love for me does now – and he used to think that he could do without human love, while now it is the expression of his whole being'.

The way to the Royal College lay through Kensington Gardens, and sometimes they went together:

We have had some exquisite spring days – and to walk across with Richard and then wander zig-zag back is as good as having a country seat of one's own. The great stretches of lawn with huge trees dotted over them and birds singing and crocuses and almond trees blooming, is worth paying double what we paid for this house. And Richard really has a country walk to and from his work which is of great value. We have a number of plants in pots in our conservatory and parlour – and have an almond tree planted in our front yard and our patch of grass at the back is a great success.[18]

Visitors came to Edith's tea parties, where they often met students from the Royal College of Art who, true to type, astonished them by their clothes and appearance. Former clients kept in touch: the Middlemores, for instance, sent them presents of grouse, and the Eustace Smiths invited them to High Coxlease. Edith created a background of cheerful domesticity, and helped in many other ways. She transcribed for the printers the hurrying, shaky script of her husband's writings, and translated material from the Deutsche Werkbund for the nascent Design and Industries Association. Because of her heart weakness, they led a quiet life: they seldom dined out, and certainly never did so in search of clients.

Closer examination of Lethaby's character shows him as a somewhat enigmatic figure, a creature of paradoxes behind the façade of the calm, well-adjusted man. Prey to perhaps not uncommon irritability and nervous depression, he was also prone to a puzzling detachment. He was a shy man of almost excessive humility; when friends or institutions wished to honour him, he protested that he was unworthy of such recognition. Yet, as proud as he was humble, his disclaiming of honours may be seen as the gesture of a man who considers himself above such trifles. Controlled and meticulous in his attention to detail and in his love of order, Lethaby was very much the product of a strict Victorian upbringing. A man possessed of an inner loneliness for much of his life, who longed for love and did not have it, his technique for dealing with this lack was to deny its existence and to direct his creative drive towards his work. In the midst of busy social activity which by no means excluded him, Lethaby remained remote: as he himself said, he felt a stranger in the world.[19]

He must have been a pray to many fears. Did these include a fear of growing up? There are testimonies (appreciative ones) to the child-like nature of his gaiety and spontaneity, but he was no Peter Pan. Rather, the child lived on in him, as it does in many artists. His own sense of this led him unaided to educational perceptions and in maturity he had realized that toys had been of fundamental importance in freeing him from the confines of his childhood.[20] It was this that made him such a firm advocate of teaching through play, very much in tune with the advanced theories of his time, from Froebel to Caldwell Cook. As a child, he himself had been anything but toy-taught. No doubt, like other children of his time, he was indoctrinated with the idea of the disciplines of work; with the notion that labour undertaken for its own sake, without ulterior motif, was an act of virtue. He also remembered constant and confusing exhortations to self-sacrifice. Isaac Watts had set forth, in his *Divine Songs for Children*,[21] the doctrine which was committed to memory by many Victorian Children:

> When from the chambers of the east
> His morning race begins,
> He never tires, nor stops to rest,
> But round the world he shines.
>
> So like the sun, would I fulfil
> The duties of the day;
> Begin my work betimes, and still
> March on my heavenly way.

It may have been these very lines that prompted one of Lethaby's little verses:[22]

> As from the mounting sun I went,
> My shadow with me stalking,
> Mine, how the time was spent –
> 'Twas my father's form there walking.

In strict Nonconformist families even very young children, who were believed to be the slaves of sin, were terrified with images of hellfire and threats of everlasting punishment for the slightest misdemeanor. The teaching was permeated with the notion of the wickedness of sexuality and the extreme sinfulness of the sex organs. The strange and disturbing drawing entitled 'The Beryl Shrine' (Plate 38) may have been an unconscious vehicle for the expression of these taboos. It is explicitly linked with the symbolism of Keats's poem, in which enchanted female beauty is withered by the unwinking stare of rationalism, and with the brooding guilt of Rossetti's; and it is itself full of overt and covert sexual symbols.

One of Lethaby's constant preoccupations was the conflict between freedom and authority, often represented in his mind by the contrast between the authoritarian architecture of the past and the free art of the future. Architecture of the past, said Lethaby, could be typified by

the stupendous temples of Egypt, at first all-embracing, then court and chamber narrowing and
becoming lower, closing in on the awed worshipper and crushing his imagination.[23]
In contrast, the message of the art of the future

will still be of nature and man, of order and beauty, but all will be sweetness, simplicity, freedom, confidence, and light; . . . the future is to aid life and train it so that beauty may flow into the soul like a breeze.[24]

For many years Lethaby's personal mark was a cross and a heart, so conjoined as to resemble a seal or brand. Taking a leaf out of his own first book, we may try to answer the question: what purpose is to be found behind the structure and form of this mark? For once, the true meaning of one of his inventions is not hard to discover. The Christian teaching of his childhood must have been ever present, a real part of himself. His cross, then, must stand for the virtues of courage, self-denial and inner discipline, his heart for affection and imagination. They are not always compatible, but the device suggests that they can be reconciled.

We have seen that Lethaby's life, outwardly for the most part so unassertive, embodied contradictions. The shy youth was immensely ambitious; the unwordly thinker enjoyed success; the plainness of a quiet man had something ostentatious about it; he attacked conformity, yet some might think his constant preaching doctrinaire in its own way; he hated controversy and avoided it, yet he held, and uttered with some eloquence, revolutionary opinions. For all his modesty he was intensely proud. He was sociable and affectionate, but he married rather late, and then only after a six-year friendship. The most remarkable phenomenon, however, is the cessation of architectural activity. Why did he shift the emphasis so completely from architect to teacher, devoting the major part of his time and energy to causes and to helping others to create? Several contributory factors and circumstances which account for the change have already been mentioned, but is it of significance, or merely coincidental, that the first year of Lethaby's marriage was also that of his last great architectural work – and most traumatic experience – All Saints' church? For although the Liverpool Cathedral Competition design was slightly later, Lethaby, though a moving spirit, was not the sole creator.

In one of his letters, Lethaby wrote:

An impeding one and an urging one are the two angels who stand on either hand of everyone.

They are inevitable – night and day, rest and labour – friends both.[25]

Did marriage and home life, together with the dauntingly full programme of hard work, offer a chance to evade the conflict which is the lot of most artists; or was his marriage the blessed and necessary reconciliation of the impeding and urging angels? There is no certain answer to a question that is relevant to the problems of more than one Victorian writer and artist.

At the end of the war Lethaby was retired, at the age of sixty-two, from the Royal College and he and Edith moved to Albion Cottage (Plate 142) in Hartley Wintney, a house found for them by Schultz Weir, who lived near by. This was a short phase; after two years, London's museums and libraries had pulled Lethaby back to Bayswater. But while in Hampshire he had done a good deal of exploring on the bicycle

PLATE 142.   William and Edith Lethaby in the garden of their house at Hartley Wintney, *c.* 1919.

presented to him by the students and had gathered much of the material which was to appear in *Home and Country Arts*.

In 1921, Beresford Pite, determined that Lethaby's sixty-fifth birthday should not go uncelebrated, told Schultz Weir: 'We shall have to do something about Lethaby. It is of no use waiting until he is in his grave; we have got to honour him now. You must tackle this.'[26] Weir at first demurred a little:

> I had organized a similar gathering in honour of the late Phené Spiers many years before, and I knew the amount of work it involved. We, however, got together a Committee, and Matthew Dawson took on the job of hon. secretary, and a small sub-committee, consisting of Emery Walker and myself, was appointed to work with him. In the end we had a delightful tea party in the Art-Workers' Guild Hall on Lethaby's 65th birthday, and had a birthday cake with 65 candles. Lord Crawford took the chair. Professor Mackail had composed, in his best literary style, an address to Lethaby, which he read, and Lethaby was presented with this address, written by Edward Johnston, with all our signatures added. We had felt that a number of his essays would be lost unless they were published in book form, and, after a great deal of trouble, we persuaded him to allow the committee to publish such essays as he would select in the form of a book. Eventually he agreed to our doing so. That is the origin of *Form in Civilization*.[27]

Aggie Strang, the wife of William Strang RA, gave a more personal and informal account of the party:

> The AWG had a delightful party yesterday afternoon to Lethaby, and the Guildroom was packed . . . There was a lovely birthday cake and 65 coloured candles all round, red, white and blue. Dear old Lethaby made a delightful speech, but was very nervous and nearly broke down once or twice. After the presentation there was a great tea party.[28]

As well as the address (Plate 143), Lethaby was presented with a portrait drawn by William Rothenstein, which was, after his death, donated to the town of Barnstaple where the town council showed its appreciation by losing it.

The drawing-in process, as Lethaby was to call it, was nearing completion. It had been a long career, with success in many different fields. He had, moreover, in these latter years an ever-increasing circle of professional friends. What more fitting than that he should at this stage enjoy the public recognition he had undoubtedly earned? But those who thought thus reckoned without their man.

In February 1924 the council of the RIBA resolved, by unanimous vote, to bestow on Lethaby its highest honour, the Gold Medal. Unfortunately, it had omitted to ask him first, and was greatly taken aback when he replied:

> I was startled, even frightened, by your notification and generous intention of the RIBA and I am most grateful for the friendliness of the brethren. There are things however that rule me out. One of these is the fact that whoever talks in going along is likely later to find himself bound

up by what he has said. In this way I have talked away my freedom of action. Just at this time of stress when so many of my fellows have not sufficient worthy work to do I should specially wish not to have a personal distinction conferred on me. Again let me assure the Council of my deep sense of gratitude for their goodwill.[29]

A delegation from the Council was unable to make him change his mind, and no medal was awarded that

PLATE 143. The Earl of Crawford presenting an address to Lethaby at the Art-Workers' Guild on his sixty-fifth birthday, 18 January 1922.

year. When the editor of the *RIBA Journal* asked the Council's secretary, Arthur Keen, who had been a delegate, the reason for Lethaby's refusal, he replied:

His decision was in no way a surprise to me: what always did surprise me was that he remained for such a number of years a member of our Institute. I suppose it was due to his personal feeling towards its members as distinct from itself.

His attitude towards affairs is such that he must necessarily disapprove of any organization of architecture as a profession because it is something that stands between an architect and his real work.

I think he is fully ready to admit the impossibility of carrying out work under modern conditions without the involved paraphernalia associated with modern architectural practice, and actually it is modern civilization itself and its methods that he is opposed to rather than any section of its activities. A system under which attention is concentrated on the individual items in a city while essential things like fine street planning and efficient services are neglected for sheer lack of strength and ability to tackle them effectively is obviously wrong, and one cannot blame Professor Lethaby if consistency prevents him from falling into line with a system of organisation that he feels to be operating on wrong lines.[30]

Another reason, however, was stated in *The Builder,* which pointedly remarked:

The bestowal of honours has been so much at random and so much the endowment of those who sought them, rather than those who sustained them, that their value has become much discounted.[31]

What Keen had said was generally true but a letter from Lethaby to Cockerell shows that the editor of *The Builder* was not very far off the mark:

About the RIBA I am disturbed, I do not like drawing back from what is intended as a generosity; but a lot of nobodies giving themselves 'distinctions' I can't abear . . . I don't like their views on 'architecture' and I find it difficult to think it is looking up.[32]

Lethaby outlived the great figures of his youth and, more sadly, many of his friends and contemporaries. His valedictory notes in various journals – on Spiers, Gimson, Sedding, Micklethwaite, Newton, Ruskin, Horsley and Sidney Barnsley – evoke poignantly and vividly a time long past.

Edith Lethaby died in 1927 and in the remaining years Lethaby was cared for by his sister-in-law, Grace Crosby. He continued to write and argue for an architecture that reflected modern times and modern materials. On his death in 1931 he was buried with his wife beneath a tombstone which he may have designed. Below Edith's epitaph 'She was wise and true and very kind' are the words 'Love and Labour are All'.

LIST OF ABBREVIATIONS

A	*The Architect*
AAJ	*Architectural Association Journal*
AAN	*Architectural Association News*
AR	*Architectural Review*
B	*The Builder*
BN	*Building News*
JRSA	*Journal of the Royal Society of Arts*
RIBAJ	*Journal of the Royal Institute of British Architects*
TEBG	London County Council Technical Education Board Gazette
TEBM	London County Council Technical Education Board Minutes

NOTES TO TEXT

NOTES TO CHAPTER ONE: EARLY YEARS
(pp. 11–36)

1   *North Devon Herald*, 21.xii.1937.
2   ibid., 3.ii.1937.
3   Census, 1851.
4   Bible Christian Baptismal Register Barnstaple, no. 409.
5   *North Devon Journal*, 28.i.1904.
6   ibid., 23.ii.1869.
7   *Harrod's Directory of Devon and Cornwall.*
8   W. R. Lethaby, *Home and Country Arts*, National Federation of Women's Institutes, 1923, p.131.
9   ibid., p.125.
10 ibid., p.132.
11 Recounted to John Brandon-Jones by a relation of Lethaby's.
12 Parliamentary Papers 1867–8, vol. xxxiii, part 14, pp.278–9.
13 Lethaby, *Home and Country Arts*, op.cit., p.125.
14 Minute Book. The Barnstaple Literary and Scientific Institute 1865. The Athenaeum, Barnstaple, Devon.
15 *Barnstaple Times*, 20.viii.1869.
16 *Parents' Review*, vol. xxviii, no. 10, October 1916, p.31.
17 Census, 1871.
18 *RIBAJ*, vol. 64, 1957, p.218.
19 ibid.
20 J.G. Hayman, *A History of the Methodist Revival of the Last Century in . . . North Devon*, London: Wesleyan Methodist Book Room, 1898, p.190. Much other information about Lauder is to be found in The Athenaeum, Barnstaple.
21 *A*, vol. 12, 1874, pp.18, 230; vol. 14, 1875, pp.214, 332, 366; vol.15, 1876, p.226; vol. 20, 1878, p. 86; vol. 19, 1878, p.64.
22 ibid., vol. 53, 1895, p.225.
23 W.R. Lethaby, *Westminster Abbey Re-examined*, Duckworth, 1925, p.65.
24 *BN*, vol. 31, 1876, p.417.
25 ibid., vol. 32, 1877, p.23.
26 ibid., vol. 34, 1878, p.23.
27 ibid., vol. 32, 1877, pp.199, 227, 299, 542; vol. 33, pp.52, 104, 135, 412, 443, 512, 534, 597, 677; vol. 34, pp.56, 141, 397.
28 *RIBAJ*, vol. 57, 1950, p.167.
29 *BN*, vol. 37, 1879, p.509.
30 *A*, vol. 20, 1878, p.208.
31 *BN*, vol. 37, 1879, p.580.
32 Information from Mrs Agnes Nash, Edith Crosby's niece.
33 *Architecture*, vol. iv, 1925, p.20.
34 Information from R. Gill.
35 *A*, vol. 22, 1879, p.334.
36 Lethaby Sketch Book No.5, *c*.1879, RIBA Drawings Collection.
37 *Proceedings of the RIBA*, 1878–9, p.57.
38 *BN*, vol. 36, 1879, p.352.
39 ibid., vol. 36, 1879, p.268.
40 ibid.
41 W.R. Lethaby, *Philip Webb and His Work*, Oxford University Press, 1935, p.69.
42 *B*, vol. 141, 1931, p.138.
43 ibid., vol. 141, 1931, p.136.
44 R.S. Weir, 'William Richard Lethaby', paper published by Central School of Arts and Crafts, 1938, p.3.

NOTES TO CHAPTER TWO: CHIEF ASSISTANT
(pp. 37–75)

1   *AAJ*, vol. 33, July 1917, p.13.
2   *Address to William Richard Lethaby with his reply*, Art-Workers' Guild, 1922, p.12.
3   Weir, op.cit., p.5.
4   *RIBAJ*, vol. 38, 1931, p.737.
5   ibid., vol. 39, 1932, p.306.
6   ibid., vol. 38, 1931, p.737.
7   Weir, op.cit., pp.6–7.

8 *RIBAJ*, vol. 57, 1950, p.167.
9 Robert Shaw, *Memoirs of R. N. Shaw*, MS, RIBA Library.
10 *RIBAJ*, vol. 38, 1931, p.737.
11 A. Saint, *Richard Norman Shaw*, Yale University Press, 1976, p.190.
12 Lethaby, *Philip Webb*, op.cit., p.71.
13 *BN*, vol. 42, 1882, p.210.
14 *A*, vol. 29, 1883, p.435.
15 H. Peacham, *The Gentleman's Exercise*, London, 1612, p.50.
16 *RIBAJ*, vol. 38, 1931, p.737.
17 *A*, vol. 29, 1883, p.435.
18 Quoted in Saint, op.cit., p.308.
19 Lethaby, *Philip Webb*, op.cit. pp.72–3.
20 W.R. Lethaby, *Architecture, Mysticism, and Myth*, Percival & Co., 1891, p.254.
21 RIBA Drawings Collection.
22 V&A Drawings Collection.
23 A. Jameson, *Sacred and Legendary Art*, Longmans, 1848, p.139.
24 *Bridport News*, 25.xii.1885.
25 J. Knight, *The Life of Rossetti*, Walter Scott, 1887, p.153.
26 *The Poetical Works of D. G. Rossetti*, Ellis & Elvey, 1891.
27 Lethaby Sketch Book, *c.* 1887, RIBA Drawings Collection.
28 *The Poems of John Keats*, Methuen, 1905.
29 Four Lethaby Sketch Books, RIBA Drawings Collection, *c.* 1884.
30 Address to W.R. Lethaby, Oxford University Press, 1922, p.12.
31 Weir, op.cit.
32 ibid., p.9.
33 ibid., p.3.
34 *B*, vol. 124, 1923, p.405.
35 Robert Shaw, op.cit.
36 R.A. Summer Exhibition 1887, no. 1074, 'The Tower of St Nicholas, Caen'.
37 Draft of letter in sketch book, RIBA Drawings Collection.
38 Lethaby's obituary of Gerald Horsley, *AAJ*, vol. xxxiii, 1918, p.13.
39 *RIBAJ*, vol. 39, 1932, p.296.
40 B. Pite to R.S. Weir, 16.iv.1932. Private collection.
41 W.R. Lethaby, *Philip Webb*, op.cit., p.80.
42 S. Cockerell, Diary, 4.iv.1890, Brit. Mus.
43 E. Gimson to W. Butler, 22.vi.1890, Leicester Mus.
44 E. Gimson to E. Barnsley, 25.vii.1890, Leicester Mus.
45 E. Gimson to W. Butler, 22.vi.1890, Leicester Mus.
46 W.R. Lethaby, A.H. Powell and F.L. Griggs, *Ernest Gimson: His Life and Work*, Shakespeare Head Press, 1924, p.6.
47 Weir, op.cit., p.6.
48 ibid., p.19.
49 Correspondence in A.B. Waters' Collection.
50 H.J.L. Massé, *The Art-Workers' Guild 1884–1934*, Shakespeare Head Press, 1935, p.7.
51 ibid., pp.82–4.
52 ibid., pp.9–10.
53 *AR*, vol. 3, 1897–8, p.239.
54 *AAN*, vol. 4, 1889–90, p.23.
55 ibid.
56 *Art Journal*, 1889, p.231.
57 ibid., p.255.
58 ibid., p.259.
59 Note in Lethaby Sketch Book, RIBA Drawings Collection.

NOTES TO CHAPTER THREE: WORKMANSHIP
(pp. 77–105)

1 Lethaby's 1889 Diary. Original lost: typescript J. Brandon-Jones.
2 Lethaby, *Philip Webb*, op.cit., 2nd ed., p.242.
3 Lethaby to Lord Manners, 11.ii.1892, RIBA Library.
4 Lethaby, *Philip Webb*, op.cit., p.1.
5 *RIBAJ*, vol. 39, 1932, p.410
6 Lethaby to Cockerell, n.d., Brit. Mus.
7 SPAB Committee Minutes, 1891.
8 Lethaby, *Architecture, Mysticism, and Myth*, op.cit., p.v.
9 ibid., p.1.
10 ibid., p.3.
11 ibid., p.5.
12 ibid., p.229
13 Architectural Illustration Society, no.230; *A*, vol. 63, 1891, p.326.
14 W.R. Lethaby, *Architecture, Nature and Magic*, Duckworth, 1956, p.15.
15 Oscar Wilde, *The Picture of Dorian Gray*, Dent, 1930, p.179. First published 1891.
16 Lethaby, *Architecture, Mysticism, and Myth*, op.cit., p.4.

17 ibid., p.208.
18 Colonna, *Poliphilo (Hypnerotomachia Poliphili)*, Venice: Aldus Manutius, 1499. Lethaby used the 1883 French edition, p.42.
19 Jameson, op.cit., p.35.
20 *AAN*, vol. 4, 1889–90, p.23.
21 *Arts and Crafts Essays*, Percival & Co., 1893, pp.410–12.
22 J. Ruskin, *The Stones of Venice*, vol. II, Smith, Elder & Co., 1853, pp.168–9.
23 W. Morris, intro. to J. Ruskin, 'The Nature of Gothic', Kelmscott Press, 1891.
24 *Arts and Crafts Essays*, op.cit.
25 L. Weaver, *The House and its Equipment*, Country Life, 1912, p.58.
26 *Arts and Crafts Essays*, op.cit., p.302.
27 Lethaby et al., *Ernest Gimson*, op.cit., p.6.
28 Ruskin, op.cit., p.154.
29 Lethaby et al., *Ernest Gimson*, op.cit., p.6.
30 ibid.
31 R. Blomfield, *Memoirs of an Architect*, Macmillan, 1932, p.75.
32 *B*, vol. 1.77, 1899, p.335.
33 Lethaby et al., *Ernest Gimson*, op.cit., p.6.
34 *Arts and Crafts Essays*, op.cit., pp.302–9.
35 A.H. Mackmurdo (ed.), *Plain Handicrafts*, Percival & Co., 1892. Later reissued as a pamphlet, *Simple Furniture*, Leicester: Dryad, n.d. Republished 1985.
36 *B*, vol. 71, 1896, p.307.

NOTES TO CHAPTER FOUR: BUILDINGS
(pp. 107–171)

1 Lethaby's 1889 Diary. Typescript J. Brandon-Jones.
2 ibid.
3 P. Henderson, *The Letters of William Morris*, Longman Green, 1950, pp.322–3.
4 Lethaby to Manners, 26.viii.1890, RIBA Library.
5 ibid., 25.x.1890.
6 ibid., 22.i.1891.
7 The present Lord Manners to the author, n.d.
8 Lethaby to Manners,. 3.viii.1892, RIBA Library.
9 ibid., 15.viii.1892.
10 ibid., 26.ii.1892.
11 *AR*, vol. 10, 1901, p.72.

12 ibid.
13 Cockerell's diary records that Lethaby was in the Orkneys the year before Middlemore purchased the estates.
14 Information from John Brandon-Jones.
15 Information from Joan Heddle.
16 J. Ruskin, *The Stones of Venice*, op.cit., p.215.
17 N. Pevsner, 'Nine Swallows No Summer', *AR*, vol. 91, 1942.
18 Edith Lethaby to Grace Crosby, n.d. Mrs John Nicholson.
19 Ruskin, op.cit., p.213.
20 Lethaby to Cockerell, 8.viii.1915. Brit. Mus.
21 Lethaby, *Philip Webb*, op.cit., p.121.
22 N. Pevsner, *The Buildings of England: Herefordshire*, Penguin, 1963, p.91.
23 Edith Lethaby to Grace Crosby, n.d. Mrs John Nicholson.
24 ibid.
25 Weir, op.cit., pp.13–14.
26 Lethaby, *Architecture, Mysticism, and Myth*, op.cit., p.79.
27 ibid., p.82.
28 ibid., p.179.
29 Rev.xxii:10.
30 Lethaby, *Architecture, Mysticism and Myth*, op.cit., p.269.
31 ibid., p.53.
32 TEBM, 2.iii.1903, p.112. GLC Archives.
33 LCC Minutes 1903, Report of the Establishment Committee, p.508. GLC Archives.
34 TEBM, 1903, p.636.
35 Lethaby to Cockerell, 9.xi.1905. Brit. Mus.
36 ibid.,15.ii.1909.
37 TEBM, 1903, p.109.
38 A.R.N. Roberts, *William Richard Lethaby*, Central School of Arts and Crafts, 1957, p.3.
39 Gimson to Lethaby, 5.vii.(?)1916. N. Jewson.
40 W.R. Lethaby, *Form in Civilization*, Oxford University Press, 1922, p.100.
41 Lethaby to A. Powell, n.d. Roger Powell Collection.
42 *B*, vol.115, 1918, p.261.
43 Lethaby, *Architecture*, op.cit., p.247.
44 Lethaby to Cockerell, 7.x.1907. Brit. Mus.

NOTES TO CHAPTER FIVE: WORK FOR THE LONDON COUNTY COUNCIL
(pp. 173–198)

1 W.R. Lethaby, 'Education for Industry', in *Handicrafts and Reconstruction*, Hogg, 1919, p.86.
2 TEBM, 1894, p.446. GLC Archives.
3 Department of Science and Art, *1st Report*, 1852, p.359.
4 A. Legros, *Royal Commission on Technical Education, Parliamentary Papers*, vol. 32, 1884, p.199.
5 H. Llewellyn Smith, *Report to the Special Committee on Technical Education*, LCC, 1892.
6 ibid., p.20.
7 TEBM, 1894, p.350.
8 R.N. Shaw and T.G. Jackson (eds), *Architecture a Profession or an Art*, Murray, 1892, p.161.
9 H. Llewellyn Smith. MS note. Arthur Llewellyn Smith.
10 TEBM, 1894, p.223.
11 ibid., 1894, p.446.
12 Lethaby to Cockerell, n.d. Brit. Mus.
13 TEBM, 1894, p.446.
14 ibid., p.447.
15 W.R. Lethaby, *Leadwork*, Macmillan, 1893, pp.2–3.
16 TEBM, 1895, p.37.
17 Lethaby, *Schools of Art*. Typescript G. Rubens.
18 TEBM, 1895, p.131.
19 *Schools of Art*, ibid.
20 TEBM, 1894, p.353.
21 ibid., 1898, p.72.
22 ibid., 1895, p.156.
23 ibid., p.157.
24 ibid., 1896, p.157.
25 TEBG, 1896, p.159
26 TEBM, 1896, p.204.
27 ibid., 1896, p.276.
28 TEBG, 1896, p.210.
29 *Punch*, 10.x.1896, p.18.
30 *RIBAJ*, vol. 57. 1950, p.169.
31 P. Johnston, *Edward Johnston*, Faber, 1959, p.97.
32 Roberts, *William Richard Lethaby*, op.cit., p.31.
33 TEBM, 1894, p.129.
34 Johnston, op.cit., p.73.
35 E. Gill, *Autobiography*, Right Book Club, 1944, p.136.
36 N. Rooke, *Woodcuts and Engravings*, Print Collectors' Club, 1926.
37 Prospectus, Central School of Arts and Crafts.
38 TEBM, 1903.
39 ibid.
40 LCC Polytechnics and Evening Schools Sub-Committee Minutes, 21.xi.1907.
41 Lethaby to Cockerell, 19.i.1909. V&A.
42 Cockerell to H. Bentinck, 17.ii.1909. Copy among the Noel Rooke papers. Celia Rooke.
43 H. Muthesius, *Di Krisis in Kunstgewerbe*, Leipzig, 1901, p.18.
44 TEBM, 1902, p.184.
45 LCC Polytechnics and Evening Schools Sub-Committee Minutes, 15.xii.1904.
46 MS Notes on Art Education. The Athenaeum, Barnstaple.
47 TEBM, 1898, p.76.
48 ibid.
49 *The Visual Arts: an enquiry*, Political and Economic Planning, Oxford University Press, 1946, pp.86–7.
50 B. Allen, *William Garnett*, Heffer & Sons, 1933, p.59.
51 Lethaby, Letter of application for Slade Professorship, 17.iii.1910. Bodleian Lib.
52 Robert Blair to Lethaby, 20.xii.1915. A. Ll. Smith.

NOTES TO CHAPTER SIX: ARCHITECTURAL EDUCATION
(pp. 199–217)

1 Gill, op.cit., p.95.
2 *B*, vol. 52, 1887, p.701.
3 ibid.
4 *RIBAJ*, vol. 23, 1916, p.334.
5 Shaw and Jackson, op.cit., p.230.
6 H. Llewellyn Smith, op.cit., p.76.
7 TEBM, 1894, p.130.
8 Shaw and Jackson, op.cit., pp.151–3.
9 TEBM, 1895, p.144.
10 ibid.
11 TEBM, 1896, p.142.
12 *AAN*, vol. 10, 1896, p.92.
13 *B*, vol. 69, 1895, p.312.
14 ibid., p.334.
15 *AAN*, vol. 10, 1895, p.112.
16 *B*, vol. 69, 1895, p.334.
17 *RIBAJ*, vol. 39, 1932, p.298.
18 *AAN*, vol. 10, p.89.
19 *AA Brown Book*, 1896–7, p.90.
20 TEBM, 1896, p.9.

21 Central School of Arts and Crafts, First Prospectus. GLC Archives.
22 ibid.
23 *AR*, vol. 15, 1904, p.113.
24 ibid., 1897, p.243.
25 *AR*, vol. 15, 1904, p.113.
26 ibid., 1907, p.268.
27 *BN*, vol. 81, 1901, p.62.
28 ibid., 1909, p.445.
29 *The History of the Brixton School of Building*, LCC, 1954, p.6.
30 *RIBAJ*, vol. 8, 1901, p.394.
31 RIBA Council Minutes, 3.vi.1903.
32 RIBA Special Committees Minutes, 1899–1908, 4.vi.1904, p.97.
33 Blomfield, op.cit., pp.105–9.
34 *AR*, vol. 16, 1904, p.157.
35 RIBA Board of Architectural Education. Syllabus 1906–7.
36 RIBA Board of Architectural Education Minutes, March 1907, p.7.
37 ibid., 16.xi.1911, p.4.
38 *RIBAJ*, vol. 24, 1917, p.252.
39 Lethaby to Pite, 23.iv.1922. Private collection.
40 S. Loweth to author, 23.v.1974.
41 Blomfield to Lethaby, 17.xii.1917. John Brandon-Jones.
42 Blomfield, op.cit., p.115.
43 H.S. Goodhart-Rendel, *English Architecture since the Regency*, Constable, 1955, p.255.

NOTES TO CHAPTER SEVEN:
THE ROYAL COLLEGE OF ART
(pp. 219–230)

1 F. Sparkes, *Report on the National Art Training School*. Ed. 23/26 PRO.
2 *Reports on the RCA*, HMSO, 1910, p.7.
3 W. Crane, *An Artist's Reminiscences*, Methuen, 1907, p.455.
4 *Reports on the RCA*, op.cit., p.40.
5 *RIBAJ*, vol. 57, 1950, p.169.
6 TEB, *Report on Art Schools*, op.cit.
7 *Reports on the RCA*, op.cit., pp.37–8.
8 *RIBAJ*, vol. 39, 1932, p.307.
9 *B*, vol. 69, 1895, p.334.

10 *Reports on the RCA*, op.cit., p.38.
11 W.R. Lethaby, 'The Teaching of Design', in F. Watson (ed.), *The Encyclopedia and Dictionary of Education*, Pitman, 1921, p.452.
12 ibid., p.452.
13 ibid.
14 P. Johnston, op.cit., p.74.
15 Lethaby, in Watson, op.cit., p.453.
16 *Reports on the RCA*, op.cit., p.48.
17 L. Day to R. Morant, 2.iii.1910. Ed. 24/87 PRO.
18 *Reports on the RCA*, op.cit., p.48.
19 ibid., p.48.
20 Parliamentary Papers, vol. 18, 1911, p.549 et seq.
21 R. Morant, Memorandum, 4.iii.1910. Ed. 24/87 PRO.
22 S. Bigge, Memorandum. Ed. 24/598 PRO.
23 Board of Education, 16.iv.1914. Ed. 24/598 PRO.
24 ibid.
25 *The Visual Arts: an enquiry*, op.cit., pp.86–7.
26 N. Rooke, *The Times*, 24.vii.1948.
27 R. Darwin, *The Times Educational Supplement*, 10.xi.1967.
28 Lethaby to Cockerell, 9.x.1915. Brit. Mus.

NOTES TO CHAPTER EIGHT:
WESTMINSTER ABBEY
(pp. 231–243)

1 W. R. Lethaby, *Mediaeval Art*, Duckworth, 1904, p.1.
2 Lethaby, *Philip Webb*, op.cit., p.145.
3 ibid., p.67.
4 W. Morris, *Manifesto of the S.P.A.B.*, SPAB, 1877.
5 Lethaby *et al.*, *Ernest Gimson*, op.cit., p.2.
6 Lethaby, *Form in Civilization*, op.cit., pp.234–40.
7 H. Muthesius, 'Peterborough and the Preservation of Ancient Buildings', in *Centralblatt der Bauverwaltung*, 10.iv.1897, p.234, SPAB.
8 Shaw to Lethaby, 28.xii.1896. SPAB.
9 Lethaby to Powys, 11.xi.1922. SPAB.
10 J.G. Noppen, 'The Care of Westminster Abbey', in *The Quarterly Review*, Oct. 1932, p.304.
11 Lethaby to Cockerell, 7.xi.1906. Brit. Mus.
12 *RIBAJ*, vol. 39, 1932, p.308.
13 ibid.
14 W.R. Lethaby, *Westminster Abbey and the Kings' Craftsmen*, Duckworth, 1906, pp.371–2.

15 Lethaby to Dean Armitage Robinson. Westminster Abbey.
16 ibid.
17 *S.P.A.B. Annual Report*, 1902. p.60.
18 Conversation with Lawrence Tanner, August 1975.
19 L. E. Tanner, *Recollections of a Westminster Antiquary*, Baker, 1969, p.90.
20 R.B. Rackham, *Anecdota Westminsteriensia*, 1907, Westminster Abbey.
21 Surveyor's Report, 1922, MS Westminster Abbey.
22 *Annual Report*, SPAB, 1930, p.6.
23 W. Morris, *Westminster Abbey*, SPAB, 1893.
24 P. Henderson, *The Letters of William Morris*, Longmans, 1950, p.312.
25 Surveyor's Report, 1926 MS. Westminster Abbey.
26 Lethaby, *Westminster Abbey and the Kings' Craftsmen*, op.cit., p.372.
27 Chapter Book, 8.xii.1927, p.62. Westminster Abbey.
28 Lethaby, *Westminster Abbey Re-examined*, op.cit., p.233.

NOTES TO CHAPTER NINE:
THEORIST AND WRITER
(pp. 245–269)

1 Lethaby, *Form in Civilization*, op.cit., p.7.
2 Shaw and Jackson, *Architecture a Profession or an Art*, op.cit., p.151.
3 *B*, vol. 71, 1896, p.307.
4 Shaw and Jackson, op.cit., p.167.
5 H.H. Statham, *Modern Architecture*, Chapman and Hall, 1897, p.15.
6 Lethaby, *Mediaeval Art*, op.cit., p.15.
7 W.R. Lethaby and H. Swainson, *The Church of Sancta Sophia, Constantinople: a Study of Byzantine Building*, Macmillan, 1894, p.247.
8 *RIBAJ*, vol. 64, 1957, p.223.
9 Lethaby, *Leadwork*, op.cit., p.148.
10 *AR*, vol. 22, 1907, p.268.
11 Lethaby, *Mediaeval Art*, op.cit., p.297.
12 Lethaby, *Westminster Abbey and the Kings' Craftsmen*, op.cit., p.vii.
13 Tanner, op.cit., p.90.
14 John Harvey to author, 8.viii.1975.
15 *RIBAJ*, vol. 15, 1908, p.215.
16 *RIBAJ*, vol. 17, 1910, pp.469, 467.
17 *B*, vol. 102, 1912, p.83.

18 W.R. Lethaby, *Architecture: an Introduction to the History and Theory of the Art of Building*, Williams & Norgate, 1912.
19 P.W. Lewis, *The Caliph's Design*, The Egoist Press, 1919, p.23.
20 *B*, vol. 115, 1918, p.261.
21 ibid., p.213.
22 Blomfield, op.cit., p.115.
23 *B*, vol. 124, 1923, p.737.
24 *B*, vol. 140, 1931, p.54.
25 C. Ashbee, 'The Masters of the Art-Workers' Guild', MS William Morris Gallery.
26 W.R. Lethaby, *Londinium: Architecture and the Crafts*, Duckworth, 1923, p.7.
27 E. Johnston, *Writing, Illuminating and Lettering*, Hogg, 1904, p.1.
28 J. Mosely, *Alphabet*, vol. 1, 1964, pp.17–48.
29 Lethaby, *Form in Civilization*, op.cit., pp.134–5.
30 ibid., p.133.
31 ibid., p.135.
32 Lethaby, 'Schools of Art', op.cit.
33 Mosely, op.cit.
34 *B*, vol. 71, 1896, p.307.
35 TEBM, 1898, p.76.
36 2nd Modern Building Design lecture (1895). Abridged accounts of these lectures published in *B*, vol. 69, 1895, pp.312, 334.
37 *RIBAJ*, vol. 24, 1917, p.252.
38 *JRSA*, vol. 45, 1897, p.855.
39 M. Arnold, *Culture and Anarchy*, Cambridge University Press, 1963, p.70.
40 Lethaby, *Philip Webb and His Work*, Raven Oak Press, reprinted 1979, p.242.
41 E. Gimson to E. Barnsley, 19.ii.1888. Leicester Mus.
42 Massé, op.cit., p.103. The text of this lecture is given in E. Le Meir, *The Unpublished Lectures of William Morris*, Wayne State University, 1969, pp.136–7.
43 W.R. Lethaby's thoughts, MS, op.cit., p.85.
44 Lethaby, *Philip Webb*, op.cit., p.240.
45 *RIBAJ*, vol. 8, 1901, p.391.
46 ibid., pp.393–4.
47 *JRSA*, op.cit., p.851.
48 Lethaby, *Form in Civilization*, op.cit., p.137.
49 Lethaby, *Home and Country Arts*, op.cit., p.45.
50 *Spectator*, 19.i.1924.
51 *Address to William Richard Lethaby*, Oxford University Press, 1922, pp.14-15.

NOTES TO CHAPTER TEN:
LETHABY – A RETROSPECT
(pp. 271–284)

1 *RIBAJ*, vol. 39, 1932, p.411.
2 ibid., p.305.
3 Roberts, *William Richard Lethaby*, op.cit., p.30.
4 Catterson Smith to H. Wilson, 20.x.1915. Royal College of Art Library.
5 P. Johnston, *Edward Johnston*, op.cit., p.73.
6 H.H. Peach, *Craftsmen All*, Dryad Press, n.d., p.15.
7 A.S. Hartrick, *A Painter's Pilgrimage*, Cambridge University Press, 1939, p.243.
8 Gimson, op.cit., p.4.
9 *RIBAJ*, vol. 23, 1916, p.334.
10 *The Times*, 8.ii.1894, p.2.
11 Information from Edith Crosby's niece Agnes Nash.
12 Ernest Crosby was appointed by the Khedive judge of the international tribunal at Alexandria, 1889-94.
13 'Of beautiful cities', in *Art and Life*, Percival & Co., 1897.
14 Marriage no.44, August 1901, Emmanuel Church, Geneva.
15 Edith Lethaby to Grace Lethaby, n.d. Mrs John Nicholson.
16 ibid.
17 ibid.
18 ibid.
19 Lethaby's thoughts, op.cit., p.55.
20 Lethaby, *Home and Country Arts*, ibid., p.134.
21 I. Watts, *Divine Songs for Children*, Reading Rusher, 1820, p.31.
22 Lethaby's thoughts, op.cit.
23 ibid.
24 Lethaby, *Architecture, Mysticism, and Myth*, op.cit., p.8.
25 Lethaby's thoughts, op.cit.
26 *RIBAJ*, vol. 39, 1931, p.309.
27 ibid.
28 A. Strang, Ashbee Journals, King's College, Cambridge.
29 Lethaby to MacAlister, 16.ii.1924. RIBA Council Minutes.
30 *RIBAJ*, vol. 31, 1924, p.282.
31 *B*, vol. 126, 1924, p.368.
32 Lethaby to Cockerell, 16.ii.1924. Brit. Mus.

THE MODERN ARCHITECTURE CONSTRUCTIVE GROUP

THE MANIFESTO

The text given here was dated 24 November 1922 and seems to have been the one that Lethaby circulated to possible members of the Group. The later version dated 23 March 1923 which may be taken as the official Manifesto of six paragraphs was presumably amended at the Group's first meeting some time between these dates. In it the text in square brackets below was omitted and the remainder of paragraph two was added on to paragraph three, which then became paragraph two. Paragraph eight was deleted.

1.   The undersigned wish to express their dissatisfaction with the lack of architectural theory and the consequent anarchy of our practice: also of the absence of any reasonable direction to the younger men who are constantly being betrayed by the false and inconstant enthusiasms of their elders.

2.   [Following the recent official assumption of the schools that the best we can do is to copy Paris 'fashions', it is now suggested that we should copy American fashions. The intention to sponge on other nations is not only undignified but it will sap any power we have (in practice it will lead to Americans being brought over to do the biggest works).] The fear of experiment and the timid copying of bolder peoples can only mean mental decay. Of course when advances have been made in any other country we should be eager to learn but this is quite different from the presupposition that the best we can do is to copy foreign 'fashions in design'.

3.   Another consequence of the lack of any agreed theory is the absence of a positive and reasonable basis for design, criticism, education or understanding: we 'carry on' in a chaos of whims and pretences.

4.   There are obvious advantages in forming groups of those who can agree on some common basis: a

sense of sympathy and understanding is helpful to one's own work, pointing to an aim and giving a sense of direction; moreover cooperation is a source of power.

5.   It ought to be easy to agree on some simple statement, for instance: *Architecture is a developing structural art satisfying the special requirements of the time by experiment.*

6.   Education should primarily be directed to developing the *constructive sense*, building power and the spirit of invention; it should be scientific, technical and practical. We should aim at closer cooperation with builders, and all young men should spend some years in builders' works and on building in progress. By 'constructive' more is implied than is usually meant by 'construction'. It means truly *constructive* construction, the proper selection and use of materials and liberty for workmansip to find a way. It means an attempt to find frank, reasonable and inventive solutions of modern problems in a developing search for organic and perfect building forms and methods.

7.   So far as may seem possible we agree to try to do our own work under the general guidance of the principle that architecture is above all sound and reasonable construction experimentally developed.

8.   If a group of ten or upwards is formed it might be desirable to meet for discussion occasionally. The main point however is agreement on a principle, letting that work out as it will. From time to time other adherents might be accepted.

LETHABY'S PRINCIPAL WORKS

EXECUTED BUILDINGS BY DATE

ABBREVIATIONS

D: date

DES: design

EXEC: executed

CL: client

CTR: contractor

C: cost

MAT: materials

DR: drawings (provenance of)

REF: references

ACK: acknowledgements

DEM: demolished

I NOTTINGHILL (NOW CAMPDEN HILL) SQ., LONDON W8

NEW STUDIO

D: 1889

CL: Heywood Sumner

CTR: Maides and Harford, Croydon, London

MAT: wood and brick, slate hung

C: £205.5s od

REF: Lethaby's 1889 diary

The studio which survives was built on top of an existing house.

2 MARLBOROUGH RD (NOW DRAYCOTT AVE), LONDON SW3

EIGHT BLOCKS OF NEW ARTISAN DWELLINGS

D: des 1889 exec 1891
CL: The Guinness Trust
MAT: brick

C: £28,000 (estimated)
REF: Lethaby's 1889 diary

Commission received by M. Macartney, but Lethaby did a great deal of work on it.

3 AVON TYRRELL, RINGWOOD, CHRISTCHURCH, HAMPSHIRE

NEW HOUSE, STABLES AND COTTAGES

D: and DES: 1890
EXEC: 1891, terrace 1900
CL: Lord Francis Manners
CTR: Albert Escourt & Sons
MAT: brick, stone dressings
DR: RIBA

REF: *Country Life*, vol. XXVII (1910), pp.846-52; H. Muthesius, *Das Englische Haus*, 1904, vol. I, p.152 and vol. III, p.116. The drawings exhibited International Exhibition of Fine Art, Berlin 1891.

Plaster work both interior and exterior designed and executed by E. Gimson. Subsequent alterations include the doubling of the height of the buildings around the kitchen court and the replacement of all plaster work by tile hanging. Some internal alterations, but generally in good condition.

4 THE HURST, HARTOPP RD, FOUR OAKS PARK, SUTTON COLDFIELD, WARWICKSHIRE

NEW HOUSE AND STABLES

D: and DES: 1893
EXEC: 1894
CL: Charles Edward Mathews
CTR: James Smith & Sons
MAT: brick, stone dressings
DR: RIBA

REF: L. Weaver, 'Small Country Houses for Today', *Country Life*, 1922, vol. I, pp.96–100; *AR*, vol. 10, 1901, pp.72–3; H. Muthesius, *Das Englische Haus*, 1904, vol. II.
DEM: 19?? The stables, converted into a small house, survive.

5 MELSETTER HOUSE, HOY, ORKNEY

VARIOUS WORKS

A Remodelling and extension of house

D: 1898
EXEC: 1899–1900
CL: Thomas Middlemore
CTR: William Firth, Kirkwall, Orkney
Survives unaltered.

MAT: local stone
DR: Elsie Seatter
REF: *Country Life*, 13.viii.1981, pp.566–71
AAJ, vol. 64, 1949, pp.167–71, 194–7.

B Chapel of SS Margaret and Colm

D: and EXEC: 1900
MAT: local stone, concrete
DR: Elsie Seatter, RIBA

REF: A. C. Sewter, *The Stained Glass of William Morris and his Circle*, Yale University Press: 1974–5.

GLASS: E. Window: Ford Madox Brown 'Nativity' (first used at All Saints', Selsey, Glos.). EXEC: Morris & Co. N. window: Sir Edward Burne-Jones 'Christ on the Cross' (first used at All Saints', Catton, Pocklington, Yorks.). S.windows: Christopher Whall 'St Colm' and 'St Margaret'. EXEC: Lowndes and Drury.
Deconsecrated. Furniture and fittings (DES: Lethaby) removed to Kirkwall Cathedral.

C   New steading

D: and DES: 1890   CTR: William Firth
EXEC: 1900   DR: Elsie Seatter
MAT: local stone

D   Reconstruction of (?) croft for agent

D: and EXEC: 1900   DR: Elsie Seatter
MAT: local stone

E   Rysa Lodge, Hoy

Remodelling and extension of croft
D: c.1900   REF: J. Brandon-Jones
MAT: local stone
Survives unaltered.

F   Orgill Lodge

Remodelling and extension of (?) croft
D: c.1900   MAT: local stone
Survives largely unaltered.

6   EAGLE INSURANCE BUILDINGS, COLMORE ROW, BIRMINGHAM, WARWICKSHIRE

NEW OFFICES

D: and DES: 1898   DR: RIBA; Birmingham City
EXEC: 1900   REF: *AR*, vol. 8, 1900, pp.51–3; H.
CL: Eagle Insurance Co.   Muthesius, *Die Englische Baukunst*, 1900, vol.
MAT: Portland stone, steel, brick and   II, p.oo.
terracotta

The Birmingham architect who was responsible for the construction on site may have contributed to the design. Recently restored when alterations were made at the rear of the building. The inscriptions on the façade have been destroyed.

7 HIGH COXLEASE, LYNDHURST, HAMPSHIRE

NEW HOUSE AND STABLES

D: 1901   MAT: brick, stone dressings
CL: Thomas Eustace Smith
Survives with extensive alterations at rear and on one side.

8 ALL SAINTS' CHURCH, BROCKHAMPTON, ROSS-ON-WYE, HEREFORDSHIRE

NEW CHURCH

D: and DES: 1901   MAT: local stone, concrete, thatch
EXEC: 1902   DR: RIBA
CL: Alice Foster   REF: *AR*, vol.130, 1961, p.354–7.
CTR: direct labour. Randall Wells was clerk of
works
GLASS: W. windows, DES: Christopher Whall. EXEC: Lowndes and Drury 1902.
S. transept, DES: Christopher Whall *c.*1916
All fittings, including the font, by Lethaby. Stalls attrib: G. Jack. Survives; wrought iron hanging lamps
removed from interior.

APPENDIX C

BIBLIOGRAPHY OF LETHABY'S PUBLICATIONS

Based on a typescript compiled by the RIBA Library Staff and others in 1950, the bibliography has now been considerably enlarged. The page references are given singly, though they usually represent articles continued on following pages. Place of publication is London unless otherwise stated.

I. BOOKS AND PAMPHLETS
(written and edited by Lethaby, alone or jointly)

In chronological order.

Architecture, Mysticism, and Myth, Percival & Co., 1891; 2nd ed, with introduction by Godfrey Rubens, Architectural Press, 1975.
Leadwork, Old and Ornamental and for the Most Part English, Macmillan, 1893.
The Church of Sancta Sophia, Constantinople: A Study of Byzantine building, with H. Swainson, Macmillan, 1894.
'Morris as work-master': a lecture . . . at the Birmingham Municipal School of Art . . . 1901, Hogg, 1901.
'The study and practice of artistic crafts': an address . . . to the Birmingham Municipal School of Art . . . 1901, Hogg, 1901.
London before the Conquest, Macmillan, 1902.
Mediaeval Art from the Peace of the Church to the Eve of the Renaissance, 312–1350, Duckworth, 1904.
'Craftwork and art', introduction in Catalogue of Exhibition Red Rose Guild, Manchester, 1921.

Westminster Abbey and the Kings' Craftsmen: a Study of Mediaeval Building, Duckworth, 1906.

Greek Buildings represented by Fragments in the British Museum, Batsford, 1908.

The Artistic Craft Series (ed. Lethaby and Archibald H. Christie) Vol I. School Copies and Examples, II. Manuscript and Inscription Letters for Schools and Classes and for the use of craftsmen. Drawn by E. Johnston and A.E.R. Gill, Hogg, 1909.

The Church of the Nativity at Bethlehem, with William Harvey and others. Edited by R. Weir Schultz (Robert W. S. Weir) (Byzantine Research Fund), Batsford, 1910.

Westminster Abbey and the Antiquities of the Coronation, Duckworth, 1911.

Architecture: an Introduction to the History and Theory of the Art of Building (Home University Library of Modern Knowledge), Williams & Norgate, 1912.

Apprenticeship and Education, Leicester: Stimpson, Art School Press, 1913–14.

'Antiquities of Ionia.' Society of Dilettanti. Part the fifth, being a supplement to part iii. (Edited by W.R.L.) Macmillan, 1915.

'Art and Workmanship.' (Design and Industries Committee, afterwards Association.) (1st pamphlet.) (Reprinted from the Imprint.) Reprinted in *Form and Civilization*, 1915.

'Design and Industry. A Proposal for the Forming of a Design and Industries Association', 1915. Reprinted in *Form and Civilization*, 1922. German translation: *Englands Kunst – Industrie und der Deutsche Werkbund*, 1916: see in III, under The Imprint.

House Painting and Funishing (Dryad Handicrafts: Dryad leaflets, No. 4), Leicester, 1920.

Form in Civilization. Collected Papers on Art and Labour, O.U.P., 1922.

Simple Furniture, reprint, with corrections, of 'Cabinet Making', from *Plain Handicrafts*, 1892 (Dryad Handicrafts: Dryad leaflets, No. 5), Leicester, 1910. Reprinted 1984.

Londinium: Architecture and the Crafts (first published in *The Builder,* 1922 – not 1921, as pref.), Duckworth, 1923.

Home and Country Arts, reprinted and enlarged from *Home and County*, the magazine of the National Federation of Women's Institutes, 1923; 3rd edition with additional essay, 1930.

Westminster Abbey re-examined (first published in *The Builder*, 1924), Duckworth, 1925.

Designing Games (Dryad Handicrafts: Dryad leaflets, No. 40), Leicester, 1926.

Art, Handicraft and Education. (Dryad Handicrafts: Dryad leaflets, No. 2) 'Education, work and beauty', from *Parents' Review*, 1916.

Philip Webb and His Work (from *The Builder*, 1925, post, revised), O.U.P., 1935 (posthumous publication).

Architecture, Nature and Magic (from *The Builder*, 1928, Reproduced with additional material 1979), with a biographical note by Alfred Powell, Duckworth, 1956.

II. MINOR CONTRIBUTION TO BOOKS AND PAMPHLETS
OF OTHER AUTHORSHIP

In chronological order.

'Of cast iron', in Arts and Crafts Exhibition Society: Catalogue of the 2nd Exhibition (p.47), 1889.

'Carpenters' furniture', in Arts and Crafts Exhibition Society: Catalogue of the 3rd Exhibition (p.46), 1890.

'The builder's art and the craftsman', essay no. 10 in *Architecture a profession or an art* (p.149) (ed. R. Norman Shaw and T. G. Jackson), Murray, 1892.

'Of beautiful cities' (lecture, mainly about London), in *Art and Life, and the Building and Decoration of Cities*; lectures . . . (1896); by the Arts and Crafts Exhibition Society, Percival, 1897.

Editor's prefaces to *The Artistic Craft Series* of technical handbooks, 9 vols, Hogg, 1901–16.

Note in *The Church of Edward the Confessor at Westminster* by J. Armitage Robinson, 1910.

Articles in *Encyclopaedia Britannica*, 11th edition 1910–11: 'Architecture: Romanesque and Gothic in France', vol.2, p.396; 'Baptistery', vol. 3, p.370; 'Byzantine art', vol. 4, p.906; 'Design', vol. 8, p.95.

'London and Westminster painters of the Middle Ages', in Walpole Society, vol. i, p.89, 1912.

'The Romance tiles of Chertsey Abbey', in Walpole Society, vol. ii, p.69, 1913.

Introduction in *L'église abbatiale de Westminster et ses tombeaux*, by Count Paul Biver, Paris, 1913.

Address in Report of Annual Meeting and Conference of the Drapers' Chamber of Trade, 1916.

Foreword in *An Embroidery Pattern Book*, by Mary E. Waring (Mrs J. D. Rolleston), Pitman, 1917.

'London architecture', in *Blue Guide to London and its Environs*, by F. Muirhead, 1918.

'The spirit of Rome', in *The Architectural Watercolours and Etchings of Wm. Walcot*, H. C. Dickins, p.43, 1919.

Introduction in *Westminster Cathedral and its Architect (J. F. Bentley)*, by W. de l'Hôpital, p.viii, Hutchinson, 1919.

'Craft and culture', in Report of the Conference on New Ideals in Education, Cambridge, 1919, p.102, Chelsea, 1919.

'Education for industry' (intro.), in *Handicrafts and Reconstruction: notes by members of the Arts and Crafts Exhibition Society*, Hogg, 1919.

'The town itself: a garden city is a town', chapter 1, p.47, in *Town Theory and Practice,* by W.R.L., G.L. Pepler and others. Ed. C.B. Purdom, Benn, 1921.

'On the teaching of art in relation to commerce', Report by a Special Committee [WRL a member] of the British Institute of Industrial Art, H.M.S.O., 1921.

Introduction in *Armenian Architecture from the 6th to the 13th Century*. Catalogue &c. V&A, 1921.

'The teaching of design', in *The Encyclopedia and Dictionary of Education* (ed. Foster Watson), p.452, Pitman 1921. Reprinted in *Training in Art and Handicraft'* (The New Educators' library), Pitman, 1922.

'Writing and civilization', foreword to Catalogue of the First Exhibition of the Society of Scribes and Illuminators, p.3., London, 1922.

'Ernest Gimson: London days', in *Ernest Gimson, his life and work*, 1924.

'Byzantine and Romanesque arts', in *Cambridge Medieval History* (ed. J. B. Bury) p.539, 1922.

'Early Christian art', in *Cambridge Medieval History*, i, p.598, 1911.

Introduction in *The Foundling Hospital and its Neighbourhood &c*, by Anne Page (Foundling Estate Protection Association), 1926.

'Industry and the notion of art', address in Report of 7th Annual Lecture Conference on Industrial Welfare, Oxford, 1926, Industrial Welfare Society, p.32, 1926.

'Medieval architecture', in *The Legacy of the Middle Ages* (ed. Charles G. Crump and Ernest F. Jacob), Oxford: Clarendon Press, p.59, 1926.

'The quest for beauty', in *The Book of the Quest* (Salford Boy Scouts, 57th), Oldham: Hanson and Son, p.22, *c*.1926.

Foreword in Catalogue of the Exhibition of the Society of Scribes and Illuminators, 1926–7.

Foreword in Catalogue of Exhibition of Wild Flower Paintings and Watercolour Drawings by A. H. Powell, Alpine Club Gallery, 1928.

Note in *This England, and Other Things of Beauty*, by F. J. Gould, Watts, p.ix, 1930.

III. CONTRIBUTIONS TO PERIODICALS, ANNUALS AND NEWSPAPERS

Periodicals arranged alphabetically; articles in each arranged chronologically.
Most periodicals cited are published in London.

Ancient Egypt, 'Alexandrian world maps', 1920, no.3, p.106.

Anglo-Italian Review, 'Italian art and Britain', i. Early Christian, July 1918, p. 241: ii. Mediaeval, August 1918, p.326, iii. Renaissance, Sept. 1918, p.46.

Archaeologia (Society of Antiquaries of London), 'Suggestions as to the identifications of the Wells sculptures and imagery', lix, pt 1, 1904, p.170; 'The Palace of Westminster in the eleventh and twelfth centuries', lx, pt 1, 1906, p.131; 'Notes on sculptures in Lincoln Minster: the Judgment Porch and the Angel Choir', lx, pt 2, 1907, p.379.

Archaeological Journal (Royal Archaeological Institute), 'The chapter-house, Westminster' (abstract of paper), lxvii, 1910, p.402; 'The Confessor's shrine in Westminster Abbey church', lxviii, 1911, p.361; 'The painted book of Genesis in the British Museum', lxix, 1912, p.88; 'Is Ruthwell Cross an Anglo-Celtic work?', lxx, 1913, p.145; 'A further note on the painted book of Genesis in the British Museum', lxx, 1913, p.162 (continuation of 1912 article); 'The Cloister of Southwark priory (St Mary Overie) and other early cloisters', lxxi, 1914, p.155; 'Archibishop Roger's Cathedral at York and its stained glass', lxxi, 1915, p.37; 'The perjury at Bayeux' (scene in Bayeux 'tapestry'), lxxiv, 1917, p.136.

The Architect, 'The English and French Renaissance', 1883, p.434.

A.A. Notes, 'Of the "motive" in architectural design', iv, 1889–90, p.23; 'Architectural (?) examination', v, 1890–91, p.115.

Continued as *A.A. Journal*, 'Travelling studies and students' drawings', xxii, 1907, p.249; 'An introduction to the study of Greek buildings', xxvi, 1911, p.73; 'Some things to be done', xxvii–xxviii, 1912–13, p.294; 'Some notes on Greek architecture', xxix, 1913-14, p.193; 'Modern German architecture and what we may learn from it', xxx, 1914–15, 1915 Feb., p.141 (reprinted in *Form in civilization*); Gerald Horsley (obit.), xxxiii, 1917, p.13.

Architectural Review, 'How they restore', v, 1898–9, p.14; 'The place of Gothic art in civilization', vii, 1900, p.17; 'The LCC new Street: Holborn to the Strand', vii, 1900, p.159; 'Westminster Cathedral', xi, 1902, p.3; 'How Exeter Cathedral was built', xiii, 1903, pp.109, 167; 'The Exe Bridge, Exeter', xiv, 1903, p.23; 'Chelsea and Holbein', xv, 1904, p.87; 'Architectural education: a discussion', xvi, 1904, p.157; 'Sancta Sophia, Constantinople', xvii, 1905, pp.118, 147; 'Inigo Jones and the theatre', xxxi, 1912, p.189; 'The Ruthwell Cross', xxxii, 1912, p.59; 'The Architecture of Londinium', xxxiii, 1913, pp.77, 90; 'The Temple of Ares at Halicarnassos', xxxvii, 1915, p.117; 'New light on Inigo Jones (as a painter)', xl, 1916, p.72; 'The Spirit of Rome and our modern problem in architecture', xli, 1917, p.1; 'Kelmscott Manor and William Morris', xlv, 1919, p.67; The late Ernest Newton, R.A. (obit.), li, 1922, p.79; 'The work of Ernest Newton' (review), lix, 1926, p.37; 'The two styles', lxv, 1929, p.271.

Architecture, 'Capharnaum et ses ruins', G. Orfali, Paris (review), vol. II, 1924, p.147; 'About beauty', vol. IV, no.1, 1925, p.20; 'Mediaeval painted medallions vaults', vol. IV, no.2, 1925, p.75; 'The engineer's art', vol. IV, no.3, 1925, p.119; 'A house in Lincoln's Inn Fields', vol. V, no.16, 1926, p.98; 'A finer common place' (review), vol. V, no.17, 1926, p.136; 'Old headstones', vol. V. no.18, 1926, p.180.

Art Journal, 'Some Northamptonshire steeples', 1889, pp.227, 254.

Arts and Crafts Quarterly (Arts and Crafts Exhibition Society), Ernest W. Gimson (obit.), vol.i, no.1, 1919 (Nov.), p.5; 'Ruskin: defeat and victory', 1919 (April), (reprinted in *Form and Civilization*).

Athenaeum, John. T. Micklethwaite (obit.), 1906, p.589; 'Colour on the sculptures of the Parthenon', 1913, p.163; 'On housing and furnishing', 1920, pp.676, 707 (reprinted in *Form in Civilisation*); 'On the Eisteddfod as a means of civilization' (letter), 1920, p.345; 'The British Museum and the Muses. Some centenary reflections', 1920, pp.479, 526; 'The English interior' (review), 1920. p.734.

The Builder, 'A note on the artistic work and life of J. D. Sedding' (obit.), lxi, 1891, p.270; 'On the Church of St John at Damascus' (letters), lxvi, 1894, pp.210, 275, 293, 353; 'Wood carving' (lecture), lxviii, 1895, p.281; 'Modern Building Design' (lecture), lxix, 1895, pp.312, 334; 'Modern architecture' (lecture), lxxi, 1896, p.307; 'Design and craftsman' (letter), lxxi, 1896, p.336; 'Cast iron' (lecture), lxviii, 1900, p.104; 'Greek art' (lecture), xciv, 1905, p.144; 'Byzantine churches in Constantinople', ciii, 1912, p.702; 'The architectural treatment of reinforced concrete' (lecture), civ, 1913, p.175; 'The structural ideal in architecture', civ, 1913, p.649; 'The designer of the Palace of Chambord and Inigo Jones', cv, 1913, p.83; 'Vaulted Norman churches in England' (letters), cv, 1913, pp.337, 425, 486, 610; 'The proposed destruction of Nelson's Column' (letter), cvi, 1914, p.642; 'A national architecture', cxv, 1918, p.213–441; 'Observations and suggestions', cxvi, 1919, p.128 to cxvii, 1919, p.565; 'Beauty of structures' (letter), cxvii, 1919, p.287; 'Records of Roman London', cxviii, 1920, p.22; 'Dynamic', cxviii, p.485; 'How shall we be classic?', cxviii, 1920, p.609; 'Greek afternoons at the British Museum', cxviii, 1920, p.19 to cxix, 1920, p.664; 'Modernism and design', cxx, 1921, p.31 to cxxi, 1921, p.749; 'Our hope for the future', cxx, 1921, p.379; 'Victorian criticism' (letter), cxx, 1921, p.119; 'Get at essentials' (letter), cxix, 1921, p.807; 'Londinium: Architecture and Crafts', cxxii, 1922, p.34, cxxiii, 1922, p.832. Reprinted as a book (1923), *See* I, *ante*; The late Mr J. Ernest Newton (obit.), cxxii, 1922, p.219; 'The earliest European architecture' (review), cxxii, 1922, pp.727–9; 'The Building art: theories and discussions', cxxiv, 1923, p.8, to cxxv, 1923, p.890; 'Clerks and artists' (letter), cxxv, 1923, p.241; 'Levelling down', cxxv, 1923, p.163; 'Hellenistic art in ancient America' (review), cxxvi, 1924, p.184; 'Westminster Abbey' (letters), cxxvi, 1924, pp.710, 940; 'Westminster Abbey re-examined', cxxvi, 1924, p.381 to cxxvii, 1924, p.939. Reprinted with additions as a book, 1925. *See* I, *ante*; 'Architecture: design, education', cxxvii, p.215; 'Pliny's Villa and Whitehall Palace', cxxxii, p.242; 'Animal spirals from Asia to Central America and North Britain' (review), cxxvii, 1924, p.311; 'Philip Webb and his work', cxxviii, 1925, p.42 to cxxix, 1925, p.922. Reprinted posthumously (1935) as a book. *See* I, *ante*; 'Pre Hellenic architecture' (review), cxxx, 1926, p.913; 'British tombs, modern and antique', cxxx, 1926, p.56 to cxxxi, 1926, p.377; The development of American architecture (1783–1830) (review), cxxxi, 1926, p.122; 'English cast iron', cxxxi, 1926, pp.537-952; 'On mediaeval paintings', cxxii, 1927, p.1007; 'Parthenon studies', cxxii, 1927, p.52 to cxxxiii, 1927, p.905; Improvement of modern building (letter), cxxxiii, 1927, p.271; 'Architecture nature and magic', cxxxiv, 1928, p.88 to cxxxv, 1928, p.984. Reprinted posthumously (1956) as a book. *See* I, *ante*; Tomb of Mausolus (letter), cxxxvi, 1929, p.459; 'Architecture as structural geometry', cxxxvi, 1929, p.52; 'Architecture as engineering', cxxxvi, 1929, pp.252, 301; 'More Greek studies', cxxxvi, 1929, p.430 to cxxxvii, 1929, p.1019; Chambers in chancel (letter), cxxxviii, 1930, p.1148; 'Art and the community', cxxxviii, 1930, pp. 55–487; 'Old St Paul's (London)', cxxxviii, 1930, p.671 to cxxxix, 1930, p.1088; 'Engineering and architecture', cxi, 1931, p.54; 'Modern church building', cxi, 1931, p.283; 'Lycian art', cxi, 1931, pp.456,627; The Palace of Minos at Knossos (review), cxi, 1931, p.1020.

Builder's Journal, The West Front of Wells Cathedral (letter), vol. 17, 1903, p.272.

The Burlington Magazine, English primitives. 'The Painted Chamber (Westminster Palace) and the early masters of the Westminster School', vii, 1905, p.257; 'Majolica roundels of the months of the year at the Victoria and Albert Museum', ix, 1906, p.404; 'The origin of knotted ornamentation', x, 1906–7, p.256; 'English primitives (cont.)', xx, 1911–12, p.4; 'The Ruthwell Cross', xxi, 1912, p.145; 'The Bewcastle and Ruthwell Crosses', xxiii, 1913, p.46; 'Byzantine silks in London museums', xxiv, 1913–14, pp.138, 185; 'The part of Sugar in the creation of mediaeval iconography', xxv, 1914, p.206; 'Some early Italian and German embroideries at South Kensington', xxv, 1914, p.298; 'Sculptures of the Parthenon. The west pediment', xxvii, 1915, pp.14, 66; (letter) *following* 'Two early Egyptian printed stuffs', by Francis F. L. Birrell, xxvii, 1915 (article), June, p.104; (letter) July, p.168; 'The Borderers of London and Opus Anglicanum', xxix, 1916, p.74; English primitives (series), 'I. Master William of Colchester', xxix, 1916, p.189, 'II. Master William of Westminster &c', xxix, 1916, p.281, 'III. The Master of the Westminster altarpiece', xxix, 1916, p. 351; 'IV. The Westminster and Chertsey tiles and Romance paintings', xxx, 1917, p.133; 'V. Matthew Paris and Friar William', xxxi, 1917, p.45; 'VI. Master Richard, Monk of St Albans &c', xxxi, 1917, p.97; 'VII. The Engish School in Sweden and Norway', xxxi, 1917, pp.192, 223; 'VIII. Master Walter of Durham', xxxiii, 1918, pp.28, 169; 'A fourteenth-century English triptych', xli, 1922, p.110; 'English primitives' (further article), xlv, 1924, p.78; English primitives, 'London painters and Opus Anglicanum', liii, 1928, p.173; 'The Ascoli cope and London artists', liv, 1929, p.304; 'Westminster portrait of Richard II', lxv, 1934, pp.220–2.

The Common Room (Educational Settlements Association), 'Art and handicraft in relation to adult education: ii . . . on handicraft' (notes of lecture), 1925 (Feb.), p.6.

Country Life, 'Restoration work at Exeter', 1906, p.857.

Devon Notes and Queries, 'Old Exeter', iii, 1904–5, p.35; 'Knights effigies in Exeter Cathedral', iii,

1904–5, p.105; 'The Conqueror's castles in Devon', iii, 1904–5, p.170; 'St Sidwell's and Exeter', iv, 1906–7, p.190; 'Leofric's Stone, Exeter Cathedral', v, 1908–9, p.294.

Hibbert Journal, 'What shall we call beautiful? A practical view of aesthetics', vol. 16, 1918, p.443. Reprinted in *Form in Civilization*; 'Towns to live in', vol. 15, 1917, p.578. Reprinted in *Form in Civilization*. 'The Royal Academy picture show and the higher criticism of art', vol. 18, July 1920, p.714. Reprinted in *Form in Civilization* as 'Exhibitionism at the R.A. &c'. 'Memorials of the fallen: service or sacrifice', vol. 17, 1919, p.621. 'Labour a manifestation of God', vol. 27, 1928, p.47. 'God or the devil in labour', vol. 27, 1928, p.535.

The Highway, 'The foundation in labour', March 1917. Reprinted in *Form in Civilization*.

Home Counties Magazine, 'The Priory of Holy Trinity or Christchurch Aldgate', ii, 1900, p.45; 'Early plans of part of the Palace at Westminster', 1593, v, 1903, p.1.

Home and Country (The National Federation of Women's Institutes), 'I. Drudgery redeemed', Jan. 1923, p.6; 'II. Drawing for everyone', Feb. 1923, p.8; 'III. Designing as a Game', Mar. 1923, p.6; 'IV. The sewing arts', Apr. 1923, p.37; 'V. Seeing London', May 1923, p.74; 'VI. Village arts and crafts', June 1923, p.114; 'VII. Farming festivals', July 1923, p.147; 'VIII. Farms and Cottages', Aug. 1923, p.182. Reprinted (1923) as a book *See* I, *ante*. 'Children make your own toys, I–IV', Jan., Feb., Mar., Apr., 1929, pp.18, 72, 124, 174. Reprinted (1930) as an addition to above book.

Illustration, Common sense code signs. n.d.

The Imprint, 'Art and workmanship', no.1, 1913. Reprinted by the D.I.A. and in *Form and Civilization*.

Journal of Hellenic Studies, 'The sculptures of the later Temple of Artemsis at Ephesus', xxxiii, 1913, p.87; xxxiv, 1914, p.76; xxxvi, 1916, p.25; 'The Nereid monument re-examined', xxxv, 1915, p.208; 'The earlier temple of Artemsis at Ephesus', xxxvii, 1917, p.1; 'A fragment of an ivory statue at the British Museum', xxxvii, 1917, p.11; 'The Parthenos (statue of Athena in the Parthenon, Athens)', xxxvii, 1917, p.140; 'Greek lion monuments', xxxviii, 1918, p.37; 'The Venus de Milo and the Apollo of Cyrene', xxxix, 1919, p.206; 'An attic cistern front at the British Museum', xlviii, 1928, p.7; 'The central part of the eastern frieze of the Parthenon', xlix, 1929, p.7; 'The west pediment of the Parthenon', l, 1930, p.4.

Journal of the Royal Institute of British Architects, 'Education in building', viii, 1901, pp.385, 399; 'The Wells Cathedral statues', xi, 1904, p.339; 'The Study of architecture', xii, 1905, p.226; Liverpool students' sketchbook (review), xiii, 1906, p.226; 'The theory of Greek architecture: an address to students', xv, 1908, p.213; 'Architectural sources in nature by Mourer' (review), xvi, 1909, p.540; Westminster Abbey (review), xvii, 1910, p.78; 'The Architecture of adventure', xvii, 1910, p.469. Reprinted in *Form and Civilization;* 'Monumental work of Cosmati at Westminster', xviii, 1911, p.81; 'Lincoln Cathedral: a new reading', xviii, 1916, pp.238, 425; Drawings of Greek Architecture at RIBA (collection of original drawings, proof plates, etc., prepared for the Soc. of Dilletanti's publications. By N. Revett. F. Bedford. J. Gandy and R. P. Pullan), xix, 1912, p.720. Report by W.R.L. 'On Early Christian Art', xix, 1912, p.60; J. Bilson, Bernay Church (review), xix, 1912, p.459; 'RIBA Records Committee Report', xix, 1912, p.431; 'Bath: a comparative study', xx, 1913, p.41; Book names for building work (letter), xx, 1913, p.448; 'Borrowing in architecture', xxi, 1914, p.309; The Temple of Artemis at Ephesus (letter), xxii, 1915, p.164; Philip Webb (obit.), xxii, 1915, p.339; Richard Phené Spiers (obit.), xxiii, 1916, p.334; 'Anarchy of styles', xxiv, 1917, p.8; 'Things to be done in architecture', xxiv, 1917, p.81. Reprinted as 'Architecture and modern life' in *Form and Civilization*. 'Education of the Architect', xxiv, 1917, pp.110, 166, 252. Reprinted in *Form in Civilization*. 'Control of street architecture', xxiv, 1917, p.181; 'Cooperation in design', xxiv, 1917, pp.272, 274; 'The function of an architectural society', xxv, 1918, p.35; 'The unity of the profession', xxv, 1918, p.51; Cecil Claude Brewer (obit.), xxv, 1918, p.246; 'Living architecture', xxvii, 1919, p.13; 'Minor city improvements', xxvii, 1920, p.32; 'On citizenship', xxvii, 1920, p.124; 'Jerusalem (Review of G. Jefferey. Brief description of the . . . Holy Sepulchre), xxvii, 1920, pp.151, 206; An outline history of Armenian architecture by A. Fetvadjian (review), xxix, 1922, p.585; 'British primitives at the R.A.: kings' portraits (mediaeval use of colour)', xxxi, 1924, p.13; 'The corporate spirit in architecture', xxxii, 1925, p.350; Inventory of Westminster Abbey (by Royal Comm. on Historical Documents) (Review), xxxii, 1925, p.391; Canon H. F. Westlake (obit.), xxxiii, 1926, p.114; 'Modernism in architecture', xxxv, 1928, p. 521; The late Charles H. Moore (obit.), xxxvii, 1930, p.337.

Journal of the Royal Society (formerly Society) of Arts, 'Cast iron and its treatment for artistic purposes', xxxviii, 1890, p.272; 'Lead work', xlv, 1897, p.452; 'Technical education in architecture and the building trades', xlv, 1897, p.851.

London Mercury, 'Architecture as form in civilization', i, (pt 2), 1920, p.574. Reprinted in *Form in Civilization*.

London Topographical Record (London Topographical Society), Pepys's London Collection (Cambridge) – (a list of engraved views of London). With A. Powell, ii, 1903, p.66; 'A note on Hollar's map of West Central London', ii, 1903, p.109; 'Wren's drawings of Old St Paul's at All Soul's College, Oxford', v, 1908, p.136; 'Notes on earliest Westminster', vii, 1911, p.21.

Museums Journal, On museum design (lecture), vol. 5, 1915–16, p.52.

North Devon Herald, 'The History of Barnstaple' (posthumous, edited by J. H. Rudd), 7.x.1937–17.ii.1938.

Observer, 'The master builder: Sir Christopher Wren and his work', 25.ii.1923. 'Save Bloomsbury',

12.xii.1926.

Parents' Review (Parents' National Education Union), 'Education, work and beauty', xxvii, no. 10, 1916, p.729.

Proceedings of British Academy, 'Medieval paintings at Westminster', xiii, 1927.

Proceedings of the Society of Antiquaries (dates of publication of volumes are years shown or after), Westminster school of painting. (Note of lecture), 2nd series, xvi, 1897, p.384; 'Early Christian and Byzantine ivories in the British and the Victoria and Albert museums', xxii, 1909, p.231; 'Some Early Christian objects at the British and Victoria and Albert museums', xxiii, 1911, pt II, p.325; xxiv, 1911, p.286; 'The Wolverhampton cross shaft', xxv, 1913, p.158; 'Fragments of a carved and painted rood from South Cerney Church, Gloucestershire', xxviii, 1916, p.17; The origin of London (summary of paper), xxxi, 1919, p.212.

Quarterly Review, 'William Morris' (with H. Steele), vol. 190, 1899, p.487.

Saturday Review, 'A London forum', 23.viii.1913.

Society for the Protection of Ancient Buildings: Annual Reports, 'Westminster Abbey and its restorations', *in* 25th, 1902, p.60; 'The preservation of national monuments. (Whitewash as a preservation of buildings and its uses in the past.)', *in* 53rd, 1930, p.5 at end.

Spectator, 'Mediaeval paintings', 7.vii.1923.

Teachers' World, 'The Place of art in education' (with portrait of W.R.L.), 27.ix.1916.

The Times (letters unless stated), Rolls chapel, 2.i.1896, p.12; Holyrood Palace restoration, 7,xii. 1906, p.4; The Civic Arts Association (Report of Meeting), 29.i.1916; Westminster Abbey, 29.vi.1920, p.26; Art in common life (interview), 23.iii.1921, p.11; The proposed loan exhibition of Early English art, 15.i.1923; Eton Hall paintings and mural remains in St Stephen's chapel, 12.xii.1923, p.14; Waterloo Bridge, 16.viii.1924, p.10; The House of Lords war memorial site, 13.i.1925, p.13; Waterloo Bridge, 23.xii.1925, p.13; Waterloo Bridge, 4.i.1926, p.13; Sidney Barnsley (obit.), 30.ix.1926, p.7; Cultural festivals, 17.viii.1928, p.13; Foundling Hospital site, 11.ii.1928, p.12; Halsey Ricardo (obit.), 17.ii.1928, p.19; Westminster Abbey and the Bayeux Tapestry (lecture), 9.i.1928, Railways and taxation, 24.iv.1929, p.12; The Abbey buildings in Westminster Abbey Appeal No., 29.vi.1929; Children's craze for amusements, 7.x.1930, p.15.

The Times Literary Supplement, 'The golden age of the Early English Church', 1917, p.569; 'William Blake', 1917, p.592; 'Middlesex in British, Roman and Saxon times', 1920, p.171; 'King Arthur's courts', 1926, p.171; 'Chaucer's tomb', 1927, p.137. The following leading articles are believed to be by Lethaby: 'Sir Christopher Wren', 1923, p.113; 'Architecture; bond or free?', 1923, p.777.

INDEX

Page numbers in *italic* refer to illustrations and captions